Horror and Hope

Horror and Hope

The Conflicted Legacy
of Christianity

———————

Dominic Kirkham

WIPF & STOCK · Eugene, Oregon

Wipf & Stock
An Imprint of Wipf and Stock Publishers
199 W. 8th Ave., Suite 3
Eugene, OR 97401

www.wipfandstock.com

PAPERBACK ISBN: 978-1-6667-1478-4
HARDCOVER ISBN: 978-1-6667-1479-1
EBOOK ISBN: 978-1-6667-1480-7

07/19/21

Scripture quotations from *The Jerusalem Bible* © 1966 by Darton Longman & Todd Ltd and Doubleday and Company Ltd.

To

The many friends, teachers, and clergy who have shaped my life,
and given me an understanding of the Christian Legacy

Contents

CONTENTS

Preface

Bois inedit by Hans Lochmann

I BEGIN WITH A digression. A digression related to the cover picture, or more specifically to the story related to the picture of the Passion that it displays. At first glance this may look like a representation of the cruci-fixion, even if taken from a slightly eccentric perspective. But a closer look at the unusual background of a ruined church and buildings, and the countless graves vanishing into the distance, indicates that it is more than a typical picture of this genre. It seems an intentionally disturbing picture, a mixture of devotional piety and anguished trauma expressed in the prone figure who fills the foreground. Not only this, but also the very medium of black ink in which the picture is composed gives a starkness and emptiness. The perspective lines of the cemetery crosses draw the eye inwards into an impenetrable blackness that envelopes everything like an all-consuming black hole of nothingness.

Probably you have never seen this picture before, as it is from a private family collection, and a copy of it has hung in my home all my life. It was once on the living room wall across the dining room table where I used to do my homework as a schoolboy and college student; it hung in the cloister of the monastery where I lived for over a decade; a copy now hangs in my bedroom. For as long as I can remember it has been like a background shadow to my life, one that seems to a pose questions: what has happened? How has this happened? How have things come to this? The answer to these questions is at the heart of my book and the explanation for its composition.

To understand this answer, a little more needs to be said of the background provenance of the picture. Perhaps you will have already noticed it has something of the resonance of the famous drawings of the great German Renaissance artist, Albrecht Dürer. This is not accidental. The artist, Hans Lochmann (1912–53), himself a German from the Bavarian village of Hilzingen near the Swiss border, was a great admirer of Dürer and styled some of his work after him. However, he was not able to pursue his interest as an artist as his parents thought it was not a reputable career and they insisted he train as a medical doctor. His training coincided with the rise of Nazism, which he loathed and opposed. As result he was interred in one of the many labor camps, *Arbeitlager*, that formed a network spreading across Germany in the 1930s like a vast web that entrapped millions of people. Though the concentration camps and death camps became the most notorious—epitomized by the infamous Auschwitz-Birkenau—this web also included, like appendages, many sub-camps: *Aussenlager* and *Arbeitlager*. It was in one of these, working on roads in extreme weather, that Lochmann contracted tuberculosis.

All this I remember from childhood conversations with an aunt. For this was also part of her story. As a young woman growing up in Manchester in the 1920s my aunt became an outdoor enthusiast, joining rambling groups that were all part of the outdoor "back to nature" movements of the time intended to promote healthier living. Such was the purpose of the "mass trespass" of Kinder Scout in 1932 by ramblers, in which she joined, led by the British Worker's Sports Federation to gain access to the open spaces of the Derbyshire Peak District. All of this was part of a much wider European cultural movement exemplified by the German *Wandervogel,* or "wandering bird," movement that gained popularity in the late nineteenth century and was itself an expression the wider Romantic movement that embraced communing with nature, seeking out old folk traditions, and songs, and reviving old Teutonic values. All of which also interested my aunt, who became a fluent German speaker, visited Germany on skiing holidays, and even became enamoured by the "virtues" of the *Jungenbund* movement that was founded in 1922—also known as the Hitler Youth! Ironically, so much outdoor, healthy living also led to her contracting tuberculosis.

At this point the life of my aunt crossed paths with that of Hans Lochmann. After the war had ended, and suffering from advanced stages of tuberculosis, she made a desperate journey to a sanatorium in Davos, Switzerland, that had an outstanding reputation for the treatment of the disease. Here she met Hans, who was also a patient and with whom she became friends. Unfortunately, he did not recover and died in 1953 at the early age of 41. But before he died, he bequeathed all his art work to my aunt for safekeeping, who, after a partial recovery herself, returned to England, where she subsequently died in 1957 at the age of forty-five. After that, some of the paintings of Hans remained with the family. Thus, by the strange alchemy of life two very different people were brought together for a brief moment of time with an unexpected outcome. This is how I have eventually come to possess the picture entitled *aus 'Passion'.*

Here perhaps a further digression is appropriate. This particular picture was one of a series of twelve similar ink drawings on which Hans Lochmann worked while he was in the sanatorium at Davos. It was number ten in a sequence of imaginary depictions of how aspects of the life of Christ might have been perceived had he lived in the current times. One picture has a figure leaving a village reminiscent of Hilzingen, another of Jesus in the midst of a very modern looking crowd in which Hans portrayed both himself and my aunt, another the torture of Jesus by two Gestapo officers, and so on. This whole sequence of pictures was passed, on the death of my aunt, to another aunt who was a member of the religious order of Notre Dame and headmistress of the convent junior school in Northampton where for thirty years they hung alongside the main stairway. When the convent closed, I acquired the pictures for the monastery in which I then lived in Sussex where they hung on the cloister wall. I have since been told they were sold to a private buyer when the order left the monastery and so they disappeared to an unknown fate that encompasses every life.

Back to the picture of our cover story. The key to understanding its meaning and purpose is the date inscribed in the top right-hand corner: 1945. This provides the crucial context, the year that the deadliest war in history, the Second World War, culminated with the liberation of Europe from its Nazi yoke. Amidst the human carnage, misery, and chaos this entailed I note here only that this year also provided the context for another event and life—that of a twelve-year-old girl also interred in an *Arbeitlagger* and forced to work on the building of railways for the Reich. Ruth Kluger described this futile and pointless work in her autobiographical work, *Landscapes of Memory*.[1] She was (having died in 2020) an unusual and caustic witness to a traumatic period of history, and she referred to the year 1945 as "the black hole at the center of the century."[2] This phrase seems to capture the context of Hans Lochmann's picture. This seems to be not a traditional portrayal but a very modern *pieta*.

I also mention Ruth Kluger here for an incident she recounts that took place previously in Auschwitz. It concerns the arrival of a woman, a high school teacher, to the camp. Even in the face of the smoking crematoria she lectured others with complete conviction how the obvious drama in which she was trapped wasn't possible, "for this was the twentieth century and we were in Europe, that is, at the heart of the civilized world."[3] To Kluger the absurdity of this view was not because the woman didn't believe in the possibility of genocide—a newly coined word that only began to enter common usage in 1945—but for thinking so highly of European culture, and that it could elevate the mind and improve conduct.[4] It is this assumption that the picture of Hans Lochmann also seems to present a challenge: can a whole cultural tradition, a civilization shaped by two millennia of Christianity, really have come to this? This is the question that has haunted my life. Trying to understand it is the reason for this book.

1. Kluger, *Landscapes of Memory*.
2. Kluger, *Landscapes of Memory*, 146.
3. Kluger, *Landscapes of Memory*, 6.
4. Sands, *East West Street*, 179.

It has been the view of some survivors and commentators that the more one studies this event—the Nazi war of annihilation and the Holocaust—the less sense it makes. Such was the view of the Polish-Lithuanian poet Czesław Miłosz.[5] In Jewish theology such an event is referred to as a *churban*, a disaster of such overwhelming proportions that it defies understanding or explanation.[6] But it happened. And it happened in the context of a cultural world and civilization shaped by Christianity. Hitler himself had a Roman Catholic upbringing, served as cathedral choir boy,[7] and his regime drew widespread support from the church.[8] Indeed, the Nazi war of annihilation was conceptualized in terms of a continuation of the medieval crusades of the Teutonic Knights and the emperors of the Holy Roman Empire, the First Reich—hence its operational code-name "Barbarossa." It was the medieval church that provided all the images and tropes—such as the obscene representations of the *Judensau*, "Jew-pig"—that incubated antisemitism.[9] In the twentieth century few places were more antisemitic than Catholic Austria, the homeland of Hitler and center of the Holy Roman Empire that under the regime of Engelbert Dollfuss became a clerico-fascist state where Judaism was seen in "traditional" terms as a "Semitic" conspiracy of powerful Jews who aimed at the subversion of the Catholic faith.[10] This was the cultural context of a particular form of hate.[11]

Just after Hans Lochmann composed his picture in 1945, a distinguished Jewish French historian, Jules Isaac, published an epochal work, *Jesus et Israel*. Having himself managed to evade capture by the Nazis and appalled at both the failure of the church to condemn antisemitism and

5. Miłosz, *Native Realm*.

6. Cohn-Sherbok, *Holocaust Theology*.

7. This was in the town of Lambach where he attended the monastery school attached to the ancient Benedictine Lambach Abbey, where above the choir stalls he saw the swastika on the coat of arms of one of the medieval abbots, and used in decorative carving on the stone and woodwork of the building. He later used it as a symbol for the Nazi party

8. On the seventy-fifth anniversary of the ending of World War ll, on May 4, 2020, the German Catholic bishops published a belated apology which acknowledged the failure of bishops to oppose the Nazi regime and went on to acknowledge, "Terrifying anti-Semitism is widespread even here in Germany" (CathNews, "Nazi Germany bishops.").

9. Wistrich, *Antisemitism*.

10. Wistrich, *Antisemitism*, 62.

11. The distinguished Austrian historian Friedrich Heer, himself a Catholic, has noted, "Measured in terms of duration, magnitude and conscious suffering, there is nothing in the history of Europe, or even the world, to compare with the martyrdom of the Jews of medieval Europe." Heer, *Medieval World*, 256.

the complicity of Christians in its imposition he set out to research the roots of this "teaching of contempt." He was researching his book before the full extent of the Holocaust, or its naming, became known. His work made clear not only the causal link between Christianity and antisemitism but also that this could not be allowed go on. In a chance meeting with Pope John XXIII in 1960 Isaac was able to present his book and case to the pope, on whom he made a significant impression. This meeting was especially fortuitous as at the time Pope John was preparing for a great church council of renewal, subsequently called the Second Vatican Council, which was intended to review the entire nature and activity of the Church in the modern world. The issue of Jewish-Christian relations was placed on its agenda. In time this led to one of the most radical documents of the council, *Nostra aetate* ("In our time"), which sought to change an almost two-thousand-year-old anti-Jewish tradition.

Since then (1965) there have been significant improvements in Jewish and Christian relations, but many of the insights and intentions of the Vatican Council have been thwarted, even reversed, and antisemitism is still a very real force in our world in both its religious and political manifestations. Indeed, this particular form of hatred is expressive of something greater than even the long history of Jewish-Christian animosity. It is expressive of the human antagonisms that lie at the heart of civilization, the shadow that accompanies every civilization. Just as every galaxy, with its dazzling array of stars, has as its center a black hole, so do all civilizations. The picture of Hans Lochmann confronts us with this often neglected aspect not only of Western civilization but civilization in general.

Ever since its origins five thousand years ago in the city-states of Mesopotamia, civilization has been characterized and made possible by powerful elites, the cult of the *lugal* ("strong man"), the organized violence of warfare, the institution of slavery, and the suppression of women. These are not the frayed edges of civilization that, as the youthful Ruth Kluger scoffed, claims to elevate the mind and improve conduct, nor unfortunate consequences, but an integral aspect of its dynamics—its heart of darkness. Technological sophistication seldom equates with moral sensitivity, and though civilization and savagery are often seen as antonyms we now understand that civilization brings its own kind of savagery.[12]

Marching out of the mists of history comes the magnificent and merciless Sargon (2360–2279 BCE), meaning "true king" in Akkadian,

12. Sarmiento, *Facundo*.

creator of the first empire, who gloried in the annihilation of all his enemies, claiming to be world-king,[13] who smashed the skulls of caged kings with a mace and commanded that any woman who spoke out of turn should have her teeth smashed with a brick. In the earliest surviving cuneiform tablets from Lagash we find reference to "the place where people die," *karas*, concentration camps where the *namr-ak*, captive women and children and prisoners of war, were interred.[14] All-consuming wars ensured not only the establishment of civilizations but also presaged their endings. In his magisterial study, *The City in History*, the verdict of Lewis Mumford was chilling: "Urban life spans the historic space between the earliest burial ground for dawn man and the final cemetery, the Necropolis, in which one civilization after another has met its end."[15] As I look at the picture of Hans Lochmann, with its prone figure, ruined church and houses, rubble-filled foreground, and infinity of graves disappearing into the distance, all this becomes graphically apparent. And the question arises: Is this a judgement on our civilization?

Clearly my digression has ominous implications for our understanding both of Christianity and civilized life. After what has been called a dark century on a dark continent,[16] gone is the confidence and conviction of our predecessors, the Victorians, with their belief in progress and enlightenment, gone is the easy assumption of cultural improvement, gone is the belief that we understand the nature and meaning of life. It is of note that the first book to describe the reality of Auschwitz—published in 1946—by survivor and Viennese psychiatrist Dr. Viktor Frankl was entitled *Man's Search for Meaning*.[17] It addressed the existential vacuum of doubt and uncertainty—that black hole—that had come to exist at the heart of Western society. As Ruth Kluger also intimated, it is no longer possible to produce a coherent and persuasive narrative of civilization: the alternative to ideological fixation is fragmentation, and the meaning of life is to be found more in our attitude to the fleeting and fragmentary moments of everyday life.

Among the titles I mulled over for my book, one was simply *Fragments*. This was also a reference to the gospel story of the Feeding of the Five Thousand, after which Jesus tells his disciple to "gather up the fragments"

13. Roux, *Iraq*, 154.

14. River, *Sumer*.

15. Mumford, *City in History*, 15.

16. Mazower, *Dark Continent*.

17. Frankl, *Man's Search*.

(John 6:12). Like the rubble that fills the foreground of Lochmann's picture the chapters of my book may, to some, seem a rough terrain, each one presenting something of a trip hazard to past convictions.

* * *

Though the chapters of my book are wide-ranging I have no ambition to repeat or even try to imitate the many great academic works on the history of Christianity and the West, even if I could. Rather, the intention of this book is more modest and personal: it merely tries to respond to some issues that I have encountered over many years in the context of the ambiguities and complex diversity that constitute Christianity.

Most of the chapters of my book have been written, and rewritten, over a period of years, as I tried to give greater focus to their content in keeping with new understanding and scholarship, insofar as I am aware of these. This is an ongoing process, as our understanding of the past shimmers and changes in the light of our understanding of the present. The exception is perhaps the first chapter, "Universal Christmas," written in a sudden burst of inspiration on Twelfth Night, 2020. It is a reflection on the Christmas imagery of the Madonna in the context of the events that unfolded in the life of the Russian writer and journalist Vasily Grossman, sometimes described as the Tolstoy of the twentieth century. Grossman's epic narrative *Life and Fate* expands the context of Lochmann's Passion and begins to address some of its questions: What has happened? How did this happen? What must we do? The seeds of Grossman's magnum opus were also sown in 1945 and his anguished journey across eastern Europe as a war correspondent with the Red Army. It was while trying to come to terms with the questions raised by this experience working on *Life and Fate* that he had a chance viewing of the *Sistine Madonna*. The imagery of the mother and child as a timeless affirmation of those universal human values of humanity, kindness, and compassion not only overwhelmed Grossman but provided a core insight for his work that is an affirmation of the timeless values that confront totalitarian ideologies.

Though Christianity was instrumental in preserving the light of civilization through the Dark Ages of European beginnings, this is not the whole story. In chapter 2, "The Christian Roots of Racism," I seek to explain why the Holocaust and Nazi era cannot be explained away simply as an aberration of German history or, as the modern right wing AfD (Alternative for

Germany party) maintain, a "speck of bird-shit on a millennium of successful German history." Why this view is very far from the truth is a theme explored further in chapter 3, "The Reality of Antisemitism," and also in chapter 4, "Christianity and Colonialism."

In further chapters I focus on the origins of Christianity, the nature of the teaching of Jesus, and try to show how this legacy has been modified, if not traduced, by historical circumstances. In chapter 5, "Between the Testaments," I seek to locate the teaching of Jesus in a wider perspective of Jewish and religious history, as we now understand it, asking the rather challenging question: Did Jesus ever intend to found a religion? In chapter 6, "Viewing the Morals of Jesus Today," I appraise what exactly were the teachings of Jesus in the light of modern critical textual scholarship, and how we can understand them in the context of our modern, secular, humanistic, and naturalistic view of the world. Taking this analysis further in chapter 7, "Rethinking Redemption," I consider the changed view of Jesus as a "Second Adam" must undergo once we realize there was no first Adam and that our modern human ancestors interbred with earlier humans, such as Neanderthals and Denisovans. It is from such origins we have emerged over a span of time and in a way unthinkable to biblical writers.

Of course, "Christianity" is a cerebral abstraction that in itself has never existed other than as the nebulous spirit of some aspirational ideals. What exists are the many ecclesial traditions that seek to keep alive the memory and teachings of Jesus as they perceive them. What often characterises the members of these traditions is the conviction that they alone are the "true believers" and their church "the One, Holy, Catholic and Apostolic church." This then sets them against other rivals. Such divisive sectarianism was already apparent in the New Testament, something I consider in chapter 8, "A Conflicted Beginning."

In the title to my book I use the phrase "the Legacy of Christianity." The use of the word "legacy" contains an ambiguity. A legacy is something that we have inherited and can now enjoy. But it also has another implication: that the giver is now deceased and so the bequest can only diminish in time as its resources are expended. This ambiguity is at the heart of the controversy, sometimes referred to as the "God wars," over whether religion has had its day and the future is now secular. But this is something of a false and unnecessary polarization. The need for a human spirituality remains and mine is not an anti-Christian or even post-Christian tract but rather a post-confessional exploration where things are seen simply for what they are and beliefs patterns in the mind.

Though the churches have made strenuous efforts in modern times to become ecumenical and overcome past divisions, still old habits and resentments linger. This was particularly true in the case of an Irish Roman Catholic priest, Fr. Sean Fagan. Though not of celebrity status he was a well-known and widely-respected theologian who had devoted his life to furthering the process of renewal envisaged by Vatican Council II and providing pastoral guidance to modern perplexed parishioners. His treatment at the hands of the Inquisition—yes, it still exists, hiding behind a name change—is little short of scandalous, and I write about his as an example of the wider issue of the abuse of power with the Roman Catholic Church (chapter 9, "Will the Sphinx Ever Smile?")

Apart from new knowledge that, over the last few centuries, has given rise to innumerable "-ologies"—such disciplines as geology, archaeology, anthropology, biology, not to mention the overwhelming presence of technology—one of the most distinctive changes to the way we understand our world has come about through the growth of historical awareness. This new consciousness of the nature of the past escalated in the eighteenth and nineteenth centuries. In conjunction with the development of the conceptual tools for penetrating textual analysis and the growth of literary critical methods our understanding of biblical and religious texts has been transformed. Ironically, it was the attempt to understand these texts that propelled the studies that so radically changed that very understanding (chapter 10, "The Religious Engagement with History"). The challenges to any form of religious engagement today and in the near future is something I consider in chapter 11, "The Global Challenge."

A final concern regarding the legacy of Christianity is with its monotheistic understanding of creation and its relation to the modern ecological crisis. The distinguished naturalist Edward Wilson has rightly noted that "the mood of Western civilization is Abrahamic" in its approach to nature. The biblical teaching about God as creator has been that "He" has handed the earth over to mankind to "subdue" it and have "dominion" over it (Genesis 1:28).[18] Though the exact interpretation of these words is now disputed, their traditional understanding has been that the earth was

---

18. "The Hebrew word *kavash*, here rendered 'subdue,' means forceful subjection: it is a word used elsewhere in the Bible to describe enslavement or rape." Trudeau, "Making Sense," 5.

there for "man's" benefit. Of the idea of "stewardship," James Lovelock, the inventor of the concept of "Gaia," was particularly scathing, saying, "The idea that humans are yet intelligent enough to serve as stewards of the Earth is amongst the most hubristic ever."[19] That an anthropocentric and functional approach to nature that derives from Christian beliefs has been a causative factor leading to the present environmental crisis that now places a question mark over the very survival of humanity is of concern; that civilizations can collapse remarkably quickly and unexpectedly is something that the coronavirus epidemic in particular has given us cause to consider (chapter 12, "Survival").

* * *

I first became aware of the general historical background to the above narrative while a college student under the direction of my history tutor, Klaus Berenzen, whose roots were (I think) in the now-lost world of East Prussia. What I remember most about him was his gaunt and haunted look that, now I come to think about it, was not too dissimilar from that of Hans Lochmann in a photo that I once saw of him, but as to what events they witnessed I can only imagine. I would like now record my debt to his learning and courtesy. Also, I should mention my Polish friend, Teresa Rakowska, who gave me an emotional understanding of Polish history and introduced me to Europe's heart of darkness, Auschwitz. Some of the chapters in this book have appeared in another form as articles in Sofia (the journal of the Sea of Faith Network, UK) and The Fourth R, the journal of the Westar Institute, USA. ("Universal Christmas," 33.2 (March–April 2020) and, forthcoming, "The Christian Roots of Racism," "Rethinking Redemption," and "Will the Sphinx Ever Smile?") I am very grateful to the editors, Dinah Livingstone and Robert Miller, for the interest they have shown in my work. Also, I am indebted to Tom Hall, who edited books for the Polebridge Press, for his unfailing support and interest in this and my previous books, and to David Lambourn for his invaluable consultation and helping with the preparation of the text, bibliography, and index.

As I began so I would like to conclude with reference to Hans Lochmann and his final testimony that my aunt translated from German and attached to his memorial card that also carried the picture of the Passion, words from a tragic past that are also timeless:

19. Lovelock, *Revenge*, 195.

One thing I now thoroughly understand—that of all the things in this world one alone is important—that is to say Love. Love to whose realisation we must contribute something of ourselves—a comfort, a pleasure or some other thing, the love of a speck of colour, an unessential part of a picture, or that we allow a flower to remain standing instead of pulling it to pieces, or that we gladly do something that costs us to overcome. All this is not new nor original, but how difficult we find it all the same to go on living. How much more difficult to die! For a good death is indeed to be found in this: that we submit what to us appears of endless importance—our SELF—which is restless, full of confidence, to a great unknown MERCY.

Easter, 2021

Chapter 1

Universal Christmas

_____

The totalitarian challenge to humanity

TWELFTH NIGHT! THE COLORFUL lights are switched off, the glittering tinsel decorations tidied away, and the shelves cleared of their joyful cards, leaving them looking bereft, forlorn and empty. The big department stores announce their Christmas trading figures and rail fares rise with their annual inevitability, so once more, with a sigh, commuters return to the daily drudgery of a dull world. Yes, the Christmas season is over once more. Oh, and if you were hoping that something of its spirit of peace and good will to all men should percolate into the coming year, President Trump ordered a missile strike! Welcome to 2020.

For myself, partly by chance and partly from the sort of person I am, my reading over the Christmas season was a new biography of the great Russian writer and chronicler of the Soviet era, Vasily Grossman.[1] Anything more remote from the spirit of Christmas would be difficult to find! Grossman's fate was to live under one of the most tyrannous regimes in history, that of Stalin. As a war correspondent he was sent to report on perhaps the most barbaric battle in history that over nine months of 1942 raged around Stalingrad. As this was coming to its grizzly denouement, he followed the advancing Red Army across Ukraine to find an unrecognisable landscape of destruction that had been stripped not only of its human population but even any evidence of their presence. Seeking out the village of Berdychiv, where he was born and had grown up, and

1. Popoff, *Grossman.*

1

news of his mother, there was nothing. Grossman was left bewildered and incredulous at the desolation that lay before him.

The totalitarian experience

Nor was this the worst of it. As he followed on the heels of the Red Army into Eastern Poland he came to new places of desolation: Treblinka, Sobibor, Majdanek . . . places the likes of which had never before existed in history. Grossman began to realize that he was also the witness to something that had never before happened in history with such a degree of brutality: the extermination of an entire people and culture. These events have led even those who tried to record them to suicide, and Grossman also fell into a deep depression. Over the coming years he strove to seek out the story of what had happened from interviews with survivors. All these events and memories would eventually coalesce into his great work, *Life and Fate*, which has been described as a modern equivalent of *War and Peace* with himself as a modern Tolstoy. A work that also led to his own destruction as writer at the hands of the Soviet censor.

It was while writing this work that Grossman was left "stunned and confused" by an unexpected event that seemed to crystalize everything he was thinking. In 1945 the Red Army art-recovery teams brought trophy paintings from Dresden to Moscow. In 1955 Krushchev gave permission for the paintings to be exhibited, which caused something of a sensation. Amongst them was Raphael's *Sistine Madonna*. When Grossman saw it he was overwhelmed, and he wrote, "As soon as you set eyes on this painting, you immediately realize one thing, one thing above all: that it is immortal." A century earlier a similarly spellbound writer, that great inquisitor into the depths of the human soul, Dostoevsky, had stood before the same painting while in Dresden declaring it to be "the highest manifestation of human genius." Whereas Dostoevsky, a deeply religious man, saw the painting as a symbol of religious faith and beauty that would save the world, Grossman, a humanist, saw it as a supreme "expression of life and humanity." Like a ray of light entering a darkened world the painting reflected the central theme of Grossman's work: that "the power of life, the power of what is human in man" is a spiritual force that cannot be enslaved or destroyed by violence or tyranny.

One of the distinctive characteristics of Grossman's writings from the outset was its characterization of individual human lives and experiences from which grew his broader reflections. It was this that gave his war reports a wide popular appeal, as they were so unlike the usual reporting of the time which emphasized party achievements and ideology. It was this characteristic that also, from the outset, would cause tensions with the state censors who had no interest other than in reporting the achievements of socialism and the Soviet state. In time this concern of Grossman became more pronounced as he was prompted to inquire further into what actually was happening to the people of his time: the Jews of Eastern Europe, the victims of the war, the great "terror-famine" (*holodomor*) of Ukraine, of the returning victims of the Gulag, the lives of the distant ethnic groups like the Kubans and Armenians. All of this was not only totally unreported and unknown but even forbidden to be known with every effort by the state to obliterate its memory from public consciousness. It was his relentless literary endeavour that would ultimately lead to the denunciation and vilification of Grossman and the suppression of his work.

Here one should pause to reflect on what Grossman found. The brutality with which prisoners of war were treated, the murderous and callous cruelty needlessly inflicted on the people of Ukraine, the total absence of any semblance of justice for those deemed politically suspect, the unbelievably extreme conditions of the Siberian camps where people simply froze to death. And the numbers involved in all of this were staggering: forty-two million war dead (NINETEEN million military and twenty-three million civilian deaths)[2]—Stalin dismissively spoke of seven million; three to seven million Ukrainians; eighteen million gulag inmates; eight million other "special exiles" such as kulaks, Poles, Balts, Tartars, Volga Germans.[3] Over seventy million people: lives destroyed, discarded, and forgotten. As one of Grossman's characters from Ukraine asks, "Is it really true that no one will be held to account for it all? That it will just be forgotten without a trace?"

The answer to that question is that no one ever has. Even today, in the malign and mendacious world of Putin's Russia, anyone who attempts to tarnish the memory of Stalin risks arrest, even those who try to place a small plaque in memory of a disappeared person—as the "Last Address" movement attempts to do.[4] In March 2021 a local historian in Siberia, Denis Karagodin, who was investigating the execution in Stalin's purges of his

---

2. Popoff, *Grossman*, 352. These statistics come from information declassified by Putin's Duma in May 2017.

3. Applebaum, *Gulag*.

4. Bennetts, "Activist Charged."

great-grandfather, a displaced Cossack farmer, was himself arrested after being accused by the descendant of the NKVD officer who signed the death warrant for the publication of false information. What Grossman realized of this era was not only that the denial was complete but it was of the very nature of totalitarian regimes that they are indifferent to individual life and human freedom, to truth and justice. And in this he was led into his greatest "heresy": that there was no difference between Hitler and Stalin, who were "mirror images." Both had banished all notions of morality and humanity. In this "wolfish time," as he put it, Grossman saw it as his task to capture his era, portray its reality, and pose the difficult questions.

The Sistine Madonna

At this point in his writing, he viewed *The Sistine Madonna*. This picture, so he reflected, had been viewed by twelve generations, over five centuries, each of which invested it with their own contemporary understanding of human destiny: the young mother who brought her child into the world where crowds roared their approval of Hitler; "It was she, treading lightly on her little bare feet, who walked over the swaying earth of Treblinka; it was she who had walked from the 'station' from where the transports were unloaded, to the gas chamber. I knew her by the expression on her face, by the look in her eyes. I saw her son and recognized him by the strange, un-childlike look on his face . . . Here she is, carrying her little son, boarding the transport train. What a long path lies ahead of her . . . And where is your father little one? Where did he perish . . . Felling logs in the taiga? . . . I saw her in 1930, in Konotop, at the station. Swarthy from hunger and illness, she walked towards the express train, looked up at me with her wonderful eyes, and said with her lips, without any voice, 'Bread.'" For Grossman, here was a symbol for contemporary humanity, "together with us—for she is us, and her son is us."[5]

Here we begin to recognize the timeless power of the Christmas icon, the mother and child. As it embellishes the greetings cards in so many different forms it reaches out to each generation with an enduring invincibility speaking of different values: kindness, compassion, fellowship, freedom. It touches the conscience and consciousness intimating the possibility of a different world. Here is something implicitly revolutionary beckoning that the mighty will be cast down from their thrones and the

5. Popoff, *Grossman*, 237.

lowly raised up. For Raphael, as much as for Grossman, the Madonna was seen, perhaps could only be seen, in the context of his own times. He was recording a belief, an idea—legend has it that its form was revealed to him in a dream—incarnated in a sixteenth-century context, accompanied by a Renaissance pope and local patron.

The world of *Midrash*

But so has it always been, even for the evangelists, Matthew and Luke, whose Gospels contain the proto-evangelium that provide the basis of our Christmas imagery. The evangelists were not writing history but weaving together a very elaborate symbolic narrative common at the time known as *midrash* that had become a feature of Jewish writing after the sixth century BCE. At that time, while exiled in Babylon, having experience a national devastation and deportation every bit as traumatic as the Ukrainian experience under Stalin, Jewish scholars entered into a period of profound meditation on the meaning of their ancestral scriptures in the light of very changed circumstances. Old stories that once had reference only to past events were rewritten, annotated and elaborated so that they would refer more explicitly to the present. As the scripture scholar Hubert Richards wrote, "To read *midrash* is to be exposed constantly to a double image, where the past is often indistinguishable from the present, and where the event being depicted can no longer be distinguished from the colors which have been used to paint it."[6] In other words, as much as anything Raphael painted, the gospel stories were verbal pictures.

What the evangelists gave us was a great symbolic narrative created of disparate elements that were mixed together, giving all the richness and density of a great Christmas cake. Unfortunately, we have persisted in misunderstanding and misrepresenting what they wrote. From the very first word of the first Gospel, we have generally set off on the wrong foot when confronted by the long list of names usually referred to as a "genealogy." But Matthew does not use this word, he uses "genesis," a far more ambitious word. This is a key "trigger word": he is offering to tell the whole Old Testament, or universal history, in the light of the birth of Jesus, seen as a second King David.

And so his "genealogy," far from being a rather tedious collection of names that can be skipped over to get on with the "real story," this is the

6. Richards, *First Christmas*, 19.

key to all that follows. It is a carefully crafted symbolic structure of three groups of fourteen names. To understand why we must understand that the background Hebraic culture that lies behind the Greek text. Written Hebrew of the time had no vowels and no numerals, so consonants were used as numbers, which in turn meant that groups of numbers could form words, which in turn gave rise to a whole popular genre of writings involving word and number play called "gematry"[7]—already this is beginning to sound arcane and complicated. It is! That's the point—but bear with me because the key, for our purposes, is simple: the name David, in Hebrew DVD, numerically adds up to fourteen! So, the list of names points to Jesus, who ends the third group, as being symbolically thrice greater than David. And there is more! Three fourteens would represent six sevens, and Jesus would mark the beginning of the seventh seven, or the fullness of time in universal history. This narrative will prepare us for the way the life of Jesus will be presented as a new Moses who recapitulates in himself and fulfils all the prophecies of the past. There is more, but so we go on, into the phantasmagorical world of *midrash*.

Despite all of this abstruse thinking, which is rarely referred to in popular presentation, we seem to have difficulty even in reading what is plainly before us. For example, everyone delights in the story of the three kings: but there is never any mention of three kings, only three gifts! More awkwardly, we like to mix the stories of Matthew and Luke into one continuous narrative: but the two are contradictory when put together and as incompatible as trying to mix the ingredients of a Christmas pudding with a Christmas cake. For Matthew Jesus is born in Bethlehem, proceeds to Egypt to escape Herod then returns to Nazareth. For Luke, after the birth of Jesus, he proceeds to Jerusalem, then returns to Nazareth. In Luke's account there is no room for a visit to Egypt and in Matthew's account no room for a visit to Jerusalem. But the tangle disappears when we recognize that we are not dealing with two historical records but two theological meditations on biblical themes. *Midrash* again!

From this brief excursion into a strange and esoteric literary world we can come to an even more strangely overlooked conclusion. Perhaps the only historical truth we can glean from all this is that Jesus was a Jew! All that Matthew and Luke have in common are three names (Jesus, Mary and Joseph), three places (Jerusalem, Bethlehem and Nazareth), and a time (the

---

7. The most well-known example is the name of the beast, 666, in Revelation 13:18.

reign of Herod the Great). And all of these indicate that the story is of a Jewish family living in a time of unprecedented political turmoil.

The sapiential experience

The post-exilic world of the sixth century BCE and after was one of expanding empires and trade networks with global reach, accompanied by a great cultural osmosis in which Hellenism was a major element—we now know, for example, that the so-called "terracotta army" of the first Chinese emperor Qin Shi Huang (259–210 BCE) was made using Greek techniques and by craftsmen trained by Greek sculptors for whom the humanist Greek statues of the time provided the artistic model. This new cosmopolitan world provided a breadth of new knowledge and urbane wisdom based on human experience that resulted in a secular humanism surprising similar to that of our own times. Also surprising to some is that writings reflecting an often world-weary scepticism should have found their way into the Bible under the title of Wisdom Literature. Distinctive among such sapiential works are the books of Proverbs, Job, Ecclesiasts, and Ecclesiasticus (also known as The Wisdom of Jesus ben Sirach). As the scripture scholar Lloyd Geering notes, following von Rad, "There is reason to believe that these represent only a small selection of what Israel's sages either collected or personally produced."[8]

It is into this tradition that Jesus was born and became a part of. As a Jewish woman of the first century BCE his mother would no doubt have been roughly contemporary with the man regarded by posterity as the greatest teacher of Israel, Hillel the Elder. Once he was reputed to have been challenged by a Gentile to repeat the whole of the Torah while standing on one leg. His reply was: "What is hateful to you do not do to your fellow man: this is the meaning of the law and the prophets." This is the now-so-called Golden Rule: the rule by which all morality is to be judged. It is a rule that Jesus would further refine in the Sermon on the Mount where he proclaimed, "Love they neighbour as thyself," thus giving an affirmative value and impetus to humane moral living. Here is an absolute ethical standard which has never been surpassed.

Yet the world in which all this was happening was one of extreme violence and brutality, particularly for Jews. Two generations before the birth of Jesus the Roman armies under Pompey had swept through Judea

8. Geering, *Christianity Without God.*

killing, enslaving, and destroying towns and villages: in one incident alone two thousand Jews were crucified at Jerusalem. Less than a century later. in 66 CE, another rebellion—the Great Revolt—led to another, even more devastating wave of destruction under Vespasian in which the whole country was systematically destroyed along with Jerusalem at the cost of one million lives, according to the Jewish historian Josephus. As if this was not bad enough, a further rebellion in 132 CE prompted the emperor Hadrian to embark on a "final solution" to the problematic Jews: the entire country was laid waste, a thousand towns and villages destroyed including Jerusalem which was levelled to the ground, over six hundred thousand Jews were killed, including by special order all scholars, and the country renamed so that there would be no further memory of it.[9]

In reciting this grim history my purpose is to show that without too much imagination we can see how closely it resembles the purges of the totalitarian states of the twentieth century: Hadrian and Hitler, Vespasian and Stalin. We may not often associate them but their works were the same: Grossman's stunned reflections on journeying through Ukraine and eastern Poland provide an accurate description of what happened in Judea two thousand years previously. "This is the murder of a people, murder of a house, of a family, of books, of faith; this is the murder of the tree of life . . . This is the murder of a people's soul and body . . . This is the murder of a people's morality, of customs, humorous stories passed on for generations to their sons, this is the murder of memories, of sad song, of people's poetry . . . this is the death of a people."[10]

In Jewish theology such events are known as a *churban*—a disaster of such overwhelming proportions that it defies understanding or explanation.[11] In Jewish history there have been three such events: the destruction of the Kingdom of Judah by the Babylonians (587 BCE), of the land of Israel by the Romans (70 CE) and of European Jewry by Hitler (1939–45).[12] Each *churban* is a catastrophe that ends an era in a holocaust. But here is the remarkable thing: what is seen as a final end never is. Life always triumphs over death, humanity over inhumanity, love over evil. It was this understanding that provided the core conviction of Grossman and the motivation to write

9. Carroll, *Christ Actually*, 46–78.

10. Popoff, *Grossman*, 162.

11. Cohn-Sherbok, *Holocaust Theology*, 28.

12. This represents the thinking of Ignaz Maybaum; other writers would add the Jewish expulsion from Spain in 1492 as a further example of a *churban*.

his works as a record that would never be forgotten; works that would show that hatred never triumphs in its designs—his reports would be used as evidence in the Nuremberg trials of the Nazi war criminals.

In this he was drawing on something central to what it was to be human, something that he saw reflect in the *Sistine Madonna* and in the ancestral sapiential tradition to which he belonged, for he was himself Jewish. For Grossman "the highest thing" a person can do is to live in accordance with his or her own conscience. It was this that was the measure of humanity and a measure against which he acknowledged his failings, buckling as many did under the pressure of totalitarianism: "We remained silent in 1937 when thousands of innocent people were executed . . . and we remained silent during the horrors of general collectivization [in Ukraine]." But he was determined that his writings, particular his master work *Life and Fate,* would not be silenced whatever the cost. As he wrote, "If a man has the strength to listen to his conscience and then act on it, he feels a surge of happiness." This is the foundation of a humanism reflected in Raphael's Madonna, embedded in the Christmas story and universal to mankind.

And the animals came too

But this is not the whole of what the Christmas story means to us today. Nor is it the only part of the modern *midrash* that we need to weave today. Though stories of wicked kings and terrible tyrants from far-away places and distant times may be seen as stories to frighten children, they are not. Herod and Hitler, Hadrian and Stalin were not aliens from another planet: they are like us and, more frighteningly even unknowingly, we can become like them. One of the features of their lives was an indifference, even unawareness of the consequences of their actions: as Stalin is reputed to have said, "One death may be regarded as a tragedy, a million is a statistic." The widespread indifference to the fate of the natural world that has typified past centuries of humanity can be regarded in a similar manner. To the crime of genocide, we must now add the crime of ecocide—the destruction of the natural world. And in this we are all complicit. Each time we turn on the car engine or switch up the heating, use our phone or apply a beauty product, our actions have consequences: the natural world is being either destroyed or exploited, with devastating consequences for ourselves: for we also are part of the natural world and depend on it for life.

The Australian fires are a graphic illustration of this reality. As I write an area the size of Belgium is ablaze and fires burn out of control across half a continent, an estimated 500 million animals incinerated. This indeed is a holocaust without parallel and for which we all bear some responsibility. Ironically this is happening in a country which is the biggest exporter of coal in the world, whose economy is based on fossil fuel extraction, and which recently voted in a government on the back of a rejection of restrictive green policies that may damage the country's economy. A handful of global companies (Exxon, Chevron, BP, Shell) have done what they please, putting corporate interest above those of the planet on the basis of providing for the market—us.

Now the natural world, our planet, is being remorselessly destroyed. We regard fish and animals merely as commodities, natural resources to be exploited: nameless and numberless, just as Stalin regarded the *zeks*.[13] In her memoir of survival in the Nazi concentration camps Ruth Kluger describes her journey to Auschwitz as a young girl in the cattle trucks.[14] As she recalls the appalling conditions no human should have imagined they would have to endure at the hands of another human she widens the scope of her reflection: Should we be putting cattle in trucks in such conditions without further thought? Seventy-five years on and the animal rights organizations, such as Compassion in World Farming, are still campaigning to stop this brutal trade in animals across the EU. Though most people like to compartmentalize or differentiate the treatment of humans and animals, the Nazi experience showed that the treatment of one elides with the treatment of the other. Before the Nazis slave traders had dismissed objections to their trade in humans as no such thing in that their cargo was no different to animals. Now Jews were being treated as animals with the same ending: mass slaughter.

It was the inspired genius of St. Francis of Assisi, who thought of putting the whole Christmas story together in the form of a little scenic model that could be viewed by all as a reminder of the love God for all creation—the first Christmas crib was created in the Italian town of Greccio in 1223. To the biblical scene he added the animals of the manger, who although not mentioned in the gospel stories, were to Francis also included in the divine love that embraced all creation, a mystical view reflected in his *Canticle of the Sun*. In a way this was also an example of an

---

13. The slang name given to Gulag prisoners.
14. Kluger, *Landscapes of Memory*, 104.

ongoing *midrash* as with the many Renaissance paintings of the Madonna, where the animals are there too. They are also part of the story. They make our lives possible and they cannot just be regarded with indifference to be discarded. This is also the Christmas message of many animal charities which this year have been pleading with people not to buy animals as presents. All too often, a few weeks after Christmas these animals are discarded, thrown out in card board boxes or just dumped at the roadside. As the slogan goes, "A dog is for life, not just Christmas."

I am reminded of this as I recently bought a puppy for a family whose pet had died. A little dog which turned out to be smaller than expected and so earned the sobriquet "Tiny Tot." But small as he is Tiny Tot has had a transformative effect on the family: his bright sparkling eyes, eager affection and boundless mischievous energy are a delight to behold, filling a room with happiness and enlivening the children's parties. He is a small reminder of how wonderful animals are, how much our lives depend upon them, how they too deserve our respect, affection, and compassion. The Christmas story reminds us of this. As the UN Secretary General admonished us all at the recent climate conference in Madrid, "We must stop this war on nature." We too must stop playing the tyrant.

And so Twelfth Night passes. Christmas comes to an end. Except that it doesn't. Already, in January, trade fairs are taking place across the world displaying all the Christmas stock that will be on sale NEXT Christmas; factories are already producing the stock for our Christmas treats several years down the road. One revealing little hiccup in all this only recently become apparent in the national calendars, which have all got the date of the May Bank Holiday wrong because last year the government decided to move it from May 4 to May 8 to coincide with the seventy-fifth VE Day celebrations.

But by the time of the announcement the calendars of all the big stationers had already been printed: they would have needed two years' notice to make the change.

So now what has become the biggest global festival there is, at least in its material preparation, never ends. So should its spiritual message. The Christmas stories and pictures of the Madonna remind us of a kinder, gentler world of compassion and care, brotherhood and peace. They shine a light of translucent beauty on a darkened world of cruelty and hate. Christmas is not just for Christmas: it is for life.

Chapter 2

The Christian Roots of Racism

How obscuring the past frustrates the future

SEVENTY-FIVE YEARS AGO, IN April 1945, war correspondent Richard Dimbleby was accompanying the British Second Army as it advanced against the retreating German troops in northern Germany when unexpectedly they came across a clearing in the woods: Belsen. The scenes of unimaginable horror that followed shocked him to the core. His report subsequently shocked the world, and TV footage has continued to do so. It has become an icon of evil, the epitome of the perversity of which humans are capable.

In dealing with the larger event we now call the Holocaust, historians and others have repeatedly looked for explanations of this genocidal act of terror. In popular consciousness it is now regarded as an unprecedented, even unique, act of evil perpetrated by the extreme right wing Nazism that grew out of the social and economic malaise of the Weimar Republic, a movement accompanied by a return to a neo-pagan nativism glorifying the German *volk* (people) and *heimat* (homeland), and bolstered by new racial theories popularized in the nineteenth century.

I believe this explanation is simplistic and dangerously misleading, for it serves as a convenient foil that distracts us from the real roots of what happened in the Holocaust, cultural elements that lie deeply embedded in European history. Thus it obscures the nature of European racism that continues to plague Western society. Lest this be dismissed as a highly provocative and unjustified opinion, allow me to offer a brief historical resume of some European colonial precedents. *The story is not always as the received historical narrative represents reality.*

A chronicle of genocide and slavery

Let us be clear, the genocidal treatment of the Jews by a European nation was neither a unique nor unprecedented event. On May 12, 1883, the German flag was raised on the coast of Southwest Africa, modern Namibia. This was the beginning of Germany's African Empire and search for what, under the Kaiser Wilhelm II, was claimed to be its right to "our place in the sun." It became a war of extermination against the indigenous Herero and Nama people, who were interned in concentration camps and systematically starved and worked to death. Approximately 80 percent of Herero people perished in what would be the first genocide of the twentieth century. Though photographic evidence of the events that unfolded in this remote wilderness existed, no widespread coverage ensued and they were soon forgotten in the context of the subsequent global war. That the perpetrators of this, an act of genocidal terror, had close links with the perpetrators of the Holocaust, and, as one said "learnt their trade there," is matter of historical record.[1]

Nor was this exceptional. Whilst this was happening, a thousand miles north in what is now the Democratic Republic of Congo, formerly the Belgian Congo, a similar but even more gruesome story was unfolding the details of which I find too sickening to repeat here.[2] Between 1885 and 1908 the Congo Free State had become the personal possession of King Leopold II of Belgium. In July 2020, the present Belgian monarch King Philippe expressed his regret that "acts of violence and atrocity were committed that continue to weigh on our collective memory." But he stopped short of a formal apology for the reign of terror and ruthless commercial exploitation that left up to ten million Congolese dead and gave rise to the term "crime against humanity." This was the systematic oppression that prompted Joseph Conrad's searing exposé of European civilization in his novel *The Heart of Darkness*. And yet Leopold was a highly regarded devout Catholic monarch who saw nothing remiss in his actions and who was described in 2010 by Belgian foreign minister Louis Michel as a "hero" who had "stimulated economic growth in the Congo."

1. Erichson and Olusoga, *Kaiser's Holocaust*.

2. Hochschild, *King Leopold's Ghost*. The publication of this book forced Belgians to come to terms for the first time with their long-buried colonial past and generated intense public debate that so troubled Belgian officials that they reportedly instructed diplomats on how to deflect embarrassing questions about the past that the book raised.

Before these events unfolded another drama had been playing out since the beginning of the century across the globe in Tasmania. Here the British had established a penal colony in 1803 that rapidly brought the settlers into conflict with the native aborigines. The initial contact led to the so-called "massacre of Risdon Cove"; and though we do not know exactly how many aborigines were killed, what we do know is that this soon escalated into a full scale conflict between natives and settlers known as "The Black War" with demands for the "utter annihilation" of the native aboriginal population—the result of which was that when the colony became self-governing in 1856 only seventeen aborigines remained of an estimated population of eight thousand that had lived on the island for over forty thousand years.[3] A commission set up to investigate the conflict under the direction of an archdeacon, William Broughton, reported that part of the problem was because the aborigines had "lost the sense of superiority of white people." Writing of these events a century later the Polish-American lawyer Rafael Lemkin, who first coined the term "genocide" in 1943 in the context of the Nazi atrocities in Europe and the pending trials for war crimes at Nuremberg, considered the extermination of the Tasmanian aborigines in the 1830s to be one of the clearest examples of genocide in history.[4]

Prior to Leopold's commercial enterprise in the Congo, a similar royally-sponsored adventure had been unfolding on the islands of the Caribbean. Here in 1672 the English Royal African Company began transporting African slaves to work on tobacco and sugar plantations. Previously in 1625 the crew of an English ship had claimed possession of the Island of Barbados in the name of James I, from whence grew a unique colony whose economy was based entirely on slavery. One should note that this was not a *slave-owning society* (as had been so many before) but the first society entirely *constituted by slavery*.[5] During more than two hundred years of relentless brutality and terror some five million slaves were trafficked for a life of remorseless work and exploitation, and regarded as no more than disposable "property."

3. Lawson, *Last Man*. Lawson notes retrospectively of this "entanglement" that "an understanding of the Holocaust has allowed us to see more clearly the moral imperatives of genocide, and as such it behoves us to ask awkward . . . questions of our national past," xxi.

4. For a detailed and fascinating account of the emergence of this now seminal concept see Sands, *East West Street*.

5. Another original feature of this economy was the introduction of a shift system of labor so that the sugar mills could be kept running continuously for twenty-four hours a day.

Going yet further back in time, another royal adventure launched in 1492 by the Catholic monarchs Ferdinand and Isabella of Spain resulted in the discovery of America by Columbus (The Latin American theologian Ignacio Ellacuria says that what was really discovered was the true nature of European civilization![6]). After the initial extermination of the Taino people on the islands of the Bahamas the Spanish presence was instrumental in bringing about the genocidal collapse of all the indigenous civilizations of the continent, an estimated 90 percent of the population and possibly 130 million people. On those who survived the Spanish imposed the *encomienda* system that had been created in Spain during the fifteenth century *reconquista* to reward the conquerors with the labor of particular groups of non-Christian people.[7] An example was the many indigenous people who were conscripted to forced labor in the Potosí silver mines in Bolivia and who, when the local labor ran out, were replaced by African slaves. An estimated thirty thousand such slaves were transported to these mines where they were worked to death. This inhuman treatment produced an estimated 60 percent of all silver mined in the world during the second half of the sixteenth century and represented the main source of Spain's wealth and prestige.

The transportation of slaves from Africa to America had in fact begun with the Portuguese. Again under royal patronage the Portuguese explorer Diogo Cao first sailed up the Congo River in 1483, making contact with the native Kingdom of Kongo. With a view to both commerce and conversion, the Portuguese soon set about exporting slaves to new sugar plantations on the island of São Tomé. Each year twelve to fifteen ships would take between five and ten thousand slaves to the island. The subsequent discovery of America and the establishment of colonies there caused the trade to be extended across the Atlantic.

The purpose of this brief resume of symptomatic colonial activity is to show that the genocidal exploitation of people was not limited nor restricted to a particular country but extented to all the major countries of Europe. It was not spasmodic but systematic across many centuries. It

6. "What was really discovered was the true Spain herself, the reality of Western culture and the church as they were then." Quoted by Jon Sobrino in unpublished lecture notes. The year 1492 is also remembered for the expulsion of the Jews from Spain: the two events are not unconnected.

7. Cervantes argues that the *encomienda* system emerged from the practice of Columbus gathering groups of natives into work parties for mining and clearing land. Cervantes, *Conquistadores*, 61.

was not accidental nor surreptitious but promoted under royal patronage. It was not exceptional behavior but typical of the European explorers who then became colonizers. It was embedded in an expression of the Christian mentality and church of the time. Also it was typically accompanied by a total contempt for the indigenous population, who were regarded as less-than-human "savages" and whose brutal exploitation to the point of genocidal extermination was normative.

From this perspective the Holocaust can be seen as but one element of a wider pattern of typical European behavior, the crescendo of an appalling history. *What makes it distinctive is that the treatment of racial groups hitherto typical in colonial lands now characterized the treatment in Europe of a European ethnic group on racial terms.* This behavior pattern was deeply embedded, persistent across many centuries, and typical of European civilization. It behooves us, therefore, now to explore what exactly were the reasons for this behavior and the attitudes that enabled and promoted it.

The doctrine of discovery

In 1521, during his attempted circumnavigation of the globe, Ferdinand Magellan landed on one of the islands comprising what we now know as the Philippines. He immediately claimed it for king of Spain and planted a cross (still preserved and treasured in the original capital of the Philippines, Cebu City), declaring this would henceforth be a Christian country, later named after the Spanish Catholic monarch Philip II. Magellan was killed a few weeks later in a battle trying to enforce the new faith on the local people, a task that he regarded as a priority. The various aspects of this incident give an insight into the European mindset of the time. Underlying this was the conviction that Christianity, or more specifically Roman Catholicism, was the one true religion, the enforcement of which represented the divine will, legitimized all temporal authority, and by implication controlled legitimacy of title to territory. Any land not under the rule of a Christian monarch was considered to lack legitimate ownership.

This mindset has been called the Doctrine of Discovery.[8] It was exemplified by the Treaty of Tordesillas in 1494 between Spain and Portugal that divided the entire new world between the two monarchs under the binding power of the pope Alexander VI and on the basis of the papal bull *Inter caetera* ("Among other [works]") of 1493. This was the resolution of a

8. Miller, *Discovering.*

dispute between the two kingdoms that had arisen from the previous treaty of Alcacovas in 1479 whereby Portugal's claim to the whole of the new world had been confirmed by the papal bull *Aterni regis* ("Eternal kings") of 1481, which in turn confirmed the decision of previous papal bulls including that of 1455, *Romanus pontifex* ("Roman pontiff"). Underlying these decrees was a belief that the Incarnation of Jesus Christ, the Son of God, had brought about a transfer of authority from God that was now handed to St. Peter and his successors. From this followed the view that infidel rulers could not rule legitimately nor rightfully possess *dominium* over other people.

I mention these now-remote and abstruse details as they are expressive of the mindset that prevailed at the moment of transition, when Europe stood on the threshold of the discovery of a whole new world. They express the mindset of Caeseropapism that underpinned Medieval Christendom as the dominant political theory, and claimed that divine legitimacy was expressed through the church to provide the basis of social order.[9] For Catholic monarchs such as Ferdinand and Isabella there was never any doubt that they were heirs to a tradition going back to the first Christian emperor of Rome, Constantine, whose conversion had providentially joined the universalism of the Christian faith to the universal aspirations of imperial of Rome.[10] This was but an expression of the natural law (*jus gentium*), applicable to all nations that any rational being could recognise and in doing so would find salvation.

It was this mentality that created the template for what has been called "a Persecuting Society" of enforced conformity to doctrinal truth through "deliberate and socially sanctioned violence [that] began to be directed, through established governmental, judicial, and social institutions, against groups of people defined by general characteristics, such as race, religion or way of life."[11] *Here we find the precedent for state-sponsored terror for ideological purposes adopted by European states as a program that would endure to the present day.*

The ambiguity of Christianity

From the outset of the discovery of the New World the treatment of its native population aroused controversy. The increasingly brutal treatment of

9. Cervantes, *Conquistadores*, 81.

10. Cervantes, *Conquistadores*, 123.

11. Moore, *Formation*, 4.

the native Taino population incited the wrath of some Dominican preachers who saw it as contrary to the teachings of the gospel to show mercy and kindess to all. Queen Isabella herself was consistent in requesting that the native people, who were now her subjects, should be treated with respect.[12] Others argued that the natives were incapable of governing themselves, lacking in morals and irrational in nature. Ultimately, the desire for wealth and territorial expansion overcame all opposition. But this did not end the controversy that revealed a fundamental ambiguity of attitudes.

Firstly, Queen Isabella's concern for the Taino people was not all it might seem. Her requirement that they be treated "in the same way as our subjects and vassals" was a view based on the understanding that they were her personal property. This was exactly how she viewed the Jews, but then that did not save them from expulsion from Spain in 1492.

Also implicit in Isabella's understanding was the view that it was only Christianity—understood as Catholicism—or the prospect of conversion that bestowed dignity and rights on her vassals. Again, with reference to Jews, it was precisely because of uncertainty over the genuineness of the conversion of some of them, the *conversos*, that led to the establishment of the Inquisition and finally their complete expulsion from Spain. More significant was the widespread influence of attitudes steeming from the classical world of antiquity, in particular Aristotle, who viewed those who lived beyond the structures of the civilized world to be barbarians and "slaves by nature." This insidious notion that some people lived in a state of "natural slavery" was ubiquitous and an assumption beyond question at the time. Even such a scathing critic as Bartolome de Las Casas, who never ceased to denounce the abuse of the Taino people, thought the solution to their exploitation lay in the substantial importation of African slaves![13]

Clearly this traditional mindset discounted the rights of any non-European and non-Christian people, deeming them an inferior people or "savages" who, like the land they lived on, were subject to expropriation. This led to the creation of the controversial document known as the *Requiremento*. This "required" all natives to submit to the Spanish monarchs immediately and in good faith. Upon taking possession of a new territory the Spanish practice was to read the *Requerimiento*—in Spanish, which would have been unintelligible to the people addressed—declaring the universal authority of the Pope, and the authority that the Spanish monarchs

12. Cervantes, *Conquistadores*, 69–89.
13. Cervantes, *Conquistadores*, 96.

had received from the Pope over this part of the New World for the purpose of colonization and evangelization. The Indians could choose to accept the sovereignty of the Spanish monarchs or suffer forcible submission. Either way their identity could not remain the same. When the Spanish Domini-can Francisco de Vitoria argued against the legitimacy of this document and procedure in his famous lectures on *De Indis* (1532), on the basis that neither pope nor emperor had any inherent right to universal dominion, he caused outrage and was denounced as heretical with calls for his im-prisonment.[14] Together with Hugo Grotius he would subsequently come to be regarded as one of the founding fathers of international law based on a recognition of the law of nations embdded in nature (*jus gentium*), the innate rights of peoples that enabled them to form natural partnerships and by implication the honor due to individuals.[15]

The modern era

From this brief summary we can see how closely colonization and the co-lonial mindset were linked to the Christianity of the time. As early modern European society moved through the Reformation to the Enlightenment attitudes towards "inferior humans" underwent a subtle change, becoming more overtly racist and discriminatory. This era reflected a cultural under-standing based on class prejudices that regarded the poor and uneducated "lower orders" as subhuman. Writing in 1693 Sir Thomas Blount typically opined, "The numerous rabble that seem to have the signatures of man in their faces are but brutes in their understanding . . . 'Tis by the favour of a metaphor we call them men."[16] Writing of the inhabitants of the African southern cape Sir Thomas Herbert noted, "I doubt [i.e., fear] that many of them have no better predecessors than monkeys." This dehumanization of Blacks helped to justify their enslavement and would in time become the basis for the maltreatment of other groups.

For educated men of letters it was above all else cultural attributes, particularly rationality, that distinguished humans from the beasts and sav-ages. In time such attitudes would become scientific and racial theories, but the original basis for this distinction, together with the basic analogue by which the world was viewed, lay in a scriptural understanding of the nature

14. Heer, *Holy Roman*, 171.

15. Cervantes, *Conquistadores*, 269.

16 Thomas, *Man*, 47.

of the "dominion" that God gave to Adam over the animals: as one Jaco-
bean commentator explained, this meant "such a prevailing and possessing
as a master hath over servants." Once this perception had taken hold it
was a short step to treating inferior humans like domestic animals—and
so as property with which one could do as one willed. As one clergyman
remarked in 1703 of the Indians of New England, "They act like wolves and
are to be dealt with as wolves."[17]

When the campaign for the abolition of slavery got under way, it was
led by devout and evangelical Christians whose core conviction was that humans could not be regarded as property. But though their motto "Am I not
your brother?" was scriptuarlly based they could not escape the ambiguity of
usage these same scriptures had given rise to. This is eptiomized by William
Wilberforce and his nemesis, George Hibbert. Both had homes overlooking Clapham Common and both worshipped at Holy Trinity Church on the
Common, even sharing the same pews. Yet it was Hibbert, a slave owner and
MP, who led the fight *against* the abolition of slavery on the basis that slaves
were property and abolition amounted to a fundamental attack on property
rights integral to a sacrosanct social order and enshrined in law, something
of which Parliament could never approve. *Though the memory of Wilberforce
has come to dominate the narrative of moral progress, it was the now-long-for-
gotten Hibbert who prevailed*! Due to his successful lobbying and campaigning Parliament would abolish slavery only if compensation was paid to the
owners, and contrary to their convictions, it was only when the abolitionists
accepted this principle (insisted upon by Hibbert) that slavery was abolished.
This resulted in the largest amount of compensation ever paid out in British
history, twenty millon pounds (£16 billion in today's money)—all of which
went to the slave owners for their personal benefit.[18]

Whilst this drama of emancipation was unfolding at the heart of the
British government in England, it seems astounding that on the other side
of the world in Tasmania this same government was conniving in an act
of genocide. There is a tragic irony in the fact that the governor, George
Arthur, who led what is now regarded as the genocidal "Black War" against
the Tasmanians, was a highly principled man with evangelical religious
beliefs who had been involved in the abolition of the slave trade and had a
real concern for the well-being of the aborigines whom he believed should
be treated with "amity and kindness." However, this concern also included

17 Thomas, *Man*, 46.
18. Olusoga, *Black and British*, 199–232.

a belief in the inevitable disappearance of "inferior" indigenous races in the wake of progressive European Christian civilization that would save the "savages" from themselves and provide a means to their eternal salvation. As the Secretary of State, George Murray, wrote to Arthur, "conciliation" was a means "to reclaim the Natives from their original savage life and render them sensible to the advantages . . . of the the religion and civilization" of the British.[19] Should this be resisted, then the alternative would inevitably be compulsion, if necessary by military force.

Such an approach had all the hallmarks of the Spanish *Requerimiento*: a "choice" between assimilation or extermination—which was really no choice at all. Accompanying the military expedition of the Black War was a concerted missionary effort that ultimately proved more successful in engaging with the aborigines and gave the whole struggle something of the religious flavour of the *reconquista*, even providing a model for further use throughout the empire. Being forced from their lands, the aborigines were "removed from danger [of being shot by settlers] and placed in safety at a suitable asylum provided for their reception and where they are brought under moral and religious instructon."[20] The ambiguity, if not contradiction, at the heart of this policy was that "the 'progress' of the island's peoples was as much a commitment to [their] eradication as the violence of the men on the Tsmanian frontier who openly practiced and preached extermination."[21] In other words implicit in the vision of progress was an understanding that was genocidal: that the "savage races" would "disappear at the approach of civilization like the dew before the morning sun."[22]

In ways that clearly anticipate Nazi attitudes, the extermination of the Tasmanian aborigines was widely welcomed in British society not only as an example of "progress" in which "inferior" people were destined to diasppear before a higher (Christian) civilization, but that their extermination exemplified an entirely natural evolutionary process—a sort of "clearing out"—destined to be repeated elsewhere in the Empire and beyond.[23] This sort of thinking became increasingly widespread across Eu-

19. Quoted in Lawson, *Last Man*, 75.

20. The surviving aborigines were transported to a settlement on Flinder's Island to the north of Tasmania. None survived what was viewed as their inevitable fate.

21. Lawson, *Last Man*, 22.

22. Quoted in Lawson, *Last Man*, 123.

23. A celebrity of the stature of Charles Dickens could write, in *Household Words* (1853), in an article entitled "The Noble Savage," that "I call a savage something that is highly desirable to be civilized off the face of the earth . . . and the world will be all the

rope—for example, the the French *mission civilisatice* and German search for *Lebensraum*—that would soon be buttressed by more "scientific" racial theories. *Within the context of such thinking an event like Belsen can be seen not as exceptional but almost inevitable.*

Racism and the Holocaust

The ambiguity in moral attititude and the assumption of the assimilation of various groups into a progressive civilization found expression in Europe particularly with regard to the status of Jews. It was the mindset of a progressive modernity that gave rise to the *haskalah* movement or "Jewish Enlightenment" among leading Jewish scholars of Central and Eastern Europe in the century following the 1770s. In essence this was an attempted acculturation of traditional Judaism to accommodate modern European thinking. A typical product of this mentality was Theodore Ratisbonne (1802–84) who together with his brother Alphonse (1814–84) saw no future for Judaism in the modern world and converted to Roman Catholicism so as to achieve fuller integration into French society, founding the Congregation of Our Lady of Sion (1843) to further this aim.[24] Whilst in many ways benign and well intentioned, such assimilationist thinking had a darker penumbra, for it assumed that there was no future outside a putative, providentially-led, progressive civilization of the West. It was this assumption that lay at the heart of the colonial mentality: that inferior native peoples would either become Westernized or cease to exist, and that resistance to such an inevitability was pointless and should not be tolerated. One could go further and say that inherent in such a way of thinking was a genocidal imperative. *It was exactly this mentality that underlay the convictions of the Nazis who sought the remaking of mankind in their own image, employing eugenics to control and transform what it meant to be human on the basis of what they saw to be scientific principles.*

So deeply buried in Western thinking are the ideological roots of genocide that their "disentanglement" has been difficult even when attempted. In a statement commemorating the seventy-fifth anniversary of the ending

---

better when his place knows him no more." Quoted in Lawson, *Last Man*, 152.

24. The congregation is now dedicated to the promotion and Christian-Jewish understanding. By the late nineteenth century confidence in the *haskalah* was being replaced by the rise of Zionism and the demands of Jews for the return of their ancestral homeland—exactly what the Tasmanian aborigines had unsuccessfully fought for!

of World War II the German conference of bishops condemned the complicity of their predecessors during the Nazi era for their failure to oppose the war of annihilation started by Germany or the crimes the regime committed: the bishops' statement acknowledged the church's "failing not only to remember its role, but also of not owning up to it." Bishop Batzing, the chair of the conference, went on to recognize that "terrifying antisemitism is widespread, even here in Germany" and warned that "those who come later must confront history, in order to learn from it."[25] A similar sentiment inspired the act of "repentance" by the Anglican Church. In an unprecedented one-hundred-page report (November 2019) the church confessed that "Christians have been guilty of promoting and fostering negative stereotypes of Jewish people that have contributed to grave suffering and injustice" and that Christian teaching provided a "fertile seedbed for murderous antisemitism."[26] As with the Tasmanians, the darker implications of belief in a "progressive" Christian civilization were not always immediately apparent and only in retrospect have they become clearer.

Many find it difficult either to express or accept these sentiments but it is exactly this reluctance that made such belated acts of atonement so necessary. As the distinguished church historian Diarmaid MacCulloch wrote, in a letter to *The Times*, "The Nazis might have been hostile to established Christianity, but all the antisemitic tropes and vocabulary, all the monstrous shapes in people's minds, had been put there by Christianity."[27] *That the Nazis were handed an entire ideological backing for the Holocaust strikes at the very heart of the traditional understanding of European civilization and, as with slavery and genocide, its responsibility.*

Seventy-five years on

We should be both dismayed and shocked that after decades and even centuries of inhumanity these present-day apologies for past evils alert us to the fact that little has really changed. That after the horrors of the Holocaust

---

25. A far more wide-ranging response to antisemitism had been made fifty-five years previously in the groundbreaking Vatican II document *Nostra Aetate* that for the first time confronted the legacy of two thousand years of hatred. Unfortunately, many of its implications have not been followed through: for example, the prejudicial terms "Old" Testament is still in common use and goes unchallenged as a normative expression.

26. Burgess, "Church's Mea Culpa."

27. MacCulloch, "Church's Apology."

antisemitism should still be widespread and rising across Europe as well as a major source of controversy within the British Labor Party. That a century and a half after the emancipation of slaves in the US and decades after the Civil Rights movement it should still be necessary to assert that "Black Lives Matter" in a society marked by overbearing and asphyxiating white privilege. That in the 1950s nurses recruited from the Caribbean in order to save the National Health Service from collapse should have been subject to discrimination and racial profiling and that sixty years later members of their families should have been subjected to the government-led "hostile environment" policy that threatened many with deportation. That in 2015 it was necessary to pass the Modern Slaver Act to address the circumstance of approximately ten thousand residents of Britain. That the Church of England should find it expedient to start checking its memorials for racism and questioning the overly "white" representation of Jesus. That despite gestures and declarations nothing much seems to have changed.

Emancipation did not lead to an improvement in the lives of former slaves, as abolitionists had intended, but rather a deterioration in their conditions as plantations closed and the former slaves struggled to provide for themselves. None of the vast amounts of compensation paid to the slave owners ever benefited their former dependents; instead it was invested for personal profit in British enterprises like the railways and thus enhanced national prosperity. Some even complained of being "victimized" by underpayment. Rather than a means of addressing a former wrong or a step in the direction of a more just restructuring of a society that English slavers had artfully contrived, abolition merely served as a symbol of self-justification and a foil to deflect further criticism as ruthless commercial exploitation continued in other forms: the Tasmanian genocide is a case in point. What was missing was any fundamental change of thinking.

In a similar way the defeat of Nazism and blaming Germany for the Holocaust conveniently exonerates the wider civilization that made it possible. It makes us feel good rather than promoting the kind of fundamental change of mentality that Bishop Batzing called for. Given all that happened in the war on Nazism, it is always a surprise to realize that the place where its racist tenets survived longest was actually in Australia and the policies of the British government towards the aborigines. In 1951 the euphemistically-titled Aborigines Protection Board—also known as the Aborigines Welfare Board—was set up with the purpose of assimilating aborigines into white society by removing children from families with the ultimate intention of the destruction of aboriginal society. This built on the well-established policy of the Christian missions, controlled by the churches, that had existed for over a century with the purpose of instilling Christian belief among the aborigines, denying access to traditional lands and sacred sites, in order to facilitate assimilation.[28] Such policies lasted up to the 1960s.[29] Though we condemn the inhuman behavior of the Nazis and their perverted ideology, the treatment of the aborigines, guided by "benign" Christian principles, had the same ultimate purpose: that a whole people should ultimately cease to exist.[30] *Quelle difference?*

This willing amnesia conveniently allows inconvenient truths to be brushed aside and old mentalities to remain unchallenged: despite the words and good intentions little really changes, as with Lincoln's Proclamation 95 emancipating all black slaves in 1862. This brought about very little real change and has subsequently been denounced as little more than a grandstanding gesture for self-serving political ends. Discrimination, brutality, and terror continued and even worsened with the end of Reconstruction and the rise of the Ku Klux Klan. And on the centenary of the Tulsa Massacre (1921) the President of the United States chose to revisit the city on his campaign trail with a message of "Law and Order," respect for property and the incongruous claim that the "Black Lives Matter" movement is a form of terrorism! *Plus ca change?*

28. The Aborigines' Protection Society that emerged in the 1830s assumed that the context of its work would be that having lost their land the Aborigines would be in settlements and separated from their children. This was the context for Phillip Noyce's brilliant film *Rabbit Proof Fence* of 2002, set in 1931, with Kenneth Branagh playing A. O. Neville, the official "Protector of Aborigines." The film caused immense controversy over the treatment of Aborigines and the children of the so-called Lost Generation. Attempts to discredit the history behind the film failed simply because it was demonstrably true.

29. The recent discovery of mass graves across Canada on the sites of former mission schools for indigenous people has shocked the nation. Many of these schools were run by the Catholic church under a government policy that only ended in 1996 and under which over four thousand children died from a combination of abuse, disease, malnutrition, suicide, and poor healthcare that has now been officially acknowledged as "cultural genocide." There have been calls for a papal apology. "Discovery of 750."

30. Nor is this merely of historic interest. Almost exactly the same policy of the extermination of indigenous people is currently being advocated for the Indians of the Amazon rainforest under the administration of President Bolsonaro with the same legitimating reasons.

Chapter 3

The Reality of Antisemitism

Uncovering the roots of the longest hatred

CONCERN ABOUT ANTISEMITISM SEEMS to be constantly in the news these days. Nationally, much of this is related to its resurgence in the Labor Party. This is both surprising and disturbing: surprising, because Jews have always had a distinctive presence in the Labor Party; disturbing, because of the party's apparent inability to deal with the issue. An expression of this concern by Jews themselves was expressed in the recent elections in the desertion of the party by many Jewish voters: seven in ten Jews who voted Labour in 2015 did not do so in 2019, and 94 percent of British Jews did not vote Labour in 2019.

But it is a bigger issue than just the Labor Party. In Hungary the government of Viktor Orban has led the attack on the financier and philanthropist George Soros and the institutes he funds that has all the hallmarks of historic Jewish conspiracy theory while resurgent antisemitism in Poland focuses on the malicious stereotypes of the money-grubbing Jew. An exhibition at the Jewish Museum in London (2019) entitled *Jews, Money, Myth*, picks up on the potent mix of ancient prejudice and political hostility which, while looking contemporary, would not be out of place anywhere in Europe over the last thousand years. In other words, antisemitism seems an endemic feature of Western society and European civilization since its foundation that continues to reoccur.

But why is this? In reviewing the exhibition for *The Times* Daniel Finkelstein reflected on its purported roots: "Towards the end of the 11th century . . . there arose a movement to reform and renew Christianity. The aim was to purify the religion, stressing 'apostolic' poverty. And Jews, already thought worldly and wealthy, became the target of this drive."[1] Having myself been a member of such an apostolic order (the Order of Prémontré founded in 1121) for nearly thirty years, and having spent much of my life inquiring into this seminal period of European history, I believe this explanation of the origins of antisemitism both misinformed and misleading: it confuses coincidence with causation and so does not enable us to get to grips with the issue.

The essential background to this period was *two* new historical developments: one was the revival of the economy of Western Europe after the turmoil of the Dark Ages, giving rise to the growth of town populations particularly along the Rhine; the second was the epic clash between the German Emperor Henry IV and the papacy of Gregory VII for the control of church lands, known as the Investiture Controversy: ultimately this was a bid for supreme political power in Europe. It was a contest in which the papacy triumphed, epitomized by the dramatic submission of the emperor to the pope at Canossa in 1077.

The apostolic movement that appeared at this time in towns of the Rhineland was a feature of the spiritual renewal taking place among new urban populations (St. Norbert, the founder of Prémontré, was himself from the Rhenish town of Xanten). It was a searching for a more authentic kind of Christianity as found in the communal life of the early church, or at least how it was imagined, but crucially it was a lay movement that grew up outside the established hierarchical structures of the church. With the power-hungry papacy set on domination of society all such movements were viewed with suspicion and deemed potentially subversive or heretical. As such their followers had an option of accepting an approved canonical form (regularization) or being suppressed. The controversial burning to death of the popular preacher Ramihrd of Esquerchin in 1077 by the Bishop of Cambrai, who Ramihrd had accused of simony and avarice, was an indication of the very real occupational hazard of dissent.[2] He would not be the last.

A persecuting society

It was in this context that an unprecedented culture of persecution developed, orchestrated by the ecclesiastical authority of the official church. The

1. Finkelstein, "Next Time."
2. Moore, *War*, 90–91.

emergence of this new reality has been chronicled in depth by the eminent medieval historian R. I. Moore in *The War on Heresy: Faith and Power in Medieval Europe*.[3] Those suspected of heresy—deemed "the enemies of Christ"—were systematically persecuted not just for their supposedly deviant beliefs but for the threat that they posed to social order. The two new instruments to enforce conformity that emerged at this time were the Inquisition and Crusades. Though the memory of the Crusades is dominated by the epochal clash with Islam, in fact, the initial purpose of its originator, Gregory VII, was to enforce conformity to orthodox Catholicism in Europe—as in the Albigensian Crusade—and the expansion of Christendom into the pagan lands of the Slavic east—as in the Teutonic Crusades. The great Austrian historian Friedrich Heer outlined this development in his book *The Holy Roman Empire*,[4] while the French historian Monique Zerner and her team of researchers in their detailed studies of the archives of the Inquisition revealed the toxic culture of suspicion that, like the later witch hunts, Stalinist show trials, and McCarthy's "exposure" of communist subversion, found what it wanted to find; so much so that the threat of the fabled Medieval Manichee can be now seen as little more than the product of clerical paranoia based on mainly imagined and fabricated sources.

The consequence of this toxic cultural mix was what Moore described in a ground-breaking book *The Formation of a Persecuting Society* as the creation of a classificatory system of "enemies": "a single account of the victim as enemy of God and society, which might be transferred at will to any object, either a class of persons already existing, such as Jews, whom it might seem desirable or convenient to persecute, or a new one, such as sodomites or witches, which, by an act of classification might be invented for the purpose."[5] Thus was created a model of persecution that came to characterise European society down to the modern times. This *started* with so called heretics but *spread* to ensnare Jews, sodomites, lepers, Muslims, and women in general. In other words, members of popular religious movements and devotees of the apostolic life were just as likely to end up being burnt at the stake or cut down by the sword as Jews and Muslims, and indeed were the primary targets of aggression.

An early example of how these various strands coalesced came in 1063 when a group of knight crusaders were making their way through

3. Moore, *War*.

4. Heer, *Holy Roman*.

5. Moore, *Formation*, 160.

southwestern France to fight the Moors in Spain. When they reached Narbonne, the archbishop left the Jewish quarter unprotected, which the knights proceeded to attack, to the dismay of the rest of the citizens. This was just a harbinger of far, far worse things to come for all in the escalation of savagery that culminated in the Albigensian Crusade of 1208. At the siege of Beziers in 1209, in response to a question as to how the heretics would be distinguished, the papal legate, Arnald-Amaury, infamously is said to have declared, "Kill them all, God will know his own"—subsequently fifteen thousand men, women, and children were slaughtered.[6]

The mentality and motivation behind such violence is difficult for the modern mind to assess. The recent global outpouring of grief over the fire at Notre Dame was an expression of concern that this monument of human creativity, expressive of the supreme capabilities of the human spirit, might be lost. But it is well to remember that this building, magnificent as it is, is also an icon of a world shrouded in dark shadows, of endemic religious fanaticism, paranoia, and extreme violence: the great western façade of the cathedral was being completed as the Albigensian Crusade reached its brutal denouement. I was going to write that this is not our world but sadly in many ways it still is.

The gothic world of faith (Christendom) was built on an understanding of a much earlier world recorded in the Gospels and New Testament that in many ways was eccentric and culturally distorted. An example is the bizarre use of the gospel parable of the wheat and tares (Matt 13:24–30), in which the weeds are gathered up at harvest time to be burnt.[7] This was used to justify the burning of heretics who were now understood as the tares and enemies of Christ. Such an allegorical reading of the parables had become widespread in the medieval church but was itself a fundamentally distorted reading of this particular Jewish literary genre.[8] Ironically, modern textual criticism disputes the dominical authenticity of this particular reading that is now regarded as a later elaboration. In origin a parable was a short, pithy saying or metaphor intended to provoke thought. Though not necessarily

---

6. Baigent and Leigh, *Inquisition*, 12.

7. Crossan, *Power of Parable*, 8.

8. The use of allegory or typology was developed by Origen, Augustine, and other early church teachers as a way of distinguishing the "new" from the "old" testaments and the truths of scripture previously hidden from view.

short there is a general acceptance that the briefer the saying of Jesus the more authentic it is likely to be—the embellishments came later.[9]

That such a distorted and perverse interpretation of the gospel teaching could be used to justify the burning of heretics was a barbarity that suddenly reemerged after six hundred years of church history.[10] It revealed an obsessive literalism and increasing obsession with the graphic details of the torments of hell that became a defining feature of the gothic world of faith. After all, if this is how God treats sinners, why should we act differently on earth? Another typical expression of the malign nature of this world are the two statues—*Ecclesia* and *Synagoga*—that stand on the great West Front of Notre Dame, as on cathedrals across Europe. The statues depict the triumphant church and a blindfolded, broken synagogue. Here is the symbolism of a prejudice that goes back to the very origins of the church and Christianity itself.

A call for change

In light of the horrendous events of the twentieth-century Holocaust we can no longer view such symbols of our civilization or its foundational religious values with a benign equanimity. In 1948, while the ashes of the Holocaust were still smouldering, the distinguished French historian, Jules Isaac, produced a six-hundred-page study of antisemitism and Christianity in which he analysed the distorted picture of Jesus' attitude towards Israel which had grown out of the Gospels in what he called "the teaching of contempt," setting Christians against Jews. Controversial as the book *Jesus and Israel* was, in 1960 Isaac was granted a private meeting with Pope John XXIII in which he presented a copy of his work. Soon after the pope put the issue of antisemitism on the agenda of the forthcoming Vatican Council which in turn led to one of its most radical and challenging documents, *Nostra Aetate,* which set out to restore the relationship of Jews and Christians after two thousand years. Among other things, this document modified the Good Friday liturgy by dropping the reference to the "perfidious Jews" and courageously exonerated Jews of the charge of deicide, for it was such a charge that lay at the heart of the enmity with which Jews were viewed. In short, for the

9. Ehrman, *Jesus before the Gospels.*

10. The Theodosian Code of 438 CE that incorporated the edict of Constantius II of 341 CE decreed that any Jew who attacked another Jew for converting to Christianity was to be burnt to death. Cf. Ehrman, *The Triumph of Christianity.* 269

first time, the Church acknowledged that it had been fundamentally wrong in its attitude to and teachings about Jews.

However, this should have only been the beginning. If the Gospels provided the basis for a hatred of "the Jews"—*hoi Ioudaioi/* Judeans—the question remains of how this came about. After all, Jesus was a Jew, as were all his first followers. Over recent decades scholars, such as Geza Vermes and John Dominic Crossan, have been reappraising not only the Jewish context of the whole ministry and life of Jesus but the way our understanding of his life has been shaped by preconceptions of the evangelists. Though generally read with a high degree of literalism, the Gospels were anything but straightforward reports of a life. Crucially they were *interpretations* of a life viewed through the lens of *midrash* or commentary on the Jewish scriptures. How this was understood was in turn guided by the context in which they were written, for, like all writing, the motivation comes from the life-situation *(sitz im leben)* and concerns of the writer.

In a challenging study of this whole context James Carroll, in his book *Christ Actually: The Son of God for the Secular Age,* has argued that the defining events shaping the formation of the Gospels were the three Roman campaigns against Jewish uprising, beginning with that of Vespasian and Titus which led to the destruction of the temple in 70 CE and culminated with the genocidal campaign of Hadrian in 135 CE, which was carried out with unprecedented ferocity leaving over six hundred thousand dead and the whole of Judea desolate.[11] This would be Rome's "final solution" to its troublesome province. Part of Carroll's thesis is that the first generation of followers of Jesus—not yet called Christians—sought to distance themselves from the Jewish zealots who had provoked the wrath of Rome. This was particularly true of gentile converts who lived in other provinces of the empire—St. Paul, for example, was very clear on the need for submission to Roman authority in his letter to the Romans 13:1–7. The result was that little or no criticism of Rome can be found in the Gospels being composed at this time that may have been seen as cause for indictment. Instead, there was a very clear rejection of Jewish practices and the cult centered on the temple, now utterly destroyed. Almost laughably, Pontius Pilate, who in a brutal age was notorious for his unrestrained savagery and was even stripped of his prefecture for his "excessive cruelty" (Philo), is presented in the Gospels as a retiring figure reluctantly swayed by the crowd.

11. Carroll, *Christ Actually.*

The tap-root of hatred

But this is not the whole story. The scripture exegete Bart Ehrman locates the animosity to "the Jews" even earlier, to the very nature of the post-resurrection community of the followers of Jesus.[12] For Ehrman the central issue is the Jewish understanding of the Messiah, the nature of the apocalyptic teaching of Jesus and who Jesus thought he was. Central to the teaching of Jesus was an understanding of the imminence of the kingdom of God that was also a central feature of contemporary Jewish apocalyptic thinking. But everything in this tradition pointed to the coming of the messianic Kingdom as a triumphant event. Insofar as Jesus thought of himself as the Messiah nothing in the Jewish tradition anticipated the failure of the crucifixion; as Ehrman writes, "The Messiah was to be a figure of great strength who overwhelmed the enemy and set up God's kingdom; but Jesus was squashed by the enemy. For most Jews, this was decisive enough. Jesus wasn't the Messiah, more or less by definition."[13]

But those who accepted there had been a resurrection event rejected this understanding and claimed that some passages of scripture, such as Isaiah 53 and Psalm 22, indicated the Messiah would suffer and die and be raised from the dead; a view rejected by most Jews, as these were not part of the messianic tradition. As a result, a rancorous division opened between different groups of Jews that soon escalated to outright hostility and hatred. So much so that by the time John's Gospel came to be written it could declare that "the Jews" were not the children of God but the offspring of Satan, murderers and liars (John 8:42–44). Thus, the foundation of future antisemitism was laid, embedded in gospel truth and teaching.

In this context the question arises of how reliable the Gospels actually are in relaying the original teachings of Jesus. Close textual readings, such as those carried out by the Jesus Seminar of scripture scholars and the scholar John Dominic Crossan (in *The Power of Parable: How Fiction by Jesus Became Fiction about Jesus*) reveal a process of editorial transformation taking place over time.[14] Whilst negative references to "the Jews" appear sixteen times in the first three Gospels, when it comes to the fourth Gospel of John this has escalated to seventy-one. Even *within* Gospels there seems to be inconsistency. In the Gospel of Matthew, for example, the serene Beatitudes of

12. Ehrman, *How Jesus Became God*, 112–24.
13. Ehrman, *How Jesus Became God*, 117.
14. Crossan, *Power of Parable*.

the teaching of Jesus at the beginning of the Gospel are later followed by the vitriolic denunciations of the Pharisees, totally negating their spirit. Similarly, the peaceful Messiah who in the Gospels rides on a donkey becomes, in the Book of Revelation, the vengeful lord of all who rides a war horse steeped in blood—incidentally, the same description as given to Hadrian's troops "who went on killing until their horses were steeped in blood to their nostrils."[15] By the time the last Gospel, John, was written, "the Jews" have become polarized into the defining oppositional antithesis of Christians; Jesus himself was no longer seen as a Jew but rather a deracinated deity. It is John who provides the Passion story read out in the Good Friday liturgy, and the Johannine writings would provide the texts read out in the Spanish public burnings (*autos-da-fé*) as Jews were led to the stake. These texts continue to poison minds with fictions presented as facts.

Building on this scriptural tradition were the writings of Justin Martyr (c. 100–165 CE) who was the first of a group of writers regarded as "apologists" for the new creed of Christianity. He is regarded as "the first intellectual and professional scholar in the church."[16] His family background was Greek and he viewed the scriptures through a Hellenic theo-philosophical mentality that posited a pre-existent *logos* that had been shaping the prophecies of scripture in preparation for a final revelation of "the word" in Jesus. This immensely persuasive view effectively stripped the Bible of its historical context and deemed the original covenant between God and the Jewish people had ended because of their failure to recognise the divinity of Jesus. In effect the Jews had been abandoned by God and superseded by Christians: the "old" covenant (testament) had now been replaced by a "new" covenant (testament). Here we find the classic rationale for antisemitism that would characterise Christianity for the next two millennia.

Time for change

What is apparent in all of this, and in the light of the new attitude encouraged by *Nostra Aetate,* is how much remains to be done in addressing the way in which antisemitism is rooted in the traditional teachings of the church and presentation of the Gospels. Rooting out this poisonous ideology needs nothing less than a radical reappraisal the foundational documents of Christianity, the Gospels. That this has not happened in the

15 Carroll, *Christ Actually*, 54.

16. Ehrman, *How Jesus Became God*, 330.

church is in part a reflection of the conservative backlash to the changes of the Vatican Council in the pontificate of John Paul II, for whom the Church was in essence a perfect and infallible institution even if some times its officiates were flawed. For him there was no need for apologies: renewal was merely a matter of representation or repackaging transcendental and timeless truth. Tellingly, his use of scripture in official pronouncements was remarkable for its uncritical use of texts, used in the traditional way as a resource for pious reflection and defence of doctrine.

But the new attitude of critical textual appraisal also raises a more challenging problem that in a time of resurgent fundamentalisms is common to all religions whose beliefs rest on texts from a distant past: how to use ancient texts in the light of modern understanding and sensibilities. The list of issues this concerns is significant: the status of women, the basis of morality, the status of alternative relationships, the nature of gender and sexuality, the relativity of multiculturalism, etc., etc. So deeply ingrained are some patterns of thought that, like antisemitism, they become opaque to us—we just don't see them. This is perhaps part of the explanation for the behavior of a man like Jeremy Corbin, who seemingly couldn't see anything antisemitic in the blatant caricature of the cabal of international financiers in the Mear One mural, or the reprinting of the book of John Hobson on *Imperialism* from 1902 that he benignly reviewed as "brilliant" without further comment of its view that this "peculiar race" of Jews controlled Europe. Similarly illustrative is the remarkable lack of judgement shown by the *New York Times* in its cartoon representation of the Prime Minister of Israel as a dog. Even the ecumenically-minded Pope Francis could reiterate offhandedly the trope of not having the courage to go against "the tide"—of Jews— "to save Jesus" during a 2013 mass in Brazil. It is a tragic irony that views that were shaped in the Roman holocaust of the first century should have survived so as to become instrumental in bringing about another holocaust twenty centuries later. Such is the potency of this hatred.

That it could last so long is in no small part due to the depth with which it has become ingrained in our ways of thinking and formative institutions, particularly the churches. Nor does it stand alone. In another of those paradoxical distortions of the original teachings of Jesus we see that with the rise of antisemitic sentiments there is a parallel rise in misogyny, of a morbid suspicion of femininity by what the scholar Elizabeth Florenza described as the "kyriarchy" of lordly male domination and even hatred towards women as a corrupting influence—"the devil's gateway," as St. Augustine would have us understand the descendants of Eve. One of the standard caricatures of Jews across the ages, apart from their love of money, was of their effeminacy, a view that also legitimated the subservience of women. In this Hitler proved very much a traditionalist for, as the historian Claudia Koonz pointed out in her extensive study of women and Nazi politics, *Mothers in the Fatherland,* two goals over which Hitler never wavered were the domestication of women and the extermination of the Jews.[17]

In the final days of Nazism one of its last victims, Dietrich Bonhoeffer, sat in his prison cell pondering what Christianity meant for the contemporary world in the light of the terrible events he was experiencing. Though he had no clear answers he realized that a seismic change of understanding of our beliefs was needed, the sort of epistemic change that rarely happens in history, such as the moral revolution that took place in the sixth century BCE in the so-called Axial period. Such a rethinking today must include everything that the Western world and its civilization has stood for, its values and way of life. The fact that antisemitism, right wing populism, nationalist exclusivity, and religious fundamentalism are still resurgent shows we have not yet succeeded in this task.

17. Koonz, *Mothers.*

Chapter 4

Christianity and Colonialism

Transformations and reclamation

WE LIVE IN A postcolonial world. The world created largely in the nineteenth century by the global expansion of powerful European states is now a thing of the past. Under the aegis of the European Union, Europe is a shadow of its former confident and assertive self as it struggles to coordinate cohesive policies and effective responses to powerful authoritarian regimes—in particular China but also Russia, Turkey, and increasingly India (China's President Xi has warned off Britain attempting to reassert colonial influence over Hong Kong and President Modi has likened the aspirations of his Hindu nationalist party, the BJP, to a "fight for freedom" from colonial domination). Indeed, just about any attempt by European states to assert an influence in foreign affairs is susceptible to the charge of "colonial meddling." This extends even to attempts to promote what may be broadly regarded as European or Western values such as democracy, the rule of law, freedom of speech, and human rights. One might also add Christianity to this list.

In the previous chapter I attempted to identify how European Christianity became an oppressive force, a persecuting society, and, with its global expansion, an incubator of racism. Accompanying the conviction of being the bearers of a divinely revealed truth was a concomitant sense of mission to make others aware of this and accept it—if necessary, by force. It has sometimes been pointed out that this program of missionary expansion was most successful when combined with military intervention, as in the Americas and Africa; but that where such military support was lacking, as in China and Japan, it failed. Be this as it may, the general attitude of both colonizers and missionaries was that the people they commonly regarded with thinly disguised contempt as "savages" needed to be saved from themselves and that in this process of salvation their own cultures and "barbarous practices" would inevitably wither away. As I have previously shown, this was clearly the case in the colonization of Australia and Tasmania.

In all of these cases religion and culture were clearly intertwined in one cohesive force: Christian beliefs and values had become inseparable from such European political institutions as the imperialism of Roman Caeseropapism, a feudal understanding of kingship, and the genesis of the nation state. In a fascinating and detailed study by the scripture scholar Bart Ehrman, on how a small Jewish sect comprising of a few dozen followers of Jesus triumphed over the Roman Empire and Classical paganism in the space just three centuries, he points to a unique and decisive feature of the new religion, its missionary zeal: "The evangelizing mission of the church was unparalleled and unprecedented . . . [it] became a standard feature of the Christian movement."[1] Whereas the focus of paganism was on the *cultus*, or ritual enactments to a pantheon of gods, Christianity was defined by its *kerygma*, its urgent and exclusive message that Jesus was the Lord and Savior of mankind, the Christ.[2]

Initially this missionary zeal expressed itself in a discrete and personalized way. This all changed with the coming of Christian emperors who united missionary zeal with imperial force. The Theodosian Code (381 CE) comprehensively outlawed pagan practices and public cults, ordering the destruction of pagan shrines and even supressing deviant or "heretical" forms of Christianity.[3] The potent combination of belief and power enhanced the status of the emperor in a way that soon became noticed by other aspiring monarchs; for example, in the Western world the Merovingians saw the political kudos bestowed by claiming "descent" from the biblical kings through the holy anointing of the Church.[4] This culminated in the formation of the Holy Roman Empire under Charlemagne (800 CE).[5] As the historian Hywel Williams wrote, "The regal milieu of the Carolingians and the nation at their command seemed therefore to be the culminating

1. Ehrman, *Triumph of Christianity*, 117.

2. I investigate in more detail the nature of this pivotal moment of transition in the following chapter.

3. Ehrman, *Triumph of Christianity*. 251–53.

4. Finkelstein and Silberman, *David and Solomon*.

5. Ullmann, *Carolingian Renaissance*.

expression of the meaning embodied in the histories of ancient Judaism, of imperial Rome and of early Christianity."[6] That this was deemed to be by providential design and a work of divine election was now part of the sacred mantra of kingship that was not to be questioned.

This understanding by Charlemagne of his divine calling to spread Christianity found one expression in the "mission" to convert the Saxons that would now be described as an act of genocide. In the end a whole country was ravaged and tens of thousands of people perished; in one massacre alone, at Verden (782 CE), 4500 Saxons were beheaded in one day. Such savagery could be amply justified by a literal reading of the Bible with reference to such texts as the Book of Judges, in which the Chosen People conquered the Promised Land.[7] This will be by no means the last reference to the providential destiny of "chosen people" in the annals of Europe's nations. Centuries later, the SS Commander Heinrich Himmler, himself a Saxon, would erect a monument to the memory of those killed at Verden. Such precedents had foreboding portents, distant events casting long and dark shadows; what began in the First Reich would be continued in the Third.

A campaigning and colonizing church

The relationship of church and state was symbiotic, benefiting both parties: the emperor conquered new territories and the church converted the inhabitants. The process of settlement and colonization was thus a shared process: "A missionary Church operating in close association with the conquering Carolingians was therefore an established feature of dynastic policy even before Charlemagne's ascent to the throne."[8] Neighboring kings, such as in Denmark and Poland, soon realized not only the status Christianity could bestow but also the security it could provide to their position; the impending threat of a militant missionary empire on their borders, should they remain pagan, was not to be ignored. And we should be clear that subsequent missionary expansion to the east was not just a matter of conversion but

6. Williams, *Emperor of the West*, 58.

7. It is important to state that, as with so much of the biblical narrative such as the kingdom of David and Solomon, that the conquest of Canaan as recorded in the Book of Judges is almost entirely fictitious. Cf Finkelstein and Silberman, *The Bible Unearthed*.

8. Williams, *Emperor of the West*, 74.

territorial expansion and colonization.[9] There was a fine line to be drawn between evangelization and extermination. As one chronicler of the time, Saxo Grammaticus, so perceptively recorded, when describing the ministry of the Danish bishop, Absolon of Roskilde (1158–92), "He acted the pirate as much as the prelate. For it is no less religious to repulse the enemies of the public faith than to uphold its ceremonies."[10]

Much of the colonization and transformation of central Europe was made possible by monasteries. This may seem paradoxical; after all, the nature of monasticism was to turn its back on civil society and withdraw to search for solitude in remote places. But the solitude and the cultivation of the wilderness would soon give way to settlements. In doing so monasticism transformed the nature of Christianity itself, and the monastic movement in Europe's so-called Dark Age, pioneered by charismatic religious leaders, led to what I call the "monasticization" of the church. As a result of the spread of monasticism in Europe, by the tenth century Christianity had been transformed almost beyond recognition from its original format. Whereas once it was an inclusive but secretive domestic urban movement it now came to be characterized by two distinct spheres or "orders" (religious and lay), monumental sacred buildings, elaborate liturgical and ritual practices from which the laity were excluded, and an all-powerful male, celibate, and sacral hierarchy. This transformation and division was epitomized by the erection of "Rood Screens" in churches to ensure the laity were kept at a distance from the sacred space of the sanctuary. Now the modest table of communion presided over by a minister or presbyter (female or male) using the common tongue was replaced by the altar of sacrifice at which a priest enacted a sacred ritual intoned in an arcane language (Latin); the "old" testament had usurped the new as the priest literally turned his back on the people who could now only stand and watch the quasi-magical rites from afar. Even the ordinary clergy increasingly became "regularized," i.e., coerced, to live as communal groups of "canons"—such was the result of the widely influential rule of Chrodegang, Bishop of Metz (c. 742–66 CE), the *Regula canonicorum*.[11]

The significance of the nature of this fundamental transformation of Christianity cannot be overemphasized, though it is often overlooked! The

9. Christiansen, *Northern Crusades.*

10. Christiansen, *Northern Crusades,* 61.

11. Chrodegang served as chancellor for Charles Martel and had significant political influence.

dichotomy in two forms of ritual and structural celebration that charac-terizes the history of human religious experience can be expressed in the difference between the communal *circle* of celebration, gathered around the table of remembrance, and ceremonial *line* of ritual enactment before the altar of sacrifice. Though I explored this difference in some detail in a previous work[12] I can do no better here than to quote a succinct passage from Bishop John Robinson: "Indeed, the very difference of position at the Communion table, so trivial a thing and apparently so ritualistic and removed from life, is in itself symbolic of much of what we have been try-ing to say. The so-called 'eastward position,' in which the priest stands with his back to the people, has the psychological effect of focusing attention upon a point somewhere in the middle distance beyond the sanctuary. It symbolized the whole way of thinking in which God is seen as 'out there' to whom we turn from the world. By contrast the 'westward position,' in which the president surrounded by his assistants faces the people across the table, focuses attention upon a point in the middle, as the Christ stands among his own as the breaker of bread."[13] This fundamental divide in un-derstanding the nature of Christian celebration still divides churches' "tra-ditionalists" and reformist "liberals." It underlines the difference between an imperial and a domestic understanding of the church.

In time the monastic cloister became a cultural repository and center of learning that mutated into the university quad, giving rise to a further characteristic of the missionary and colonial ecclesiastical juggernaut, its overbearing intellectual confidence. The way Christianity understood and expressed itself in Hellenistic thought forms, especially the Neoplatonism of its theology and later the Aristotelianism that underpinned scholasti-cism, gathered together the sum of human knowledge available at the time and cast it as the only valid way of understanding the world as well as being the path to the truth and salvation that was believed to lie beyond it. How—if at all—this vast amalgam can be related to the actual teachings of Jesus is a moot point.[14] I mention it now only to note what formidable learning and confidence underpinned the expansion of Christian Europe on the eve of the discovery of the New World in the fifteenth century.[15]

12. Kirkham, *Our Shadowed World*, 83–94.

13. Robinson, *Honest to God*, 89.

14. Crossan, *God and Empire*.

15. Cervantes, *Conquistadores*, 69-92.

Imagining a "chosen people"

Whilst the Carolingians were crafting an imperial future on biblical foundations an even more potent myth was being fashioned in a remote monastic scriptorium in Northumbria by a Benedictine monk named Bede (c. 672–735 CE). Sometimes called "the father of English history," Bede was remarkable in many ways, but most notably for his book *The Ecclesiastical History of the English People*,[16] which has good claim to be the first and most seminal work of English history.[17] One of the most intriguing things about this work was that at the time of its composition there was no such thing as an "English people" nor was there a place called England. What existed were several Angle and Saxon kingdoms (retrospectively known as a Heptarchy), often at war with each other, striving for dominance in the land that the Romans had previously called Britain.

So why was Bede pretending there was a *gens Anglorum*, an English people? The simple answer is that he thought there ought to be, or rather it was the intention of Divine Providence that there should be, such a people. The antecedent to this belief relates to the circumstances of the first Christian mission sent to this island by Pope Gregory the Great in 595. After an encounter in the Roman slave market, so legend has it, with some fair-haired slave-boys of remarkable angelic countenance, on inquiring who they were Gregory was told that they were *Angli,* to which he quipped, "*Non Angli sed angeli*" (Not Angles but angels) and determined to send a mission to their land. Reflecting on the outcome of these events over a century later and in the light of the successful conversion of the various Angle and Saxon kingdoms Bede envisaged a people who would become a divine agency for a Roman Christianity. As the historian Diarmaid MacCulloch wrote, this people would be "a covenanted people like ancient Israel, a beacon for the Christian world."[18]

Unlike other nations that often traced their roots to a specific ethnicity of culture, the English would be different. But why "English"? It could just as well have been Jutes, Saxons, Mercians, or, as it had formerly been, Britons; after all, the dominant king of the Heptarchy at the time of Bede was known as *Bretwalda*, "Britain ruler,"[19] and the sixth-century

16. Bede, *Ecclesiastical History.*
17. Wood, *In Search of the Dark Ages.*
18. MacCulloch, *History of Christianity*, 341.
19. Wood, *In Search of the Dark Ages*, 63–64.

Welsh monk Gildas in his saga of post-Roman times, *The Ruin of Britain*, provided a perfectly adequate conceptualization of these islands. Clearly Bede thought otherwise; he was not interested in a British past so much as an English future. That Pope Gregory's "angels" were predominantly Saxons was beside the point. "Bede had depicted a single race called the English . . . [he] gave this 'people' a pride in their common and special destiny."[20] Roman Christianity—as distinct from Celtic Christianity of which Bede disapproved—would now be a central thread of England's national identity and historic destiny.

Because "the English" was primarily an idea, with the actual people—whoever exactly they were—only its expression, it had an adaptability that could survive traumatic change. Danes could be added to the mix and then Normans, who would grasp its crown, contemptuously replace its language—which they likened to the barking of dogs—and its governance with a wholly alien feudal nobility. But in time it was England that would swallow Normandy, and much of France, and "Englishness" would become a fearful force to be reckoned with: as the fifteenth century diplomat Philippe de Commynes noted, "Of all the people in the world [the English are] the most inclined to give battle."[21] But territorial expansion was not to be the only goal. Central to Bede's thinking was his allegorical understanding of Solomon's temple as representing obedience to God's word and the healing of the divisions resulting from the building of the Tower of Babel, thus inaugurating a cosmic unity at the end of time. All this anticipated a New Jerusalem "builded here" in this green and pleasant land, or as Blake subtitled his famous poem, "The Emanation of the Giant Albion." Here was an identity with universal, or at least global, implications.

This understanding had undergone some modification with the coming of the Reformation and Henry VIII's break with Rome. Now the idea of a "chosen people" became interlinked with the idea of a reformed Christianity and of being an island set apart, with Henry even being depicted as a new Moses![22] Already in the court of Elizabeth there was talk of an "Empire of Britain," a concept formed by the Queen's imaginative adviser, John Dee.[23] English antiquarians like Aylett Sammes now saw "this Ancient and Renowned ISLAND, once a hanger-on, or part of the Continent . . . that

20. MacCulloch, *History of Christianity*, 340.

21 Goodman, *Fatal Colours*, 179.

22. Longley, *Chosen People*, 125.

23. Parry, *Arch Conjuror*.

its Empire is preserved entire and as it abounds in all things, both for the necessary delight and support of Man, and needs not the World to sustain it . . . [is] a distinct WORLD by itself."[24] By the seventeenth century the perspective of England's divinely-appointed destiny had been augmented by a geographical chauvinism. Sammes elaborated how the English were also exceptional in being descended from the lost tribes of Israel.[25] In his *Britannia Antiqua Illustrata* of 1676 he helpfully provides a map of the exact journey the Lost Tribes took to Britain across Europe from the Black Sea after the destruction of the Kingdom of Israel by the Assyrians.[26]

Though this may sound fanciful—as indeed it is—such beliefs became widely popular and gave rise in the nineteenth century to the movement of British Israelites. Here was a country, and people, that strongly believed in their being exceptional in every sense and whose royal family was, as the Carolingians had claimed, the occupant of a Davidic throne, and whose empire was little short of the fulfillment of biblical promises to become a light to the nations. This understanding was neatly encapsulated in a drawing that appeared in *The British Worker* magazine of 1859 where Queen Victoria is depicted handing a copy of the Bible to a grateful Indian ambassador: here was the secret of our success.[27] Christian conviction in a divinely-ordained salvific destiny underpinned an overbearing self-confidence and buttressed by technological innovation all contributed to belief in a progressive civilization that would transform the world.

Though much of this may now be forgotten, what it indicates is that the core of English identity and concept of empire is to be found in its understanding of Christianity. Biblical beliefs provided the foundation for a self-understanding that would become inextricably linked with the nation's "mission" or manifest destiny to colonize the world.

From "Manifest Destiny" to genocide

A further consequence of this belief was to be found in the New World where it was taken to the English colonies by the Pilgrim Fathers and would become seminal to the American self-understanding.[28] The myth

24. Pigott, *Ancient Britons*, 19.
25. Pigott, *Ancient Britons*.
26. Pigott, *Ancient Britons*, 104.
27. Brown, *Wisdom of Science*, 156.
28. Longley, *Chosen People*.

of a "special providence" and "manifest destiny" of a nation set apart that lived according to a moral ideal (or "higher law") was believed to supersede other considerations and bestowed a unique entitlement. As Carlos Fuentes wrote, "The philosophy of manifest destiny had already been formulated by Thomas Jefferson and John Quincy Adams. In a letter written in 1821, Adams wrote to Henry Clay, "It is unavoidable that the remainder of the continent shall be ours."[29] This assumption was elaborated by politicians and writers, such as John O'Sullivan, to justify the annexation of neighboring and indigenous Indian territories in order to provide living space for "our yearly multiplying millions."

The concomitant of this belief was to be found in the American Indian genocide that culminated in the massacre of Wounded Knee (1890). But this "higher law" reached even further afield, across the Pacific Ocean, as with the deposition of Queen Liliokalani of Hawaii in 1898. This was little more than a naked land grab led by Lorrin Thurston, himself from a an American missionary family, opposed to the constitutional change that would have recognized native land rights.

At the same time in Germany a similar presumptive understanding was implicit in the claim to *lebensraum*, "living space," that motivated the imperial expansion of the Second Reich into Africa that also culminated in genocide. It was a work that the Third Reich would continue in its crusade against Bolshevism and annexation of the countries of eastern Europe. In both cases, in the Wild West and Slavic East, the outcome was genocide. Thus, we see a somber outcome, if not truth, of historical "progress," ideological beliefs, and national mythology: what is destiny for some is destruction for others.

Should this statement seem unduly contentious perhaps I could here, in parenthesis, make a reference to the Nuremberg trials that followed the ending of the Second World War. One of the most significant things about these trials of Nazi war criminals is what it *didn't* do. The Allied judges, from Britain, France, the USA, and USSR, had the choice of two charges: genocide and crimes against humanity. As the distinguished human rights lawyer Philippe Sands makes clear in his detailed account of the trials, the judges chose to use the latter charge only, as with the charge of genocide it seemed more difficult to attribute individual responsibility.[30] But there was another, largely unspoken, reason for this hesitancy. Each of the Allied

---

29. Fuentes, *Buried Mirror*, 278.
30. Sands, *East West Street*, 183–89.

countries had skeletons of their own from the not-too-distant past of which an able defendant like Hans Franck (himself a lawyer and former Governor of Poland who oversaw the implementation of genocide) was all too aware.[31] In particular, only just before the war the Soviet Union had instigated the *Holodomor,* "terror famine," in Ukraine between 1932 and 1933, in which between seven and ten million people died (the true figure can never be known, though this estimate was agreed by the United Nations in 2003) and had all the features of a genocidal act. As the witness, journalist, and novelist Vasily Grossman wrote: "Is it really true that no one will be held to account for it all? That it will just be forgotten without a trace?"[32]

The Renaissance *ur*-myth

Important as all of this is in seeking to understand the assumptions, beliefs, motivations, and behavior of Europeans with regards to other people beyond the confines of their continent it is not the whole story. Of central importance was the humanism that came to characterize the period we refer to as the Renaissance, or re-birth, of European culture. It is important to note that this humanism was not averse to Christian beliefs but, as in the works of one of it most prominent luminaries, Erasmus, the basis for a renewal of Christianity by championing rationality and challenging obscurantism. A walk round any Italian art gallery or along the corridors of the Vatican reveals walls bursting with incomparable representations of the glory of the human form, pedestals bearing sculptured figures in every pose imaginable, but generally naked. The subject matter derives primarily from both classical literature and scripture, in the latter case with the depiction of biblical figures and events in classical pose.

A crucial theme was the creation of the first man—pristine and complete, noble and serene, from the outset set apart from and above all of nature. The imagery is compelling in its simplicity and potency. And it has become even more so through innumerable visual images. Who can think of Adam other than as depicted by Michelangelo in the Sistine Chapel or in the glorious portrayal by Lucas Cranach the Elder, now in the Uffizi? This is the figure destined to march through human history as civilization

31. Sands, *East West Street,* 358.

32. Popoff, *Grossman.* Grossman, a Soviet journalist, was among the first to record events in Ukraine, his homeland, and the Nazi genocide. His testimony was used as evidence in the Nuremberg trials.

unfolded, flawed perhaps but peerless in might and cunning, godlike in ambition and destiny. Notice also the obvious assumption and implicit message of the iconography: how very white and European all these heroic figures appear. This is the dominant image—the crypto-Aryan white Caucasian depiction of biblical figures and even of God "himself"—that long before modern racial theories arose shaped the notion that white supremacy was the natural order of things. Of this the historian R. I. Moore has commented, "The master narrative of European history . . . presented the Renaissance and Enlightenment as, on the one hand, the heirs of classical antiquity, and, on the other, supplying the rational foundations of the modern world—and hence the basis, and more or less explicitly the justification, for the hegemony in the nineteenth and twentieth centuries of European and neo-European industrial power."[33]

Just how powerful these images are, both consciously and subliminally, I can testify from my own experience of growing up as a Roman Catholic. One of the books I most clearly remember, and which I still have before me now, is an illustrated Bible History, by I. Schuster published in 1913 and specified for use in Catholic schools.[34] My mother used it as a child and in turn used it to teach me. Most memorable are the illustrations: God in heaven, Adam being cast out of Eden, Moses with the commandments, and many others—all of them bearing the imprint of the great Renaissance works. Whatever I may have come to understand since, these figures are so etched in my mind that the very mention of God inescapably carries the mental image of an elderly bearded male, white skinned, always referred to as "He." So, when the archbishop of Canterbury in the context of Black Lives Matter referred to our image of Jesus being too white and European, I knew exactly what he was referring to.

The modern normative "white supremacist" view became iconic with the creation of a now universally-recognized "scientific" image of human progress, Rudolph Zallinger's *The March of Progress*, now hanging in the Peabody Museum of Natural History. It shows our early relatives, beginning with a chimpanzee striding purposefully across the page, becoming more modern with every step and giving the impression that human evolution involved the linear and progressive ascent of man. Its visual message is clear: the cultural and evolutionary process culminates in the modern white male. This beguiling image, in a way comparable to and

33. Moore, *Formation*, 191.
34. Schuster, *Illustrated Bible History*.

perhaps subliminally influenced by the many Renaissance paintings of Adam, is almost impossible to dismiss from consciousness. It constitutes a prism through which we unconsciously view "the facts" about diverse peoples. And though it is little more than a myth, it may be the *ur*-myth of modern Western civilization.

The crusading mentality of the West

The beginnings of the Renaissance are generally related to the Turkish conquest of Constantinople in 1453. Both a cataclysmic and symbolic event, this defeat signaled the demise of the Byzantine Empire more than a thousand years after its foundation by the first Christian emperor, Constantine. It also marked the triumph of Islam. Amongst its consequences was an exodus of scholars and scholarship from this center of classical learning to the safety of the West. This migration took place along trade routes controlled by Italian cities such as Venice and was of incalculable importance: one cardinal alone brought over eight hundred Greek codices from Constantinople.[35] As the church historian Diarmaid MacCulloch notes, "Before this event, Medieval western Europe had access to remarkably little Greek literature . . . Few scholars had any more than the vaguest knowledge of the Greek language . . . Western humanists needed Greek if they were to make use of the texts suddenly available."[36]

But this was only the last chapter of a much longer history in which the year 1204 is pivotal. In that year the Frankish knights of the Fourth Crusade appeared before the walls of Constantinople. Their plan to help the Byzantine prince Alexios Angelos restore his deposed father Isaac II as emperor was thwarted, however, by a popular uprising during which the crusaders ransacked and plundered the city. The resulting devastation was followed by the fragmentation of the Byzantine empire into three states. Understandably, this saga of betrayal, duplicity, and incomparable destruction is remembered with bitterness even today and has rendered the word "Frank" a term of contempt. And because the fatally weakened city never really recovered, its conquest by enveloping Turkish forces became almost inevitable.

Though the crusades are now remembered mainly as the attempt of Christianity to repel the expansion of Islam, the events of 1204 indicate that

35. Fisher, *History of Europe*, 450.
36. MacCulloch *History of Christianity*, 575.

this is not the whole story. Even more they were the expression of a militant Christianity—Roman Catholicism—that was intolerant of any diversity of belief. Within Europe internal crusades such as the Albigensian Crusade against deviant sects and the institution of the Inquisition to root out heretical belief continued the symbiotic relationship of church and state that had been present at the outset of the Holy Roman Empire. In the fifteenth century, as the *reconquista* (the crusade against the Moors and Jews) gathered pace in Spain, and in conjunction with the ambitions of the Catholic monarchs of Spain and Portugal, Christianity became allied to commercial expansion and overseas exploration in the person of the *conquistador*.[37]

Thus began a rather grim history. Though we now tend to prioritize the commercial aspects of the voyages of discovery they were also a product of the crusading mentality and seen as a continuation of the *reconquista*. This was certainly how both Columbus and Ferdinand and Isabella seemed to have regarded his voyage, as a way of circumventing Muslim lands via the Orient with a view to the liberation of Jerusalem thus enabling the Second Coming of Christ and the end of the world. This millenarian mentality provided a crucial motivation for his voyages.[38] In a similar state of mind, in 1498, Vasco da Gama sailed round the southern tip of Africa to the Swahili Coast of East Africa on his way east. Here he encountered a number of prosperous city states that were part of a long established and sophisticated Islamic trading culture that encompassed the Indian Ocean and reached as far as China, a network that had been prospering for over five hundred years. Da Gama's first meeting with the Sultan of Mozambique ended with the Portuguese firing their cannons into the city, destroying the sultan's palace and other buildings. They then turned to attacking the unarmed Arab trading ships and looting them. In short, the Portuguese entered the African world as crusaders (or "pirates" in the sense of Bishop Absolon!) intent on its destruction—much as with the knights of the Fourth Crusade or the great Teutonic crusades.

Meanwhile, a similar pattern of events was unfolding on the other side of the globe, when the Spanish ravaged the Americas with similar catastrophic consequences for local cultures. All of this loathsome behavior derived from a sense of superiority and entitlement based on an absolute conviction that they alone possessed religious and cultural truths others must accept,

37. Cervantes, *Conquistadores*.

38. Cervantes, *Conquistadores*, 13. Also Fernandez-Armesto, *Columbus* and *Before Columbus*

a mentality summed up in the "three G's": God, Gold and Glory.[39] Seen from a distance this broad spectrum of events reveals a very clear pattern: a self-righteously superior culture (European) was impelled by a missionary conviction derived from its beliefs (Catholicism) and the desire for wealth, the acquisition of which was often seen as divine confirmation of its aims. The underlying assumption was that the European value system and way of life were of such unquestionable benefit that their adoption would lead to universal progress and the advancement of civilization.

The reality was rather different. What one sees unfolding is an immensely destructive cultural force destabilizing settled cultures and causing their collapse, together with the imposition on a subsequently impoverished or enslaved people of a belief system and way of life that were essentially European. This would become ever more apparent as the Portuguese pressed on to India and the Far East. For with them came missionaries, in particular members of the newly formed Society of Jesus, which had been founded in Spain in 1540 by a former Spanish soldier, Ignatius Loyola, for the propagation of the faith. The society became a by-word for the efficiency and dedication with which they approached their task.

An example of their uncompromising proselytization was evident when Jesuit missionaries went to Ethiopia in the 1554. Here they encountered another ancient Christian tradition that goes back to the very earliest days of Christianity: in the Acts of the Apostles 8:26–38 we find mention of an Ethiopian convert. Thus, it is no less than bizarre that they set about seeking to "convert" its members to "true" Christianity—the form practiced by Roman Catholics. Underlying this difference was an arcane dispute over the two natures of Christ, divine and human, that had evolved in the West but was unknown in Ethiopia. The net result of the Portuguese attempt to impose the Catholic faith on Ethiopia was a civil war that in 1622 overwhelmed and devastated the nation. That it was the home of the only precolonial sub-Saharan church in Africa seems to have made little difference to the way it was viewed by Europeans.

Outstanding among the members of the new Society of Jesus was Francis Xavier who in 1542 embarked on a prodigious missionary journey to the Far East that would earn him canonization and the designation of patron saint of missionaries. Not only was little appreciation paid to native cultures but the unexpected encounter with Christians of the long-established Mar Thoma Church of southern India merely led to their

39. Elliot, *Imperial Spain*, 65.

denunciation as "crypto-Hindus" and Xavier's recommending the introduction of the Portuguese Royal Inquisition to Goa.

A more nuanced and far less tragic example of the cultural change ef-
fected by colonization was that of the Parava people of southern India, an
impoverished caste who were facing extermination in the early sixteenth
century due to an alliance between their local rulers and Arab merchants.
The appearance of the Portuguese offered them a chance to survive by
converting to Christianity and invoking Portuguese protection. This they
did in a mass conversion of twenty thousand Paravas, who came to constitute a loyal base for Catholicism in southern India and Ceylon—much
as similar "strategic conversions" had in earlier centuries provided the
foundations for Christendom in Europe. So successful was this strategy
that when Dutch traders captured Ceylon in 1658 they were unable to
establish a Reformed Church.

A disastrous decision

As missionaries and traders pushed eastward, they eventually encountered
a wholly new challenge: China. This ancient and formidable empire had
little interest in anything the Portuguese could offer, including their beliefs, and would provide the ultimate challenge to European aspirations for
commerce and conversion. The Jesuits quickly recognized that to make any
impression they must begin to adapt themselves to Chinese customs and
that presuming cultural superiority or the use of military power would be
pointless. So, dressing as Confucian scholars and in all ways determined
to show the depth of their learning the Jesuit missionaries attempted to
engage with the Chinese court through dialogue.

Outstanding in this strategy was Matteo Ricci, who managed to engage the emperor's interest in clocks, a technology in which Europeans
were becoming increasingly proficient.[40] Yet the adoptive accommodation
of Chinese rites—what we would now call "acculturation"—was fraught
with difficulties. Attempts to follow traditional Chinese funerary rites, in
particular wearing robes of white, the traditional color of mourning in the
orient, were at best problematic. And that, together with the language of the
rites and how to name God, led to furious controversy within the church
and with other religious orders that denounced any such accommodation.
This controversy over the Chinese Rites rumbled on across the seventeenth

40. Cronin, *Wise Man.*

century and became enmeshed in highly complex theological and post-Reformation disputes about the nature of grace, justification, and salvation. The final decision by Rome, given in 1704 by Pope Clement XI, was that there could be no such accommodation.

This decree was reaffirmed in 1742 by Benedict XIV in the decree *Ex quo singulari* which forbade any further debate and was emphatic that the matter was closed for good. "Peter had spoken." The strength of his prohibition was underlined by an apostolic constitution of the previous year which affirmed that popes, past, present, and future, were infallible. Dialogue and respect would now be replaced by suspicion and rivalry, a situation that was to endure down to the present time—even though in 1939 Pius XII surreptitiously annulled this teaching in the light of its disastrous consequences not only for the future of Christianity in China, but in the wider history of the church.

Not only did this Eurocentric approach raise obstacles to the need for understanding foreign cultures, but it also showed that Catholicism had failed to understand its own history—in particular the origin of its own funerary rites. In this a decisive influence over understanding our interaction with the world of the dead had been that of the Cluniac monastic reform movement of the tenth century—previously mentioned as being of seminal influence in the formation of medieval Christendom—from whence arose such rites associated with the dead as the feasts of All Saints and All Souls, the roots of which stretched deep into Europe's dark pre-Christian Celtic past.[41] Little of this tradition, with its solemn Latin liturgy and black vestments, related to anything in early Christianity, and certainly not to its traditional Jewish matrix which had no settled concept of an afterlife. Indeed, Jesus was reported to have given the subject a blunt dismissal: "Leave the dead to bury the dead." In short, the problem in China resulted from the imposition of purely Eurocentric cultic practices under the pretext that they had a unique divine legitimacy.

Ricci himself was captive to the theological and cultural traditions of Europe. As Hans Kung notes, "Ricci, who was so tolerant on the 'natural' level, was as intolerant when it came to baptism as any Tridentine Catholic: he demanded a complete break with the Confucian, Taoist, and Buddhist

---

41. The reason these feasts are at the beginning of November is that this was the time of the year when the great Celtic festival of Sanhaim had been celebrated that marked not only the ending of the year and beginning of the "darker half" of the year but the time of visitation by the ancestral spirits.

past, hence the burning of Buddha figures and tablets."[42] Surprisingly, in Ricci's "catechism" the name of Jesus is mentioned only once in the margin! Rather than delve further into these complex and contested issues, let it suffice to highlight the wider point: what missionaries were presenting was not some timeless truth but a set of beliefs that were culturally specific to a very particular place—Western Europe. Unfortunately, this practice was not restricted to Roman Catholicism, but all too soon came to characterize other church missionaries and the colonial mentality in general.

The story of Hoa Hakananai'a

The fate of the people of Rapa Nui, or Easter Island as it became known in the West, is symptomatic of the colonial tidal wave that swept the globe after the discovery of the New World. Fragile indigenous cultures were overwhelmed by sophisticated technology, powerful ideas, and dedicated missionaries: they never stood a chance.

The most distinctive element of Easter Island culture is its great stone giants or Moai that represent the heads and torsos of ancestors. Almost a thousand of these are still scattered about the island, either on the mountain sides where they were quarried or on the remains of the stone platforms, *ahu*, where they were once erected and venerated. Perhaps the most famous of these moai has a name, Hoa Hakananai'a, but he is no longer on the island; he stands in the British Museum, a silent witness to a lost—or rather, intentionally destroyed—culture. But it is not a simple story.

When the Dutch navigator Jacob Roggeveen discovered the island on Easter Sunday 1722 (hence its European name), he merely noted its existence and passed on. At that time the island had an efficient agricultural system with ingeniously engineered micro-climates that enabled it to provide a surplus of food for an estimated population of fifteen thousand.[43] The next visit was by a Spanish expedition in 1770 that noted the Moai were standing, but the subsequent visit by Captain Cook in 1774 found that they had been toppled. Something had prompted a dramatic change in the population's belief system. Subsequent belief seem to have been centered on the so-called Birdman cult that was witnessed and described by the first missionary to the island, Fr. Eugene Eyraud

42. Kung and Ching, *Christianity and Chinese Religions*, 239.

43. Soza, *Official Handbook*, 50. This understanding has resulted from later archaeological investigation.

(1820–68).[44] Though initially they were resentful of his presence, in 1864 he baptized all the islanders and many traditional practices were abandoned, thus bringing their culture to an end.

Eryaud also brought tuberculosis to the island. An epidemic killed a quarter of a population that had already declined significantly since the first European contacts. This initial decline can now be seen as the result of disease, for, as happened with many "first encounters," it is likely that a considerable portion of the original population succumbed to the silent killer diseases from Europe to which natives had no immunity. Such a catastrophic loss of life could well have been the explanation for the abandonment of the Moai, which recent research has shown were not "toppled" but laid to rest as communities collapsed. It is in this context that original beliefs were replaced, perhaps as a matter of desperation, by the new Birdman cult.[45] As well as disease, Europeans introduced sheep farming which decimated the landscape, making survival for the Rapa Nuians precarious. The population was reduced still further due to their "enslavement" by merchants seeking workers to remove guano from the islands off the mainland of Chile.[46] Though slavery had been abolished by the British in 1833 the Pacific region was plagued by "Blackbirding," a practice involving entrapment and bonded labor that was slavery in all but name.

Thus, when the British frigate *HMS Topaz* arrived off the island in 1868, the year that Fr. Eyraud died, only a few hundred islanders were left, living pathetic and impoverished lives. Now converted to Roman Catholicism, with some moai already sold to Europeans, one of the requests made to the captain was that he remove a moa that was concealed in a former initiation hut. Here it was buried up to its chin in the ground and used for initiation rites linked to the Birdman cult, signs of which had been

44. Fr. Eyraud belonged to a French missionary congregation of the Sacred Hearts of Jesus and Mary that had been founded in 1792 in the wake of the French Revolution and was particularly active in Oceania. Its history is quite typical of many such missionary religious orders from that time.

45. The change of traditional practices and beliefs as a consequence of colonization has been observed as a factor in the collapse of the social cohesion of the native Taino population of Hispaniola with the coming of the Spanish in 1492. Cervantes, *Conquistadores*, 83.

46. This trade was controlled largely by the English businessman William Gibbs who made a huge fortune from supplying the fertilizer from bird droppings to country estates and was able to build himself a magnificent country house at Tyntesfield with its own chapel. He was a devout high church Anglican. See Kirkham, *From Monk to Modernity*, 99–104.

carved on its back. Because it was concealed from view in a stone hut that could only be entered through a small entrance to the rear of the statue by initiates this moa was named Hoa Hakananai'a, "our hidden friend."[47] Though this translation and the exact significance of the statue have been questioned, it was clearly an embarrassment to the islanders now to have such a figure in their midst as they had no doubt been made fully aware by Fr. Eyraud that in keeping with the decree of Benedict XIV in 1742 any ancestor worship or other cultic devotions were incompatible with Christianity. This was the same issue that had confounded Ricci but of which missionaries in China at the time had no power to enforce—this would change in the nineteenth century.

All these details are important in the subsequent story of Hoa Hakanani'a, for he was not stolen, as now widely claimed, but given away and then taken to the British Museum, where he began a new lease on life attracting numerous visitors by his mysterious and impressive presence. Amongst these visitors was a Victorian proto-anthropologist Katherine Routledge, who was so captivated by the statue that she sought out its origins, funding a private trip to Rapa Nui (she was from a very wealthy Quaker industrialist family of Gurney Pease in Darlington) and in doing so managed to record much of the ancient Rapa Nui culture and people that were then on the point of extinction. She was a little too late to be able to decipher the writing system known as *rongorongo*, but thanks to the widespread public interest in Britain that her work generated through her best-selling book *The Mystery of Easter Island*, there was a change in fortune for the island people. Since then, a sustained revival of Rapa Nui culture has taken place, as inhabitants have tried to piece together the story of their ancestral past. But it seems that it is only when the point of extinction is reached that we stop to ponder "the mystery" of what has happened and, when it is almost too late, realize a change of mentality and behavior is necessary. In 2016 the governor of the island, Tarita Alarcon Rapu, made an impassioned plea at the British Museum for the return of the Hoa Hakananai'a, claiming the "We are just a body. You, the British people, have our soul."[48]

47. van Tilburg, *Among Stone Giants*, 129. These details were recounted to Katherine Routledge by a local woman, Victoria Veriamu.

48. This sentiment is misplaced insofar as this particular moa was *given* to the British captain of HMS Topaz to take away by a people newly converted to Catholicism and to whom its presence was now an embarrassment; such an act was also an expression of their commitment to their new faith that forbade ancestor worship.

I have mentioned this story in some detail because it is a discrete example that in many ways encapsulates and epitomizes the global drama of colonialism and Christianity that was being played out over several centuries: the sheer destructiveness of the European presence, both unintended (by disease) and intended (by enslavement); the persistence of uncompromising missionary efforts antithetical to the native culture; the subsequent abandonment and destruction of native identity and its near final obliteration. Today we would regard such a series of events as genocide. Then there was a slow but growing realization on the part of some Europeans as to the devastating consequences of their actions prompting a change of heart and pioneering attempts to curtail the unbridled commercial exploitation and cultural obliteration that had taken place. From this conflicted history the indigenous people in a postcolonial era now seek to rediscover and revive their ancient heritage that is a challenge to the colonial powers that destroyed it.

Pioneers of a changed consciousness

Whilst this tragic scenario was unfolding another scarcely-noticed drama was taking place on the other side of the world in the remote sands of the Sahara Desert that in its own way expressed the change of sentiment and sensitivity that was beginning to take place among European colonial missionaries. It featured the French cavalry officer Charles de Foucauld (1858–1916) who renounced military service to become a Trappist monk.[49] As a cavalry officer he had been stationed in Algeria, and it was to there, after a period of spiritual turmoil, he returned in 1901 to live a life of prayer as a silent recluse. Deep in the Sahara at Beni Abbes, on the Moroccan border, he built a small hermitage of "adoration and hospitality," seeking merely to be a loving presence among the Tuareg, and there he lived until his assassination in 1916. But his legacy lives on in the Little Brothers of Jesus, a fraternity who, inspired by his life, likewise seek to live anonymous lives in silence among the poor and marginalized, imitating the hidden life of Jesus at Nazareth.

---

49. The Trappists were a reformed branch of the Cistercian Order. It is ironic Foucauld chose to join this order that had been involved more than any other in the twelfth century colonization of central Europe and also the crusades of which one of the founders, Bernard of Clairvaux, was a notable advocate.

I mention this not just because as a young man I too was inspired by his example to attempt to join the Trappist order (this didn't work out) but because his life and mission reflect a rejection of colonialism and traditional missionary Christianity: a recognition that a different future was necessary. De Foucauld epitomises the changed spiritual commitment that needs to take place that involves an attitude of humble deference, of respect and acceptance that goes beyond mere words and dialogue to taking up shared life and action for the good of others.

By coincidence, while de Foucauld was in the northern Sahara another European figure moved to the south, to Gabon, and the trajectory to whose life also indicated one of a dramatic change of understanding. It was Albert Schweitzer (1875–1965), a celebrated Lutheran theologian, organist, writer, humanitarian, philosopher, and physician. His great work of scholarship *The Quest of the Historical Jesus* (1906) had sought to set Jesus free from the shackles of ecclesiastical dogma and in doing so had led Schweitzer to understand the essence of Jesus' teaching as a certain "spiritual force" that found expression in the "religion of love" and a "reverence for life"—a message that remained essentially the same for all regardless of time, place, and varying world views. This "ethic of active love," as Schweitzer called it, led him to train as a medical doctor and embark on a ministry of healing in the remote village of Lambarene in French West Africa. Though Schweitzer has since been sharply criticized by the Nigerian writer Chinua Achebe and others for colonial, racist, and paternalist attitudes, he himself said, "I try to follow Jesus and his way of loving generosity and justice, but I accept none of the doctrines laid down by the Early Church or any other Church." His worldwide recognition stems from a missionary programme focused on humanitarian support rather than traditional attitudes of European colonialism.

Some decades before Schweitzer's departure for Africa the life of another scholar and missionary, John William Colenso (1814–83), had been unfolding in South Africa in again a rather unpredictable way.[50] A Cambridge scholar, he left England in 1853 to become the first bishop of Natal, a position he held until his death thirty years later. During those years he twice attained a degree of public notoriety for views that antagonized his fellow colonialists and disconcerted the authorities in England. Like

---

50. For the details of his life and work I am indebted to a lecture by Dr. Nathan MacDonald given in 2014 at St. John's College, Cambridge, to celebrate to two hundredth anniversary of Colenso's birth. See MacDonald, "John William Colenso."

Schweitzer, he was a controversial biblical scholar and in his 1861 commentary on Paul's Letter to the Romans espoused a universalistic theology in which the free grace of the gospel did not require faith to effect salvation. He also insisted that there was no such thing as eternal punishment and that the sacraments were a sign of divine blessing rather than rites essential for salvation. Such views prompted cries of heresy but they were nothing compared to the views Colenso would express in his major work *The Pentateuch and Joshua Critically Examined.* This was a full-frontal attack on the veracity of the scriptures, one that used the new tools of critical scholarship being pioneered in Germany to show that the Pentateuch was a composite work, lacking in both coherence and historical accuracy. Colenso was convinced the revolution in scriptural exegesis then gathering headway required a radical change in Christian preaching and practice.

This new attitude was reflected in his support for the king of Hlubi, Langalibelele, who had been banished to Robben Island after a travesty of a trial. Colenso was soon drawn into resisting the attempt to establish a federation in South Africa and the annexation of Natal, opposing the invasion of Zululand against the express wishes of authorities in London. Instead, he took up the cause of the Zulu king, Cetshwayo, exposing the scurrilous conduct of leading colonial administrators and going on to use the skills he had honed in analysing the Pentateuch to piece together official reports to create a detailed criticism of colonial policy. Needless to say, he became an increasingly isolated figure and received no further ecclesiastical promotion, but to the people of Natal and Zululand he was known as *Sobantu*—father of the people.

I have presented the lives of de Foucauld, Schweitzer, and Colenso as a glimpse of how in the nineteenth century Christianity was beginning to be reinterpreted and become critical of colonization, leading in time to a wider change of European consciousness. Colenso's universalist beliefs allowed him to see the humanity and dignity of native Africans and to testify that truth, mercy, and justice should be the core values embodied in the British Empire. Though at first regarded as eccentric, even subversive, the views expressed by these three men continue to be heard and acquire increasing influence. It was the missionary bishops who provided the main impetus for the great reforming Vatican Council II of the Catholic Church and insisted on its radical agenda to reexamine its the place in the modern world. It would also give rise to the radical liberation theology movement, whose critique of capitalism and Western power structures calls for a radical option in favor of the poor—the controversial work of conscientization.

A radical view of Christianity

I have focused on the links between colonialism and Roman Christianity because that is the tradition with which I am most familiar. I am aware, of course, that numerous similar links exist between other churches and colonialism, perhaps most notably the Puritans in North America and British evangelicals in nineteenth-century India. Although these are often lumped together under the heading of "Christian" I would contend that, while this designation may be well-established, it is both misleading and wrong. What we have in reality is various church traditions *claiming* to be Christian, and that is quite a different thing.

At the heart of this distinction lies the difference between the ethical teachings of Jesus and the cult of the divinized Christ, itself the subject of bitter dispute among and even within churches. Nineteenth-century theologians expressed this difference as the contrast between the Jesus of history and the Christ of faith. This was the subject the ground-breaking work of the German scholar David Strauss whose 1835 book *The Life of Jesus Critically Examined* outraged public sensibilities and was denounced by Pope Gregory XVI as "demonical." It also ruined any prospect of his future career. Yet he was fully aware that though his work "annihilated the greatest and most valuable part of that which the Christian has been wont to believe concerning his Savior Jesus," this did not deny the possibility of a new dispensation that viewed religion as a human creation and found its highest expression in the teaching of Jesus.

The many and considerable differences between the teaching of Jesus and much of what would come to be termed Christianity have more recently been explored by the distinguished biblical scholar John Dominic Crossan in his challenging book *God and Empire*.[51] Here he focuses on the radical difference between the human pursuit of power that finds its apogee in empire, and the spiritual teaching of Jesus in which power is expressed through service and healing. This is the crucial difference between the power/*potestas* of Rome, which crushes all opposition, and the power/*dynamis* to heal and make whole, that we are told "went out of Jesus" to cure the sick

---

51. Crossan, *God and Empire*.

(Mark 5:30). The attribution of imperial "Lordship" to Jesus is something that is still of ongoing concern to scholars.[52]

Almost immediately, the original teachings of Jesus were subverted by a cultic focus on the nature of the messenger rather than on his message. This distraction is one that Jesus himself is reported to have brushed aside: "Why call me good; only God is good." Yet soon after his death claims of his divinity began to reshape how he was remembered. One of the most interesting aspects of Crossan's book is his account of how quickly the imperial titles of Roman emperors were transferred to Jesus in the devotional understanding of his followers. And in like manner the whole panoply of imperial administration was absorbed by the pontifical caesaropapism that created the Roman Catholicism we know today. So persuasive has this *cultus* of an imperial ultramontane religion become that we now take it as quite normative.

Yet when we study the gospel stories, we see a different world. It is a world that evokes a compelling range of emotions—compassion, forgiveness, mercy, tenderness, simplicity, service, self-denial, fellowship, hospitality, humility. Particularly in Luke's Gospel all these virtues and dispositions cluster around the central concept of justice, which is constitutive of the kingdom of God. This remains as a sign to this world of a radical departure from the kingdoms men are wont to create. It is because such feelings are so deeply embedded in human nature that we can claim that central to Christianity is a humanistic and ethical creed detached from any cultic or ritualistic power system.

Years ago, while I was pondering my religious vocation, Ingmar Bergman's classic film of 1957, *The Seventh Seal,* made a tremendous impression on me. Its title refers to the opening of the seventh seal in the Book of Revelation (Rev 8:1), after which a long and deep silence in heaven anticipated the pronunciation of judgement. The movie's plot tells of a disillusioned crusader knight, Antonius Block, who rejects an early religious and ideological fervour that had driven him to become part of a disastrous crusade that has now left him seeking to understand the meaning of life. Such a state of bewilderment had indeed followed that the historical failure of the Second Crusade. In the end Block discovers that meaning is not conferred by belief—for God remains silent—but by simple acts of compassion and communion.

52. Scott, "Jesus the Lord: It's Dangerous."

The Jesus of history who proclaimed the "radicality" of God bore little resemblance to the devotional Christ of faith purveyed by Europeans. Jesus had no desire to create a cult following, but as Schweitzer put it, sought to inspire a new spirit of love. The ethical standards Jesus set have yet to be improved upon—or, for that matter, widely adopted. As with many other popular leaders the growing number of Jesus' following attracted the attention of the Roman authorities and helped lead to his death. It was this that prompted the quip from the Roman Catholic writer and apologist, G. K. Chesterton, that Christianity had not been tried and found wanting, but rather had been seen to be difficult and left untried. There is still time to try again.

Chapter 5

Between the Testaments

Exploring the matrix of Christianity

Now HERE'S A CONUNDRUM: Who founded Christianity? Did Jesus really intend to "found" a religion after the manner, say, of Buddha or Mohammed? When I was studying at the seminary in the 1970s an interesting book came out that caused quite a stir: *Jesus the Jew* by Geza Vermes. He argued that Jesus should be seen as a Jewish holy man (*hassid*) and that Judaism defined all that he was and taught. Some Roman Catholics thought this was blasphemous and there were attempts to block its publication. About the same time this work appeared (1973) another life of Jesus appeared by another distinguished scriptural scholar, C. H. Dodd, with the unequivocal title, *The Founder of Christianity*; obviously it took quite a different line. So, what are we to make of all this? Or, as Vermes asked, if the picture of Jesus the Jew clashes with "traditional, dogmatic . . . Christianity, what are we to do?"[1]

One of the problems in answering this question is how little information we have to go on and how opaque what we do have is. Between the estimated composition of the Book of Wisdom in the mid first century BCE—the last book of what has to known as "The Old Testament"[2]—and the mention of the first identifiable complete text of the New Testament (by Athanasius in a festal letter written in 367 CE), there is a gap of four centuries. Of course there were numerous texts in circulation among the Christian communities long before then but many were of uncertain provenance or authenticity even among those that made it to the official New Testament. For example, six of

1. Vermes, *Jesus in the Jewish World*, 7.

2. The phrase "Old Testament" is a Christian (and derogatory) term for the Hebrew Bible that Jews call the Tanakh.

the thirteen letters of St. Paul are now regarded as pseudopigripha (forgeries!) while the attribution of works such as the Gospels to specific authors only came much later to their origination.[3]

And this is only a part of the problem. When looking for an understanding of who Jesus was and what he taught, the Gospel texts show evidence of a prolonged period of composition and modification. Examining the different surviving manuscripts has given rise to endless controversy, particularly during the Reformation when people were desperate to be certain of exactly what was the "Word of God." To the horror of many in 1707 one of the truly great works of New Testament textual scholarship was published by the Oxford scholar John Mill, who had spent thirty years amassing all the variant textual readings with a view to establishing an original authoritative text; he found some 30,000 variations! As church authorities at the time were quick to point out, such a degree of textual corruption "seems quite plainly to render the standard of faith insecure."[4] So they attempted to discredit it.

In the following centuries further anomalies appeared as scholarship and critical studies developed. Problems also arose from new discoveries such as the discovery in 1945 of an almost complete text of the *Gospel of Thomas* in a rubbish heap outside the Egyptian village of Nag Hammadi. That such a text should have survived almost two thousand years undisturbed and unknown in the dry desert sands until dug up by two scholars working in the area was sensational. But its content was even more so. This gave a very different range of teachings and understanding of Jesus to the four canonical Gospels, and it may well have been buried or discarded in the fourth century for this very reason, in that it did not conform to the orthodoxy being demanded in the church under Athanasius.[5] Today it is often classified under the vague and pejorative name of "gnostic"—a term which like "protestant" or "pietist" is something of a catch-all term. This was often the lot of non-canonical works.[6] Yet despite this, its dating puts it to the middle of the first century CE and so alongside the earliest New Testament Gospel (Mark). In other words, from the very beginnings of Christianity, this Gospel reflected the beliefs and understanding of some Christian communities that went to the trouble of recording these memories.

3. Ehrman, *Forged.*
4. Erhman, *Whose Word,* 85.
5. Pagels, *Gnostic Gospels.*
6. Ehrman, *Lost Christianities.*

And it was not alone. The opening words of St. Luke's Gospel indicate as much: "Seeing that many others have undertaken to draw up accounts of the events . . ."(Luke 1:1). These words were written probably towards the end of the first century at least fifty years after the death of Jesus—in those days a lifetime. But the comparison is illuminating for its difference. A feature of the *Gospel of Thomas* is just how tedious it is to read. It is little else but a collection of "the hidden sayings that the living Jesus spoke"—114 in total, many opaque and gnomic—but with no narrative, as in the canonical Gospels, and from which no character portrait emerges. As with most New Testament texts the attribution of apostolic authorship was only a later appendage to give authority and authenticity. What makes the canonical Gospels so different is the dramatic interpretation and representation of a life that is the work of writers of considerable literary skill and obvious extensive Classical learning—about which more shortly—from which a challenging and heroic figure emerges.[7] Each of the canonical Gospels is a carefully-structured text presenting a unique character study, from a new Moses (Matthew) to an unknown son of man who insists on secrecy (Mark), and from one who *must* suffer and be killed (Luke) to one who has power over his persecutors and destiny as the preexistent *logos* of Greek theo-philosophical though who freely manifests himself (John).

Writing several generations after the events, the attempt of the four evangelists to recount what happened in a compelling way is not too different from the challenge that has always faced dramatists, from Shakespeare writing of Yorkist kings like Richard III to today's TV historical dramas such as *The Crown*, which portrays the lives of members of the British royal family—often with considerable controversy. The challenge for the dramatist is not just to record history but to make the characters "come alive." Speaking of his new dramatization of the life and times of Catherine the Great—*The Great*—the Australian producer, Tony McNamara, admits it is "an occasionally true story," one that "we don't always tell . . . in the right chronology, but we tell it in the right spirit."[8] This is clearly also true of the evangelists. We see, for example in the birth narratives of Matthew and Luke, incompatible chronologies as well as conflicting places and characters, and there is nothing to suggest that Jesus was born either at Christmas or in Bethlehem other than to fulfil "the spirit" of prophecy (Mic 5:1). Where necessary this telling could even stretch to making up the prophecies, as, for example, "He will be

7. Dodd, *Founder*.

8. Pottan, "We're Not Slavish to History."

called a Nazarene" (Matt 2:23). All this was well understood at the time as an acceptable form of storytelling, that went by the name of *midrash*—a story that could be told to fill in the gaps in our knowledge but was not necessarily true. Even so there is still a gap of some three decades from the death of Jesus for which we have no records. It is a gap that was filled by the collective memory of disciples and communities.

But how accurate was this memory? This is a field of speculation that has been investigated in fascinating detail by New Testament textual scholar Bart Ehrman.[9] As is generally the case, memory was shaped by the needs and circumstances of the various communities of believers with their own understanding of who Jesus was: the distinguished church historian Diarmaid MacCulloch writes of "a cacophony of opinions and assertions" among the first Christians.[10] I mention all this now as an indication of just how uncertain our knowledge is of Jesus and how far it is from the dogmatic certainty of established ecclesiastical tradition. It was this tradition that at a much later date accredited the apostolic authorship of the Gospels and gave them their four symbols from the vision of Ezekiel 1:10—the faces of a human, a lion, a bull, and an eagle—that at once set them aside from other Gospels and linked them to the fulfilment of Old Testament prophecy. Whatever the identity or intentions of Jesus, these become inextricably linked to the interpretations of those who came after him.

The coming of "the book"

But in the search for clues about the origins of Christianity the *Gospel of Thomas*, with its unimaginative list of sayings, can help to throw some light. Of particular interest is the medium in which they were recorded—on manuscript parchments. The word for such documents is *codex*, plural *codices*. This is a Latin word for which there is no Greek equivalent (the language in which the Gospels were written), indicating that this was a Roman development. Originally a codex was just like a small tablet or scrap book of single sheets of paper that could be stitched together for jotting down short messages, easy for storage and distribution—Julius Caesar may have been among its first users on his campaigns. And it is not just a coincidence that when this medium became available it became significant in the first Christian communities in the Roman Empire.

9. Ehrman, *Jesus before the Gospels*.

10. MacCulloch, *History of Christianity*, 81.

In fact, the codex became the distinctive medium of Christian writings that differentiated them from the scrolls used previously by the Jews in the Old Testament writings, and perhaps this was also part of the purpose. It also indicates that the precursors to the Gospels, we now know, were probably fragmentary records of the sayings and deeds of Jesus (also hymns, prayers, and creedal statements, such as those quoted by St. Paul in his letters) that were jotted down, circulated, and stored so as not to be forgotten. Such "notes" were not books and certainly not works of literature. They are a category of writings know to the Greeks as *hypomnemata,* or mnemonic aids to memory. These "tools for remembrance" lacked authorship, textual finality, and textual intention.[11]

But *hypomnemata* also had another meaning as funerary inscriptions or tomb epitaphs by which the dead were remembered that facilitated interaction between the living and the dead. As such the primary importance of such a textual object among the Christian communities would have been as a memorial to the missing Messiah: "The rendering of Jesus stories as text established a means of memorialization for a group or groups responding to a situation of absence."[12] This accords with the nature of what we know of the canonical Gospels, as in origin primarily accounts of the Passion and events that led up it. This is particularly clear in Mark where over one third of the Gospel is devoted to this as a kind of extended epitaph.

The codex also has another significance. This cheap and basic medium of communication, as with the common form of Greek in which the contents were written (*koine*), reflected a community of humble social composition with few resources and limited literary capabilities. This would indeed have fit with what we know of the earliest Christian communities.[13] It is these "accounts" (Luke 1:1) that would provide the materials for later, more sophisticated, works that in time would become proper books.[14] Thus, the book would become the distinguishing form of the new Christian testament and among its most enduring legacies.

11. Vearncombe, "Gathered Around."

12. Vearncombe, "Gathered Around," 19–21.

13. Ehrman, *Forged,* 70–73.

14. The book we now call the Bible, comprising the Old and New Testaments, was first referred to at the end of the fourth century by St. John Chrysostom

A wider religious context

Despite the obscurity of the three decades after the death of Jesus, these are perhaps the most significant in the whole history of Christianity. The German scholar of the New Testament, Martin Hengel, has written that "with regard to the development of *all* the early Church's Christology . . . more happened in the first twenty years, than in the entire later, centuries-long development of dogma."[15] It was in this period that the focus of attention moved from the teachings of what Jesus said to the personality of who he was. An early example of this is the hymn quoted by St Paul in his letter to the Philippians 2:6–11 that is a succinct summary of a new form of belief—presumably he was copying this down from a copy! The Jesus of history would become the Christ of faith, his earthly presence transfigured into a divine emanation. This would become the essence of the new religion of Christianity that would come to change the Roman Empire and transform the world.

But before pursuing this theme further, I would like to make a detour to broaden the perspective and see the issue of the inter-testamental period and Christian beginnings in a wider historical context of religious change that had been happening across the ancient world. In a modern evaluation of the significance of Christianity, the noted theologian Lloyd Geering places it in the context of the human religious quest crucial to which was the threshold of religious consciousness crossed in the middle of the first millennium BCE.[16] So significant is this period that it has been called the Axial Age or The Great Transformation.[17] This was a period "of radical cultural transformations in several major civilizational centers, unfolding during four or five centuries around the middle of the last millennium BCE."[18]

In the Bible, this transformation is reflected in the emergence of the prophets of Israel, such as Amos and Micah with their denunciation of traditional ritual practices bereft of any ethical content or conviction. Their search for universality of belief and personal transcendence, such as we also find in Plato and Buddha, was the hallmark of this religious transformation.[19] In the Bible these "axial transformations" spread from the

---

15. Hengel, *Studies*, 383.
16. Geering, *Tomorrow's God*; also Geering, *Coming Back to Earth*.
17. Armstrong, *Great Transformation*.
18. Stramousa and Shuman, *Axial Civilizations*, 1.
19. van Hagen, *Agnostic*.

prophets to the priesthood and gave rise to the so-called "Holiness Code" of Leviticus 17–26 that strongly resembles the teaching of the prophet Eze-kiel.[20] This code seems to have been inserted into an older text during the time of the Babylonian Exile in the sixth century BCE. The Holiness Code expands the understanding of ritual from temple and cultic practices to the whole life of the people, addressing such issues as the treatment of slaves and redemption of property (Lev 25). This was a tradition that was clearly still in the process of development at the time of Jesus and to which he referred as continuing: "Do not think that I have come to abolish the Law and the Prophets, I have come not to abolish but to complete them" (Matt 5:17). The parable of the good Samaritan that is located on the road to Je-rusalem is clearly a reflection on the tension between the demands of ritual conformity and personal humanity (Luke 10:25–37).

Indeed, it is noteworthy that, like the prophets before him, a central feature of the teaching of Jesus was opposition to the uncritical assumptions of established tradition. In his opening presentation in the synagogue at Nazareth we see him picking up where the prophet Isaiah left off by claim-ing he has come "to bring good news to the poor" (Luke 4:18). Here Luke is also reiterating a theme previously announced in the radical sentiments of the Magnificat, which pictures God dethroning princes and exalting the lowly (Luke 1:52). This is all potentially seditious, but still does not go far enough. Continuing with this theme of the dawn of a new era of justice, Luke begins Jesus' "inaugural discourse," often called "the Sermon on the Plain," by describing "the poor" as possessors of the "kingdom of God" (Luke 6:20). But what exactly does "the poor" mean? Who are they and what is "the kingdom of God"? Generally, we may take this term to refer to the impecunious or impoverished. But elsewhere in scripture we find an-other word, *anawim*, that has an altogether different meaning. The ending of the Second Book of Kings reports the utter destruction of Jerusalem and the deportation to Babylon of the population in 598 BCE (2 Kgs 25:8–12). This would be the end of the kingdom of Judah. We are told that Nebu-zaradah, the commander of the king's guard, left behind only "some of *the humbler people of the land* (anawim) as vineyard workers and ploughmen." In other words, "the poor" are the stateless, despised non-persons who have no kingdom. It is such whom the prophet Zephaniah urges to prepare for the final Day of the Lord (Zeph 2:3)[21]

20. Knohl, "Axial Transformations," 201–24.

21. Cf. The accompanying Note "E" in the Jerusalem Bible provides thematic

In the context of the New Testament message, it is from the stateless *anawim* that a new people will arise—a people without ethnic or national defining features who therefore possess a moral equivalence and equal status. This will be "the kingdom of God." St. Paul depicts this new dispensation very concisely when, in words that probably reflect a baptismal creedal statement of the early church, he writes, "For all baptized in Christ . . . there no longer exist distinctions between Jew and Greek, slave and free, male and female . . ." (Gal 3:28). This statement is so radical that two thousand years later an American theologian wrote of his experience of the church in the United States as being "the last truly segregated public space in America" that did not reflect the "ancient Christian credo declaring solidarity across ethnic lines, class division, and gender difference" but rather had become "more a symbol of social ills than idealistic utopian dreams."[22]

The Jewish matrix

If the discoveries of so many ancient texts at Nag Hammadi in 1945 excited the world of scholarship it was as nothing compared to the international sensation that followed two years later with the discovery of what came to be known as the Dead Sea Scrolls in some caves overlooking the Jordan valley not far from Jerusalem. This led to further investigations at the remains of a nearby settlement just below the caves at Qumran. The two appeared to be linked and it seemed as if, according to the lead archaeologist Fr. Roland de Vaux, after two thousand years, a whole new aspect of a world we thought we had thoroughly understood was suddenly opened up almost with the force of revelation.[23]

As the scrolls and settlement at Qumran were contemporaneous with the times in which Jesus lived a whole host of questions arose as to the possible links. For example, did John the Baptist live at Qumran? Was the baptism of Jesus an indication of his acceptance of the apocalyptic teaching reflected in the scrolls? Did he also preach the imminent end of the world, a final battle between good and evil, and the coming of a righteous ruler, the Messiah that the scrolls predicted? Immediately after his death, two disciples on the road from Jerusalem expressed the view of Jesus that "Our own hope had been that he would be the one to set Israel free" (Luke

---

references.

22. Patterson, "Forgotten," 10.
23. From a lecture I attended personally in 1967.

24:21). This is an expression of the earliest belief and hope of the disciples of Jesus that he was indeed the Messiah, or anointed one (in Greek, *Christos*, for the Hebrew *Masiah*). That this was also the self-understanding of Jesus was also the clear belief at the core of the teaching of St. Paul and that the end of time was here: "We can tell you this from the Lord's own teaching . . ." (1 Thess 4:15.) As the archaeologist Herschel Shanks, who was involved in the publication of the scrolls, wrote, "What the scrolls show is that in almost every respect the message of early Christianity was presaged in its Jewish roots. And even the life of Jesus, as told in the Gospels, is often prefigured in the scrolls."[24]

Whilst there are a variety of clear apocalyptic statements by Jesus in the synoptic Gospels—notably Mark 13:24–27, citing the prophet Daniel's vision of the Son of Man coming on the clouds of heaven and that "before this generation has passed away all these things will have taken place" (Mark 13:30)—with the passage of time the problem for the early Christians was how to explain them when clearly life continued as normal. By the time the fourth Gospel, entitled John, came to be written, apocalypticism had disappeared to be replaced by a very different teaching of the nature of the Messiah with an understanding that the end of time had been realized in the resurrection of Jesus so that the final end of all things was temporarily deferred. It was this core belief that now separated Christians from the majority of other Jews, who held the traditional teaching of Judaism that the Messiah would be a triumphant figure that would once again make Israel into a great kingdom. This difference of view engendered increasingly bitter hostility between the two groups that would become the tap root of antisemitism and a hatred of "the Jews" that would be a distinctive feature of the legacy of Christianity.

What the discovery of the Dead Sea Scrolls confirmed was a view of who Jesus was and what he taught that had become increasingly widespread among scholars over the previous century: that he was an apocalyptic preacher convinced of the imminent end of the world. Some, like Albert Schweitzer, went on to say that this was an illusion that cost him his life.[25] But when Schweitzer wrote of Jesus belonging to a world whose ideas were quite different fromours, and so he "will be to our time a stranger and enigma,"[26] he was only partly right, for ever since the

24. Shanks, *Mystery and Meaning*, 64.

25. Schweitzer, *Quest*.

26. Schweitzer, *Quest*, 397.

"deferred ending" of apocalypticism has been enthusiastically anticipated by millenarian movements across the centuries, both religious and secular.[27] They plague us still![28]

But the Dead Sea Scrolls have a further feature of interest in our exploration of the context of the New Testament. Though analysis of the 981 scrolls and twenty-five thousand fragments has been painfully slow and ongoing; ever since their discovery new and often unexpected insights have been gained into the nature of biblical textual composition. In 2020, for example, Professor Noam Mizrahi, of Tel Aviv University, published the results of research on fragments of four versions of the Book of Jeremiah that he was able to date to the late third and second centuries BCE.[29] As the versions differed, what this indicated, according to Mizrahi, was that the Hebrew Bible was still "evolving" and that its holiness did not rest on precise wording. That such textual variants should exist is something that, as with the variants in the Gospel texts, some now find shocking—just as centuries ago with the work of John Mill—yet points to the different manner in which texts were handled and understood in these times.

It was textual variations in the Bible that gave rise to a distinctive genre of Jewish writing: *midrash. Midrash* was the solution to a crisis that beset Judaism in the sixth century BCE following the destruction of Jerusalem and the subsequent Babylonian exile in which Jewish culture faced extinction. In fact, one could even say it was a crisis that made Judaism into the religion we know today, as the ruins of its Israelite past were reshaped by spiritual leaders such as Ezra and Nehemiah. Part of their work of reclamation was to compile the many traditions and legal codes that had existed before the exile into one compendium, the Torah. That they did just that, without seeking to harmonize or excise all the many inconsistences or differences in these traditions, is what prompted the need for *midrash*, a form of conjecture or explanation that provided answers whereby scriptural conundrums and seeming contradictions could be resolved.

And the answers could be highly imaginative, perhaps playing on words or applying old texts in new contexts or conflating the past with

27. Cohn, *Pursuit.*

28. Perhaps the latest expression of this mentality is the conspiracy-theorist followers of "QAnon" who led the assault on the US Capitol, January 7, 2021, who believe they are in a life-and-death struggle with evil forces; that Nancy Pelosi, the Speaker of the House of Representatives, is Satan; and that they alone can save the freedom of the world. Aaronovitch, "QAnon Cultists."

29. Blakely, "Dead Sea Scrolls."

the present. The content of this body of literature would become known as "halakic" if it dealt with matters of law, from the Hebrew word *halakah* (law), or "aggadic" if it dealt with wider traditions and prophecies, from the Hebrew word *aggadah* (stories).[30] The fact that these have become largely forgotten and now entirely detached from the Bible has led to the widespread deception, common among fundamentalists, that the Bible can be read for "just what it says" by anybody. Yet the "aggadic tradition" shows that the interpretation of the Bible is also part of the fabric of the Bible. As Howard Schwarz wrote, "The aggadic tradition is a continuing process of the integration of the past into the present. Each time this takes place, the tradition is transformed and must be reimagined. And it is this very process that keeps the tradition vital and perpetuates it."[31]

The gospel story

All this was familiar in the Jewish world in which Jesus lived and also to the Gospel writers who shaped our memory of him. Indeed, some of the best examples of *aggadic midrash* are to be found in the infancy narrative of Matthew. So, Matthew's Gospel tells us, Jesus settled in Nazareth, helpfully adding that "in this way the words spoken through the prophets were to be fulfilled: 'He will be called a Nazarene'" (Matt 2:23). Of course it means nothing of the sort. Not only does this quotation not belong to any text found in the Old Testament but refers to a dedication service known as the "nazirate."[32] This is an adjective derived from an Aramaic word *nasraya* and now applied retrospectively, in a totally different context, to explain an event and place name in another language (the common Greek of *koine*) that we now read in English. Quite a tangled process!

And it's not alone. Other "translations," such as the term "virgin" when applied to Mary (Matt 1:23), expresses a similar manner of midrashic thinking.[33] In fact, the whole Gospel of Matthew is constructed in terms of *midrash*: a new universal beginning or *genesis*—the opening word of the Gospel (not "genealogy" or ancestry as it is usually translated!)—presents Jesus as a new Moses giving a new law (the Sermon on the Mount) and leading a new people to salvation. Quite a story!

30. Davidson and Leaney, *Pelican Guide*, 199.
31. Schwarz, *Reimagining*.
32. Richards, *First Christmas*.
33. Miller, *Born Divine*.

The deeper one enters into this phantasmagorical world the more fascinating it becomes; for instance, the *gematria* discussed on page 6. Subsequent cultural transformations mean that for us Matthew's opening chapter—the key to the whole Gospel—is either read as fact, dismissed as fiction, or skipped over as irrelevant. It is none of these. It is a magnificent symbolic piece of writing, call it myth or *midrash*, that ties together a whole cultural worldview that gives a universal religious meaning to life that has beguiled people ever since. It is in such details that the nature of our conundrum as to who Jesus was and what he taught is really hidden.

The Classical matrix

Significant though Jewish traditions and beliefs were in shaping the gospel story, perhaps even more so was the cultural matrix of the classical world and Roman Empire. After all, it was within this pagan or gentile culture that most Christians lived. As with the Jewish world of *midrash* this was a world where the cultural assumptions were vastly different from our own. Because of this, though such assumptions were formative in the minds of those who wrote the Gospels, they are overlooked or not even noticed today, often with very distorting consequences for our understanding.

I would like to illustrate this assertion with reference to the Gospel accredited to Luke. There are two possible beginnings to this Gospel. One that we have already mentioned comes at, well, the beginning: chapter 1:1. But this is widely regarded by scholars as the beginning of a distinctive section now called the infancy narrative or *proto evangelion* ("before the Gospel"). This is a stand-alone literary piece that was a later addition to the main body of the Gospel that begins at chapter 3. At this point the opening sentence begins, "In the fifteenth year of Tiberius Caesar's reign . . ." That the mention of Tiberius Caesar is not just accidental or trivial can be gleaned from the fact that already the birth of Jesus has been introduced as being, "Now at this time Caesar Augustus . . . ." (Luke 2:1). Clearly Caesar and Rome will be significant in the story that is to be related in the Gospel and the succeeding narrative of the *Acts of the Apostles*. The plan of this narrative will be to show how the Son of God was born on the remote fringes of the Roman Empire, preached the coming of the kingdom of God, was killed by Roman authority but whose messenger, St. Paul, takes the message of the kingdom of God to the center of that empire, where the church is established in Rome. Thus, the kingdom of God confronts the empire of

Caesar and prevails. The third part of this story, continued in the Roman church, will be when the emperor becomes a Christian and the pagan gods are once and for all overthrown.

But this is not the whole story, or even the most significant part of the story. Simple and clear as this outline may seem to us, to anyone in the Roman world reading or hearing this story they would note something far more significant but not explicitly mentioned: something startling, seditious and even shocking. The title "Son of God" was the proper title of Caesar! It was Julius Caesar who had been declared, on his death, to be divine by decree of the Roman Senate and so his heir and adopted son, Octavian, was considered to be divine even while alive. That Caesar Augustus, as he became known, was also understood to be the Son of God, was a status recognized across the empire commanding respect and obeisance. Thus, the Gospel is setting up an antimony between *two* Sons of God, an unspoken *agon* ("contest") or antagonism. The radical and seditious implication is that only one will triumph.

Nor is this all that should be noted of significance about Caesar's adopted son-ship of Octavian. This was a practice in the Roman world that was understood in a very different way to that of today. As Bart Ehrman notes, "It was in fact often the case that a person who was a son by adoption in the Roman world was given a greater, higher status than a child who was a son at birth."[34] After all, who now remember Caesar's natural son, Caesarion? The fact that the adopted son was seen to take over the status of the adoptive father was crucial to how the first Christians understood the status of Jesus after the resurrection. In this understanding Jesus was seen to have been exalted as a heavenly Messiah who ruled the kingdom of his Father as Lord of all. In this, the earliest Christology of the Church, the first Christians expressed their belief in terms of the imperial Roman cultural world in which they lived. As Ehrman notes of this parallelism, "The emperor was the son of God; Jesus was the Son of God. The emperor was regarded as divine; Jesus was divine. The emperor was the great ruler; Jesus was the great Ruler. The emperor was lord and sovereign; Jesus was Lord and Sovereign."[35] In short, *Quibus imperavit Augustus, imperavit Christus*— the only legitimate successor to Augustus (Caesar) is Christ.

We may choose to see all this as a very clever literary conceit or narrative structure—one of many in the Gospels—but it should alert us

34. Ehrman, *How Jesus Became God,* 233.
35. Ehrman, *How Jesus Became God,* 234.

to something more significant about the classical world that provided the matrix of the gospel story. This was a world in which the divine was understood to be part of the world in a seamless continuum; a world in which a multitude of divine agents, gods, angels, and diabolic powers were constantly affecting its every aspect. St. Paul, for example, refers to the invisible Thrones, Dominations, Sovereignties, and Powers with which we have to contend (Colossians 1:16). In this world, heavenly annunciations, transfigurations, and ascensions into heaven were regarded as quite *normal* events in life. This is unlike the normal modern understanding of the world that is seen to function according to impersonal empirical forces conforming to rational scientific laws.

The classical world was a world in which, as the title of the Roman poet Ovid's great work *Metamorphoses* indicates, nothing was quite as it seemed: everything was malleable and liable to merge into something else.[36] In this world not only could humans become divine, like Caesar, but gods could become human, a fact that was never doubted by the general populace. Such was one of the stories of Ovid concerning the visitation of the gods Jupiter and Mercury disguised as mortals, to the region of Phrygia (now Turkey) where, having received no hospitality, they bring destruction upon it. This story anticipates and explains the story recounted in the *Acts of the Apostles* of the visit of Paul and Barnabas to Lystra where, having healed a crippled man, the locals insist that "the gods have come down to us in the likeness of men" (Acts 14:11). Determined not to be caught out a second time, they insist on worshipping them and preparing a feast.

Even more significant for our purposes here is that the whole outline of a well-known figure throughout the empire whose life was announced by angels and celestial phenomenon, deemed to be the incarnation of a god, who growing in wisdom became a famous teacher and healer, then, being killed, was taken up to heaven from whence he guided his followers. This is not just the outline of the gospel story of Jesus it was also the story of an equally famous contemporary, Apollonius of Tyana (c. 15–100 CE), a neo-Pythagorean philosopher. Not only were the stories told about Jesus and Apollonius remarkably similar, but there was a real rivalry between their numerous followers, as attested by the church historian Eusebius. Regardless of the truth behind any of these stories, the significance here is that they

36. Warner, *Fantastic Metamorphoses*. Ovid (43 BCE–17 CE) was roughly a contemporary of Jesus.

illustrate an understanding of life that was common to the time. But it is an understanding that is alien to us.

Apart from the way that Jesus is presented in the Gospels in a manner common for the time, competing with the earthly power of Caesar and pagan wisdom of Appollonius, what is also of interest is the speed with which he is accorded the regal status of the imperial cult. In view of the contempt Jesus expressed for those seeking status and power (Luke 14:7–10) and his self-definition as one who serves (Luke 22:27), this may seem incongruous. Yet almost immediately his followers are referring to him as "Lord" with increasingly imperial overtones. The ambiguity of this title was pointed out by the scripture scholar Michael Goulder. Both Jews and Jewish Christians commonly used "Lord" as a title of honor or respect; whereas later St. Paul used this term to depict Jesus as a *divine* Lord, "an eternal being alongside God in heaven, who became a man at his conception."[37] This would have struck the Jewish Christians as blasphemous, for "to them Jesus had been a normal human being of exceptional virtue and wisdom, on whom God had sent his divine spirit at his baptism."

The irony of all this is that the more exalted Jesus becomes as a divine incarnation with all the trappings of the Roman imperatum the more detached he becomes from any specific ethnicity or historic identity as a Jew. Rather, like the emperors, he becomes a divine being with a universal cult, so much so that in time the radical, apocalyptic preacher from Nazareth becomes eviscerated. Ironically, as noted by the distinguished historian of Late Antiquity, Peter Brown, that later "when the 'governing elite' of [the] officially Christian empire presented themselves . . . to the world at large, as being 'in truth governing,' the 'set of symbolic forms' by which they expressed this fact owed little or nothing to Christianity."[38]

Conclusion

The Christianity that has come down to us has been shaped by numerous cultural, linguistic, and historical factors that in many ways were arbitrary and coincidental. When Mark wrote the first Gospel some forty years had elapsed since the death of Jesus; this is a period of which we know virtually nothing. How were his words transmitted; how were they to be interpreted or translated; how was he himself to be understood? Answers

37. Goulder, *Five Stones*, 98.
38. Brown, *Authority*, 11.

to these questions would be decided by the significant developments in understanding that had taken place in the different Christian communities.

In the above narrative we can perhaps see how the teaching of Jesus, and indeed Jesus himself, can be located in the penumbra of the so-called Axial Age; that age of charismatic individuals who propelled human thought to new levels of moral understanding with a transcendental view of life, individuals who seemed to define themselves in contrast to the earlier ritualistic cosmologies that reached back to the dawn of human time.

More specifically, we can locate both Jesus and those who formulated his memory—the evangelists—in the religious world of post-exilic Judaism in which returning Jews sought to create a new national and religious identity that gave order to their experience and aspirations. This was a world that was shaped by a gathering together of memories, vague and half-forgotten, arranged and interpreted so as to give meaning to the present by providing a coherent story that makes the Bible at once both so fluent and persuasive, so easy to read but difficult to understand and interpret. A world shaped also by Hellenic and Roman culture that spread across the Near East, the imprint of which is to be found both in the Septuagint and the New Testament, both of which were written in Greek. It was in this world that Geza Vermes located the *hassid* or holy man from Nazareth.

By the time the New Testament was collated in the third century CE not only had the teaching of Jesus been significantly edited but the Hebraic cultural world of which he was a part had been destroyed: Jesus the Jew had become apotheosized into an Imperial Roman Lord and divinized as God. As for the historical Jesus, the Jewish *hassid* or holy man from Galilee who challenged and inspired his audiences with a radical message beyond expectation—well, one might say that much of him has been lost in translation and the memory of him that has lived on has been a mirage susceptible to endless interpretations.

Chapter 6

Viewing the Morals of Jesus Today

Ideals, attitudes, and misrepresentations.

THE CORONAVIRUS QUARANTINE HAS caused unprecedented changes to habits and lifestyles. It has also provided time for a deeper reflection on our values that have brought us to this point. Amongst its more positive consequences I have noticed a willingness among friends to share books, which arrive unexpectedly by post. For me one such surprise was a copy of *The Morals of Jesus* by Nicholas Harvey.[1] The gift was from a friend who was a former Anglican minister.

Though not a new work—it was published in 1991—it has a perennial theme. Harvey, a former Benedictine monk and lecturer in ethics, thinks morality has loomed large in Christian history primarily because of the Church's fear of individual and social disintegration. But he contends that this totally misrepresents what Jesus was about since "there is little evidence to suggest that Jesus was all that interested in morality."[2] In a more recent book the philosopher Julian Baggini expresses a similar opinion, that Jesus was not a great moral thinker with a moral system, but primarily a "moral challenger": "His teachings offer a much-needed challenge to our moral thinking that shakes us out of any complacency."[3]

Though a number of his sayings and parables are difficult to classify, taken together they certainly don't seem to add up to a coherent "moral system," while many are rather gnomic: "Leave the dead to bury the dead,"

---

1. Harvey, *Morals*.

2. Harvey, *Morals*, 6.

3. Baggini, *Godless*, 168.

"He who does not hate . . . ," "I do not come to bring peace but a sword," "Why call me good?" etc. Some parables, such as the laborers in the vineyard, even seem an affront to natural justice, while the chap who is invited to the wedding feast only to be thrown out for not being suitably dressed seems a bit harsh (Matt 22:1–14) and has left commentators confused over its meaning ever since. Rather than premeditated moral enlightenment, many of the sayings of Jesus seem more like off-the-cuff *repartee* that arises from close encounters, forcing the listener (reader) into self-reflection and self-questioning: one thinks of his doodling in the sand (John 8:7) or asking about Caesar's coin (Mark 12:17).[4]

But even before we get into evaluating what Jesus is reported to have said there is another problem that might not at first seem apparent: Do the Gospels actually give an accurate record of what Jesus said? Did he actually say what he is reported to have said? Take, for example, anger—generally regarded negatively as an emotional loss of control. We normally tend to think of the message of Jesus as one of compassion and kindness and his ministry as one of compassion. Yet the Gospel of Mark, the first Gospel to be written, frequently shows Jesus getting angry, for example, when he cures the man with the withered hand (Mark 3:1–6) or the leper who started telling others he had been cured (Mark 1:40–45). Of course, explanations can and have been given to justify this negative attitude, but that is not my point. In numerous manuscripts this negative expression has been toned down or changed completely, with the Greek word for "becoming angry," *orgistheis* (quite a strong word with the same root as "orgy"!) being changed to "a feeling of compassion," *splangnistheis*. In the Gospels of Matthew and Luke, even when drawing on Mark and recording the same stories, they elide the expression of anger.[5] As Mark's Gospel is generally thought to have been composed in the seventh decade CE, followed by Matthew and Luke in the following decades (with evidence of Luke continuing to being modified into the second century) and, as both used Mark's account, or at least his sources,[6] for their own Gospels, we can

---

4. His reply "Give to Caesar what is Caesar's . . ." would arguably become the most important principle of European political theory for over a thousand years, providing as it did the cornerstone of caesaropapism and the political structuring of medieval Christendom until it was replaced by the new order at the Treaty of Westphalia (1648) that introduced the principle *cujus regio ejus religio*.

5. Ehrman, *Whose Word Is It?* 133–39.

6. Perkins, *Introduction*.

see that from the outset the teaching and image we have of Jesus was being modified or interpreted for popular consumption.

The textual background

Such concerns show how modern textual studies have significantly changed our understanding of the Gospels, often in ways that are quite disturbing.[7] In order to better understand the New Testament its texts have long been scrutinized and analysed in immense detail by innumerable scholars of great distinction, but in the last century the depth and detail of textual analysis has been characterized by ever-more-penetrating analysis.[8] Now even computer algorithms are used to analyze word use and compare manuscripts (stemmatology). If anything can be concluded from this research it is that not everything is as it seems at first sight. Not only do we now know that the New Testament has an extremely complex origin and took several centuries to compile, it is still not at all clear how it was compiled or by whom, and the attribution of authorship to the texts is often arbitrary and anachronistic with many not by the people who they are supposed to have written them. For example, six out of thirteen letters of St. Paul are generally now regarded as not authentic, as are many of the New Testament texts.[9] This whole subject is extremely controversial, but then it was controversy that provided the catalyst that created the New Testament in the first place, just as it surrounded the teaching of Jesus himself (Luke 4:28).

When we get into individual Gospels, textual interpolations raise further questions about authorship. For several decades scholars of the Jesus Seminar have been examining the gospel sayings, seeking to establish a scale of authenticity that is also color-coded: red being definite, pink possible, grey unlikely, and black definitely not.[10] Their conclusion is that combining the red and the pink elements ("Jesus undoubtedly said this or something very like it" / "Jesus probably said something like this"), 18% of the sayings can be taken to constitute the voiceprint of Jesus.[11] Apart from these whole sections of the Gospels can be seen as later additions, such as the infancy

7. Shah, *Changing.*

8. Davidson and Leaney, *Pelican Guide.*

9. Ehrman, *Forged.* For a traditional evangelical view of the authenticity of scripture that rejects the interpretations of Ehrman and others, see Shah, *Changing.*

10. Funk, *Five Gospels.*

11. Funk, *Five Gospels,* 36.

narrative in Luke and the resurrection narrative in Mark. The parable of the wedding feast, for example, in Matthew (22:1–14) seems to post-date the destruction of Jerusalem in 70 CE when hopes of an apocalypse had all but faded and antisemitism was on the rise in Christian communities as they distanced themselves from "the Jews."[12]

What did Jesus actually say and mean?

This textual background impinges on any attempt to formulate a view of Jesus and his authentic or original teaching. As an example of the need for caution when approaching any assumed saying of Jesus perhaps I could focus on an issue central to the lives of many: marriage and divorce. The dominical saying recorded in Matthew 5:32 and 19:9 seems pretty straight-forward: if a man divorces his wife, except on the grounds of sexual immo-rality, he "makes" her commit adultery. The caveat aside, and the ambiguity of how the man's behavior "makes" the woman an adulteress, this quote provides the cornerstone for one of the most important moral teachings of Christianity: the indissolubility and sanctity of marriage. Like many clergy-men over the years, I had to deal with awkward pastoral cases of marital breakdown to which there seemed no humane solution by finding some sort of exemption from the often extremely distressing consequences of this teaching. Often for people who wanted to rebuild or "regularize" their lives within the church after a marital breakdown, for whatever reason, there seemed no hope. The aspirational idealism that Jesus undoubtedly preached was perniciously being used to underpin canon law that frustrated the very compassion that is held as the hallmark of his ministry. But did Jesus really say or mean what the Gospel of Matthew records?

After a detailed textual analysis of this particular teaching, in which he exposes the various complications, Bart Ehrman concludes that "this is a real tangle."[13] The reason for this conclusion is not only the discrepan-cies that arise when this this text is placed alongside others but that these discrepancies indicate that Jesus was *remembered* as teaching different things about divorce by storytellers "who were remembering those precise teachings [but who] could well have been influenced by the views of di-vorce in their own communities, or that . . . they *wanted* to have in their

12. Ehrman, *Jesus before the Gospels*, 203.
13. Ehrman, *Jesus before the Gospels*, 201.

communities."[14] If this sounds somewhat contentious the Jewish scripture scholar Geza Vermes provides further insight by locating the teaching in its Jewish context.[15] Jesus is here seen to quote the well-known position of the Pharisee Shammai that divorce was permissible only for "*erwat debar*," "something sinful," without ever saying what the "something" was. So, Jesus was repeating a teaching of the Mishnah regarding Deuteronomy (24:1–4) which, as Vermes notes, was deliberately left vague: "If the Law-giver had wished to impose a more severe rule, he would have done so."[16] Interestingly, the explanatory note to this verse given in the Jerusalem Bible (the authorized version for the Roman Catholic Church) is that Matthew "creates a special category for cases of infidelity in marriage." In fact, he does no such thing, as this was but one of numerous examples of rabbinic *midrash* that in post-exilic times (after the sixth century BCE) tried to clarify lacunae or contradictions in the written text of the Torah.

Looking back on this now makes me quite angry for several reasons. For one, despite all the moral idealism of the Sermon on the Mount, within which this teaching appears, the Church chose to take a legalistic view of divorce that is far more restrictive than even the "old" law of Deuteronomy and with no redress. Furthermore, as Ehrman notes, the foundation text for such a view is not as absolute as it may first seem and could well reflect other factors in the early Christian communities. But above all, I think of those couples whose hopes of a brighter future together had been dashed by the necessity of me as a pastor repeating canon law constructed on questionable exegesis that was deaf to the truly dominical saying that the Sabbath, and thus the law, was made for man, not man for the Sabbath. This attitude of Jesus that reflects a willingness to challenge certain boundaries of the law also comes across in the aforementioned healing of the man with the withered hand (Mark 3:1–6) that took place on the Sabbath. This was not seen by Jesus as an attempt to transgress the law so much as to transcend it on the basis of a higher principle of compassion. As with the beatitudes, it is the expression of a moral view that did not discount the law but went beyond it, a view expressive of ideals not constrained by the precision of law.

In his book Harvey argues that as the gospel unfolds it "presses beyond all systems and puts all securities in question," and thus is quite at odds with "the current of biblical fundamentalism now running in most

14. Ehrman, *Jesus before the Gospels*, 202.

15. Vermes, *Jesus in the Jewish World*.

16. Vermes, *Jesus in the Jewish World*, 55.

churches and the new papalist fundamentalism in the Roman Catholic church both [of which] find their security in the notion that the moral life is already decisively chartered for us." (He was writing during the pontificate of John Paul II).[17] For those so minded texts can be cherry-picked to bolster any argument or admonition.

The Jewish background

When viewing the moral world of the Torah with which Jesus was familiar it is worth noting how distinctive and ancient the Jewish tradition really was. The recent discovery of an inscribed ostracon (fragment of pottery) at the site of Kherbit Qieyafa, a fortress some twenty miles southwest of Jerusalem, has been dated to about 1000 BCE and is among the oldest and most extensive pieces of writing in the proto-Canaanite script ever found and from which would come our phonetic alphabet. Though the exact translation of the text is disputed some words and phrases stand out: "Do not oppress . . . serve God . . . judge the slave and the widow . . . the stranger . . . protect the poor and slave . . ." Such sentiments immediately remind us of gospel sayings and the sentiments of the Magnificat (Luke 1:46–55), not to mention the letter of St. James that true religion is "coming to the aid of orphans and widows when in need" (Jas 1:27). The significance of this tradition is that morality is seen not as the pursuit of individual perfection—such as with Stoicism or the later Catholic view of "saving one's soul"—but in the enrichment of the life of the community. As Richard Trudeau remarks of the tradition behind the story of Cain and Abel, "The sin of Cain was to be self-centered in an ecologically fragile environment . . . Cain's ultimate sin was to endanger his community."[18]

The importance of understanding the Jewish context of the life of Jesus has been increasingly affirmed in modern scholarship as essential for understanding who he was.[19] All he said and did lay within this religious tradition, as passages from the Gospels indicate—such as Matthew 15:24: "I was sent to the lost sheep of the House of Israel"—and from the fact that after his death the first community of his followers in Jerusalem happily continued Jewish practices and rituals, attending the temple services daily (Acts 2:46). Insofar as he was a radical and challenging preacher then the

17. Harvey, *Morals*, 6.
18. Trudeau, "Making Sense."
19. Vermes, *Jesus the Jew*

nature of his radicality can only be understood by a close reading of his statements *within* the context of an ancient biblical tradition. But then as the former Chief Rabbi of Great Britain, Jonathan Sacks, wrote in his engaging book *The Dignity of Difference,* "The Hebrew Bible is a book whose strangeness is little understood."[20]

The creation of the book that we now know as the Bible together with the emergence of the alphabet and alphabetical scripts in conjunction with Israelite proto-history is a fascinating and unique story.[21] Suitably enough, the book begins with a creation story, though it should be noted that this was among the later parts of the Bible to be composed (in the sixth century BCE). Nor is the word "creation" what it might first seem. The Hebrew word used, *bara,* is about the ordering and fixing of destiny through organising and assigning roles and functions. Doing this entails separation and division, *hivdil,* much as a trader might separate out his wares—and, indeed, this was the purpose for which writing originally evolved.[22] So we read of God dividing light from darkness, land from sea, day from night (Genesis 1), always in pairs. This polarization will continue in the laws that separate the daily usage of things, of the good from the bad, but above all in the separation of a "chosen people" from the rest of humanity. So, the foundational principle is laid, common to many religions, of what is permitted and forbidden, clean and unclean.

When we have understood all of this, we are in a better position to understand how sensational a mild observation by Jesus referring to the divine intention becomes: "He [God] causes his sun to rise on bad men as well as good, and his rain to fall on honest and dishonest men alike" (Matt 5:45). This aphorism is perhaps the most radical it is possible to make, as it challenges the entire order of creation and morality based on separation and division. As the scripture scholar Robert Miller has noted, it "is radical because it calls into question what is perhaps the most fundamental of traditional biblical values: that God rewards righteousness and punishes wrongdoing."[23] Not only would many hearing these words have found them to be profoundly disturbing, if not blasphemous, but the manner in which they were delivered epitomizes the manner in which Jesus taught. As Miller goes on to say, "The aphorism is remarkable not only because

20. Sacks, *Dignity,* 50.

21. Sacks, *Dignity,* 130–31

22. Schmandt-Besserat, *Before Writing*

23. Miller, "Free Rain."

HORROR AND HOPE

it dares to doubt a bedrock belief [of Judaism], but because it does so in perhaps the most disconcerting way imaginable: gently." There is no argument or denial, no theological or philosophical reasoning, no quoting of authority or scripture, but simply an observation and affirmation that really only points out the obvious and what anyone can see who has eyes to see with: yes, the sun does indeed shine on everyone alike and the rain falls on all without distinction or discrimination. Such was the art and manner of the moral radicalism of Jesus.

An existential attitude

Having said all this, however, I have always had a sense that this is not the whole story of the teaching of Jesus and that, as Harvey so clearly exposes, there is something much deeper and more radical behind this. For the Gospels seem to express a sense of divine immediacy and dependence that makes life fundamentally benign—of the sun shining on all alike, of not a sparrow falling unseen, of the flowers in the field that neither labor nor spin . . . As the distinguished scripture scholar C. H. Dodd once wrote, "This sense of divineness of the natural order is the major premise of all the parables, and it is the point where Jesus differs most profoundly from the outlook of the Jewish apocalyptists with whose ideas he had on some sides much sympathy."[24] The difference being that whereas apocalypticists looked forward to some future divine intervention, with Jesus there was a sense that "now" was the moment of divine immanence. *What matters is how we act now, and what Jesus offered was a way of living in the immediacy of the present; it is in the present reality that our lives unfold and become meaningful, not in some imagined future*

Even without the specifically theistic element this attitude translates easily into a modern sense of the "givenness" and "embraciveness" of nature/existence, of the glory of life and the need for an underlying gratitude, sensitivity, and respect for this cornucopia: that life is embracive of everything. Such sentiments have been the fare of nature mystics throughout the ages and became part of the spiritual ferment in the seventeenth century that fed into the nature mysticism such as that of Jacob Boehme's *The Divine Signature of All Things* (1621),[25] the pantheism of Spinoza's

24. Dodd, *Parables*, 21.

25. Jacob Boehme (1575–1624) was part of the post-Reformation religious ferment that swept across central Europe in the seventeenth century seeking a divine immediacy

84

Deus sive Natura (God or/as Nature), and thence inexorably onwards to the poet Wordsworth with his sense of the human spirit coexisting with nature from whence it emerges, the "natural supernaturalism" that presages modern eco-awareness.[26]

This new sensitivity to the power of nature that arose in the eighteenth century found expression in a new word "sublime" that had come into vogue in the writings of the third earl of Shaftesbury, who referred to the classical work *On the Sublime* ascribed to Longinus. That this work should have come from the first century CE and shows an awareness of Jewish scripture is not without interest. The usage of the word "sublime" was to capture a sense of awe and veneration felt in the presence of such natural phenomena as Alpine terrain or in the childhood experience on the lake recorded by Wordsworth in the *Prelude* that was overwhelming and awe-full, immediate, and compelling. The purpose of the sublime was not persuasion but, as Longinus wrote, to inspire as sense of ecstasy. This was closely linked to a sense of religious transcendence, that all life deserves respect, that we are but part of it and that now our survival is a matter of salvation as we strive to "save" the planet. What were once theological terms have now become natural dispositions: "Warblers I heard their joy unbosoming . . . chant in full choir their innocent Te Deum," writes Wordsworth in "Rydal on May Morning."

This post-theistic understanding of nature was well expressed by the Catholic priest and ecologist Thomas Berry when he wrote, "Awareness of an all-pervading mysterious energy articulated in the infinite variety of natural phenomena seems to be the primordial experience of human consciousness, awakening to an awesome universe filled with mysterious power."[27] Such a sense was certainly present among primordial people but has tended to be lost in the hubristic confidence that has accompanied growth of civilization. But with the threatening consequences of

---

and emphasizing the "Inner Light" that now goes by the name of Pietism, cf. the excellent chapter in Clark's *Iron Kingdom*, "Protestants"; also Knox, *Enthusiasm*. This vastly influential movement would reach beyond Europe to become a significant influence in the new colonies of America.

26. Bate, *Radical Wordsworth*, 158; also Abrams, *Natural Supernaturalism*. The pivotal work in this change of understanding is Spinoza's *Tractatus Theologico-Politicus*, where he expresses the radical view that "God's decrees and commandments, and consequently God's providence, are in truth nothing but Nature's order." Nadler, *A Book Forged in Hell*, 34.

27. Berry, *Dream of the Earth*, 24.

this hubris becoming all too apparent is an understanding that nature deserves respect and also has rights; that we have responsibilities not just for fellow humans but for our planet.

Accompanying all of this is an *attitude* of how we must respond to the world and its challenges. Recently a new freshmen course at Yale to help undergraduates settle in and cope with the stresses of their new life has been gaining much wider notice and acclaim—for it focuses on cultivating a sense of gratitude as the key to human happiness.[28] An existential attitude toward reality—a feature of the present pandemic—focuses the mind on the possibilities of life *in the present moment* as the only moment of worth. Life confronts us with its challenge of what we will make of it, *now*.

What strikes me about this is its essential similarity to what the Viennese psychiatrist Dr. Viktor Frankl wrote about in his reflections on the much more extreme circumstances of the Auschwitz death camp, an ordeal he recounted in *Man's Search for Meaning*. As Frankl so often watched human life ebb away in the most horrific circumstances he realized that each day there are three things our existence calls upon us to achieve if we are to find fulfilment and meaning: we must do a deed of generosity or create something of value; we must appreciate something of value such as a work of art or the natural beauty of the world that takes us beyond ourselves; we must carry a burden or endure suffering positively, reminding us that life is never easy or to be taken for granted. Using the Greek word *logos* to imply meaning, Frankl sought ways to focus patients beyond themselves: "Thus, the typical self-centeredness of the neurotic is broken up instead of being continually fostered and reinforced."[29]

The development of "logotherapy" as a psychoanalytical tool based on Frankl's own experiences was an attempt to address the moral vacuum in the lives of many people, but particularly the young.[30] A feature of his and numerous other "survivors'" experience was that the core issue in survival was one of attitude: a determination to remain positive and grateful for life, even in the face of suffering and death—and this is a point with which Harvey also wrestles. I believe that this attitude of existential confrontation/living similarly underlies all that Jesus said and did. It is an attitude reflected in his challenging words and teaching (Matt 19:21).

28. Santos, "Happiness Lab."

29. Frankl, *Man's Search*, 98.

30. Frankl, *Man's Search*, 99.

The kingdom of God and the Golden Rule

In the Gospels this attitude finds expression in the nature of "the kingdom of God." It is a term that is used 162 times in the Gospels and seems to lie at the heart of Jesus' teaching. It comes at the top of the list of intercessions in the Lord's Prayer. Yet the exact meaning of this term remains enigmatic and has been much debated by scholars and writers.[31] Whatever else it might mean, the American writer Paul Gilk argues that the kingdom of God embraces a radical understanding of servanthood and a radical stewardship. "That is, the 'kingdom of God' is both profoundly *ethical* and profoundly *earthly* in its humble 'Taoist' spirituality. It is not some grand cosmic vision of extraterrestrial salvation but, rather, a yearning for deep and unflinching ethical committedness on *Earth*—sharing a coat or a meal, being the least, laying down your life for your friends. It's about personal, social, cultural, and political transformation."[32] Here Gilk is closely following the view of the scripture scholar John Dominic Crossan, who writes, "Jesus is not just announcing to his audience that God's kingdom is now present. He is announcing that it is only present *if and when* it is accepted, entered into, and taken upon oneself. If discussion and debate, agreement and disagreement, argument and contradiction do not arise from and because of his challenges, then no change in consciousness can take place, no paradigm shift can occur, and no kingdom of God can be present."[33]

When it comes to the ministry of Jesus, I must confess that I have generally been happy to go along with the view—dismissed as inadequate by Harvey—that "Jesus offers distinctive moral teaching clearly superior to what is available elsewhere."[34] The gathering of his teachings in the so-called Sermon on the Mount does stand out as a very high moral standard indeed, epitomized by what is often referred to as the Golden Rule of morality: to love thy neighbour as thy self (Matt 22:39). Of course, I realize this is not unique—Hillel said something very similar, as did Confucius and Buddha, and it is on this basis that recently the writer Karen Armstrong has been campaigning for the world religious to sign up to a

---

31. Gilk, *Picking Fights*, ch. 11.

32. Gilk, *Picking Fights*, 141

33. Crossan, *Power of Parable*, 134. Crossan also notes how our very understanding of the nature of parables has been distorted by our failure to understand their original Jewish context and the usage of Jesus.

34. Harvey, *Morals*, 32.

"Charter of Compassion," toward which, in their better moments, they are or should be trending.

I will always remember a little incident that took place many years ago when as a newly ordained priest I was running an ecumenical gospel study day in the parish in a small village in Sussex. Most of those present were formidable retired women of vast experience and acumen. When the dominical injunction of "loving thy neighbor as thy self" (Matt 22:39) came up, one woman stood up and caused not a little consternation and amusement by forcibly stating, "But I don't love myself—in fact I hate myself—so how can I love my neighbor?" The ensuing turmoil and discussion produced no resolution.

Thinking about this, as I have often since done, I have concluded that, like the rest of us, she was a product of the long Christian tradition of teaching on original sin: that we are fallen creatures; that there is no goodness in us; that our works are useless (a theme even stronger in the Protestant tradition); that the world is "a dirty little place" (one even stronger in Augustinian and Platonist tradition); and that we're all heading for damnation. The consequence of this foundational and pernicious teaching is a self-denying asceticism which demands self-annihilation.

This is the Christian tradition of morality or "moralism" that Harvey refers to as a long list of "shoulds" and "should nots" that is so focused on social control that our lives often remain unlived and suppressed—some might say "sublimated"—as a result of fear and guilt. Such "heteronomous" or command morality that justifies itself simply by the authority of an arbitrary pronouncement—"the Law"—is not only oppressive and unpersuasive but was indeed dismissed by Jesus: "You have heard it said . . . but I say . . ."; "The Sabbath was made for man, not man for the Sabbath." In contrast to ecclesiastical demands, the words of Jesus are spoken in and emerge as exhortations and ideals out of human encounters in specific situations, not as binding commandments or expressions of "natural law" that can be read off as literal injunctions—like ripping out one's eye to avoid temptation (something I never heard of having actually happened). Moral values do not drive a person; rather, as Frankl wrote, they "do not *push* him, but rather *pull* him."[35]

35. Frankl, *Man's Search*, 101.

Two types of morality

This distinctive characteristic has been described (by Paul Tillich and John Robinson, among others) as "theonomous"[36]—something that reaches beyond supranaturalism and naturalism to a third position in which the transcendent is nothing external or "out there," but encountered in the *Thou* of finite relationships as their ultimate depth and ground. Such thinking was very much at the heart of Martin Buber's existential human-ism—drawing as it does on a long tradition Jewish wisdom—according to which "All real living is meeting" and in that meeting we find the holy, the "Eternal *Thou*."[37] This would seem to give real insight into the life of Jesus, who lived in companionship and whose teaching arose from many such meetings and encounters. These encounters were marked by a refusal to stand in judgement of others. As Julian Baggini writes, "Although we have to judge *what* is right or wrong, we have no right to say *who* is good or bad. When we remain in judgement and don't move on to forgiveness we become distracted from our primary task of reforming ourselves and we become too fixated with reforming others."[38] Refraining from judgement leads to the re-establishment of relationships; the refusal of forgiveness merely perpetuates broken relationships.

It is partly because of this dynamic or emergent sense of the innate possibilities of life that I have come to reject the foundational ecclesiasti-cal doctrine of original sin and the whole soteriological edifice that has been built upon it, including the Pauline rhetorical tropes of Adam, sin, and death with their artificial chiasm of the Second Adam—there never was a first![39] The church delivers this in a ready-wrapped, rule-dominat-ed, prescriptive form of morality that completely misreads and distorts the aspirational—and unachievable!—attitude of Jesus. Yes, he may have condemned divorce, but he also said "Love your enemies," "Give to all who ask," and "Sell all you have and follow me." But it is curious that usu-ry, condemned alongside sodomy for a thousand years with unspeakable disgust (Dante places those guilty of these sins together in the seventh circle of hell), was quietly dropped with the emergence of new attitudes

36. Kee, *Roots*.

37. Hodes, *Encounter*, 17–30.

38. Baggini, *Godless*, 174.

39. Remarkably there is no such understanding of "the fall" in Jewish tradition, in which the real story of Adam and Eve is one of moral freedom and responsibility for the choices we make. Cf. Pagels, *Adam, Eve, and the Serpent*, xxiii.

toward the use of money and the arrival of modern banking practices. Why then if one "unspeakable" practice can be rehabilitated—as we reach for our cheque books—can the other not?

In place of injunctions against perversities I see the morals of Jesus as the aspiration of possibilities; as pointing not to the inevitability of perdition, but rather of the chance of better outcomes. It is in the endless possibilities of openness, of what the radical theologian Don Cupitt called "solarity"[40] or "solar living" (emulating the endlessly shining benignancy of the sun), reaching beyond ourselves to the unattainable goal of perfection—"being perfect as your heavenly Father is perfect"—that I see the true understanding of the "morality" of Jesus—embracive, uncensorious, unequivocal, radical almost beyond rational comprehension.

40. Cupitt, *Creative Faith*, 77.

Chapter 7

Rethinking Redemption

The Palaeontological challenge to soteriology

WHEN I WAS A seminarian, some fifty years ago, pursuing my theological studies in anticipation of ordination, the course of studies spanned, in what sometimes seemed never-ending tedium, six years. Towards the end of the course in the fifth year we were introduced to one of the key modules: the Atonement or Redemption. Presumably it was left late so that students could first mature in their studies and become conversant with scripture, church history, and other theological prerequisites for the understanding of this core doctrine, a doctrine that stands at the heart of Christian revelation and provides the key to everything the church stands for. In view of the seemingly endless controversy that surrounds the expression of the doctrine, this was perhaps not a bad thing.

The nub of the issue is simple enough to state: what was/is the significance of the death of a man by crucifixion which took place outside Jerusalem sometime in the fourth decade of the common era? If the question is simple enough, the answers are anything but. First up was St. Paul writing a letter in explanation to the Romans. There he refers in a key text to "the redemption which is in Christ Jesus, whom God put forward as an expiation by his blood, to be received by faith" (Rom 3: 24–25). The meaning of this text hinges on the word "expiation."[1] Indeed, is this the right translation of the Greek word *hilasterion* (which only appears once in the Bible), or should it be "propitiation"? But what does this mean and where did it come from?

---

1. Komonchak, *New Dictionary*, 836–51, "Redemption."

The Pauline tradition

For elucidation no doubt one must look to the Jewish context, with which Paul would have been familiar, where *hilasterion* refers to the lid of the Ark of the Covenant which on the day of Atonement (Yom Kippur) was sprinkled with sacrificial blood as part of the ritual to propitiate or appease God's wrath and for which God's forgiveness was granted. If it's "propitiation," then this means the turning away of wrath, but if it's "expiation," this means the taking away of sin. The text does not suggest that Christ placates God's wrath so much as that God puts forward Christ for the remission of sin. But, these subtleties aside, it is exactly in this former sense that atonement came to be understood for centuries to come. It is most graphically expressed in that wonderful eleventh-century Easter hymn, *Victimae paschali laudes* (aka, "Bring all ye dear bought nations bring") which praises, "That guiltless Son, who bought your peace/ and made his Father's anger cease."

In the early centuries of the church this grand soteriological drama of salvation became understood as a cosmic battle in which God and Satan were engaged in a battle over the human race. The neoplatonic tradition envisaged redemption as the emancipation of humans from the devil's power in which Christ's body was used as a kind of bait by which the devil was caught like a mouse in a trap (cf. Augustine, *De trinitatae,* 13:19). In some versions God offered Jesus as a ransom to the devil. It was this tradition that Anselm of Canterbury disowned in his great work *Cur Deus Homo* ("Why God Became Man"). His answer was set in another cultural context, that of feudalism and the sociopolitical world in which Anselm lived. Now redemption was presented as the restoration of the order of creation that had become distorted by sin. An order manifest in the hierarchy and structure of the church, exemplified physically in the majestic structures of the medieval gothic cathedrals

So the controversy and diversity of opinions rumbled on through the Reformation down to modern times. In each period theology reflects, even if inadvertently, some of the cultural tensions of the time in an ongoing process of elaboration. It is in this context that I remember reading a work by John Saward, *The Mysteries of March: Hans Urs von Balthasar on the Incarnation and Easter.*[2] This work, as the subtitle indicates, seeks to elucidate the work of one of the theological giants of the twentieth century and favorite

---

2. Saward, *Mysteries of March.*

theologian of both Pope John Paul II, who made him a cardinal, and Joseph Ratzinger (later Pope Benedict XVI). This patronage itself gives a clue as to the theological orientation of Balthasar, who wrote in resistance to the reductionist accommodation with Western modernity, which seemed to be threatening large areas of theological thinking.

Balthasar, a Swiss Jesuit priest with a biblical-sounding name, is an interesting character who fled Nazi Germany for Basle where he met the mystic and stigmatist Adrienne von Speyr. In 1945 they set up their own religious institute for men and women while his writings took a profoundly mystical turn in attempting to elucidate the vast cosmic "theodrama" (his term) of salvation. The focus of his work was to draw attention to the nature of Jesus' own faith who has "total fidelity to the Father": Critically, Jesus allows the Father to control everthing. Drawing on numerous patristic works from the early church Balthasar elucidates such themes as the "Harrowing of Hell" on Holy Saturday when Christ the new Adam descends to liberate the old Adam from his thraldom to the devil. As with all such works they tend to become a vast phantasmagoria of imagery in which one is left struggling with ideas just beyond the horizon of intelligibility. Despite my best intentions I never did manage to finish even Saward's introductory work, let alone Balthasar's originals!

The new perspective of Teilhard de Chardin

At this time, and while myself studying the doctrine(s) of Atonement at the seminary, one was aware of another significant if rather enigmatic figure, also a Jesuit, hovering on the margins of theological speculation but never quite recognized: Pierre Teilhard de Chardin. The story of this mystical palaeontologist, his enforced silence and posthumous fame, is now well known. But not quite as well-known, as many think, as it is only quite recently that the documents at the heart of this drama have become known.[3] These documents from 1925 are the "six propositions" to which Teilhard had been made to assent. They state that Adam had been created with original holiness, which he lost; that his sin damaged not only him but his descendants; and that this sin is transmitted by propagation and is therefore in all of us.

This theological content—the official teaching of the church—came wrapped up in further demands that faith must be placed above reason

3. Grumett, "Let His Fire Burn," 7–8

and that Catholic dogma could not be reinterpreted in the light of modern knowledge. All of which Teilhard accepted. It was only at the sixth proposition, that affirmed that the whole human race is descended from Adam, that he demurred and added a handwritten codicil that he was doing so "in the full sense that the Holy Church gives them." In this he was referring to the earlier patristic tradition that used Adamic imagery *allegorically* to portray the shared human condition and in doing so distancing himself from the neo-scholastic (and relatively modern) view that linked original sin to a single event. Paradoxically, this "official" view, as with many neo-scholastic positions, unduly restricted if not misrepresented the full scope of Church dogma.

In contrast to this latter view Teilhard regarded sin as something of a cosmic event, that could now be expressed in the second law of thermodynamics, through which decay and disorder were intrinsic to life and from which there was never a time this did not apply. From this perspective Teilhard saw paradise not as a place of past perfection but an image for future spiritual unification (his so-called "omega point"). Redemption could now be viewed as part of the grand drama of evolution, the motivating force of which was embodied in Christ. Though all this seemed to skip ambiguously between many disciplines and would be contained in his writings, notably *The Phenomenon of Man* (begun in 1925), he would have no control over its interpretation as they were not published until after his death in 1955. In the meantime, he had to endure the patronising disdain of his religious superiors who were rather dismissive of what one called his constant "rhapsodizing."

One thing that should be coming clear from even this cursory and fragmentary narrative so far is that there is no one view of redemption. Pauline, patristic, neoplatonic, Anselmian, Teilhardian—none are without their ambiguities, contradictions, and ensuing controversies; none are explicable outside the context of their times; none, even the most mystical, are wholly satisfying. However, with Teilhard there is a sense that one is entering a new domain, for his views are not just theological; they also claim to have a foundation in science. It is his peculiar blend of evolutionary science, philosophy, and theology which, as seen in *The Phenomenon of Man,* gives his work a distinctive if not enigmatic nature, leaving people beguiled but perplexed. Even the militant atheist Richard Dawkins admitted to being "captivated when I read it as an over-romantic undergraduate." It is as if we crave something more than scientific reductionism alone, some grand "theodrama"!

And it is this that Teilhard provides, *par excellence*. What he was looking for was some overall plan or process that revealed itself in the history of the planet and gave coherence and purpose to life. The word he singled out as central to this quest was *"orthogenesis"*—the property of living matter to form ever more complex forms; as he wrote, "Without orthogenesis life would only have spread; with it there is an ascent of life that is invincible."[4] Here, in the notion of ascent, was what he called the "Ariadne's thread" that led through the maze of life; it provided a direction "and therefore proves that evolution has a direction."[5] Furthermore, as his thoughts unfolded, it became clearer where the "axial" direction was leading: it was leading to us, or *hominization*: "But because the specific orthogenesis of the primates . . . coincides with the axial orientation of organized matter . . . man, appearing at the heart of the primates, flourishes on the leading shoot of zoological evolution."[6]

But the process doesn't stop there. Crucially, this whole process of increasing complexity gives rise to consciousness—hence Teilhard's fundamental law of "complexity-consciousness"—which becomes possible through the development of the human mind (by way of *noogenesis*) which in turn leads to the possibility of a new terrestrial threshold for the planet—the *noosphere*, the realm of thought. Of this new realm of interactive human thought Teilhard waxes lyrical: should there be "a Martian capable of analysing the sidereal radiations psychically not less than physically, the first characteristic of our planet would be, not the blue of the seas or green of the forests [the biosphere], but the phosphorescence of thought."[7] When written such "rhapsodizing" may have seemed speculative, if not fanciful, but it was remarkably prophetic of the modern world wide web of interactive thought and the virtual world of electronic media which now increasingly consumes our lives.

It is at this point that for Teilhard science gives way to religion, "in the conjunction of reason and mysticism.[8]" His mystical view of future is the gathering together of personalized thought in the "hyper-personal"

4. de Chardin, *Phenomenon*, 120.

5. de Chardin, *Phenomenon*, 161.

6 de Chardin, *Phenomenon*, 200.

7. de Chardin, *Phenomenon*, 203.

8. de Chardin, *Phenomenon*, 313.

Omega point. This point is not some "ideal focus destined to emerge at the end of time" but already here in embryonic form in the expression of love which brings people together; "Thus something in the cosmos escapes from entropy."[9] Finally, in the Epilogue, Teilhard locates the Christian phenomenon with its spirit of personalism and love expressed in the life of Christ as a "principle of universal vitality." In words that echo the Pauline paeans, this is presented as "indeed a superior form of pantheism" when God is all in all—*en pasi panta Theos*. Such is "the prodigious biological operation—that of the Redeeming Incarnation."[10]

Surprisingly, in this vast theodrama of cosmogenesis, no mention is made of Adam nor original sin. This omission outraged religious traditionalists who denounced the work as heretical and a new form of Pelagianism. Nor were reactions from the scientific world, which didn't quite know what to make of it all, more positive. In one particularly scathing review the biologist Sir Peter Medawar dismissed the whole thing as "tipsy, euphoristic prose poetry which is one of the more tiresome manifestations of the French spirit."[11] But the work still became a publishing sensation.

The timing of its appearance together with his other works in the late 1950s also proved propitious insofar as it contributed to the great theological tsunami which was building up in the Catholic church that would lead to the Vatican Council. Not only did his writings chime with the sense of optimism and radicalism that characterized the 1960s but, in an intangible sort of way, they would contribute to the mindset which of many participants in the Vatican Council and shape some of its key documents, such as "The Church in the Modern World" (*Gaudium et Spes*, 1965), which sought to break out from the attitude of suspicion and fear that had characterized much of the previous hundred years, engaging more positively with the spirit of the times. This new spirit of optimism was certainly my memory of conferences run by the Teilhard de Chardin Association, which I joined in 1968, and was again one of those intangible influences that led to my pursuing a religious vocation.

One of the first expressions of this new spirit was the so-called Dutch Catechism, published in the Netherlands in 1966 as "A New Catechism of the Catholic Faith for Adults." Though it became an international best seller it also ran into fierce opposition from traditionalists for a number

9. de Chardin, *Phenomenon*, 298.

10. de Chardin, *Phenomenon*, 321.

11 Dawkins, *Unweaving*, 184.

of reasons. Not only did it not mention angels (!), it chose not to focus on the historical nature of Adam and Eve or original sin but rather a Christo-centric narrative. The denunciation from a Roman consistory of cardinals was not long in coming. This stated unambiguously that man's fall from grace lost him God's sanctity and justice, and he entered a state of sin that propagated throughout human nature. One of the cardinals who took a dim view of both Teilhard's influence and the pernicious teaching that flowed from it was Karol Wojtyla, soon to become Pope John Paul II. One of the things he would do as pope would be to promote a new *Catechism of the Catholic Church* which would clearly state the traditional teaching of redemption, and much else besides.

A new understanding of human origins

It was at this time that I was becoming increasingly disturbed by the status of those archaic humans who had preceded *Homo sapiens*, particularly the Neanderthals. As the eminent palaeontologist Chris Stringer wrote in *In Search of the Neanderthals*, "No other group of prehistoric people carries such a weight of scientific and popular preconceptions, or has had its name so associated with the lingering traits of savagery, stupidity, and animal strength."[12] Evidence revealed, as at the Shanidar cave in Iraq, that here was a people who buried their dead, scattered flowers on the bodies in some sort of ritual, hunted with skill, and decorated their bodies as well as cared for the infirm. Here in fact was a sensitive people like us, but how did they relate to us? What was their place, if any, in the grand theodrama of redemption, or were they just to be cast aside?

At the time I still accepted a primal human couple as having some form of historical reality with *Homo sapiens* having a distinct status. But what if humans had mated with Neanderthals from the outset: this would surely have implications for that primal state of "sanctity and justice" in which it was claimed that Adam had been created. Evidence for some kind of interaction mounted. Then in 2008, Svante Paabo and his team of geneticists at the Max Planck Institute for Evolutionary Anthropology in Leipzig pulled off the master stroke of teasing DNA out of millennia-old Neanderthal bones in sufficient quantities compare with the modern human genome.[13] The conclusion was that early humans had interbred with Neanderthals and

12. Quoted in McKie, 150.

13. Paabo, *Neanderthal Man*.

that every one of us, but not Africans, carry between 2 and 4 percent of their genes. What the historical evidence was implying was that if there was interbreeding or hybridization then, by definition, we were not dealing with two species but one broader, diverse human population.

And that is not all. More recently, in August 2018, Paabo and his team released further DNA evidence that had been extracted from a recently found bone of another prehistoric people that had been found in the Denisovian caves in the remote Altai Mountains of Central Asia. The DNA analysis revealed not only that this was an entirely new group of archaic humans which had split from a common Neanderthal ancestor some five hundred thousand years ago but that it had also mated with the Neanderthals some thirty to fifty thousand years ago. Other genetic comparisons have shown that Denisovan genes are widespread in the population of Asia, indicating that they ranged widely over Siberia and Southeast Asia. At least one of their genes helps modern Tibetans to live at high altitudes.[14] Genetics is revealing that our ancient ancestral "cousins" did not become extinct but live on *in us!*

Clearly, what is emerging from all this genetic evidence is a completely new and unexpected understanding of human origins. It was while excavating at Choukoutin near Peking in 1926 that the team with whom Teilhard worked discovered the so-called "Peking Man." At the time this fossil, dated to about seven hundred thousand years ago, caused a sensation. It was believed to represent a distinct species, named *Sinanthropus pekinensis,* that had migrated to Southeast Asia from Africa some 1.8 million years ago. Its discovery also prompted Teilhard to begin the first pages of *Le Phenomene Humain* together with other notable works such as *Le Milieu Divin.* Since then, numerous other, similar fossils have been found in China with the same curious mix of ancient and modern human features, prompting the understanding that these are not so much a distinct species as "transitional forms." The evidence suggests that early modern humans were in southern China at least one hundred thousand years ago, with the further radical

14. Barras, "Genes of the Undead," 74–77. The recent discovery (2021) of so-called Dragon Man in northeastern China as being a closely linked "sister species" to modern humans has dramatic implications for our understanding of human evolution in that *Homo sapiens* as the apex of an evolutionary tree is replaced by an understanding that we are simply the last species to remain from a network of many other, often overlapping and inter-breading, hominids who walked the earth. This is a view confirmed by the newly excavated site in Israel at Nesher Ramia that was shared by other ancient humans 140,000 years ago.

implication that they continued to evolve there. This suggests a form of "multiregionalism" as the context of human origins. This once maverick idea has now become more respectable, undermining the prevalent palaeontological model of human evolution that *Homo sapiens* emerged from Africa as a single population—the "Out of Africa" model.[15]

Apart from anything else, all this suggests that the conclusions that Teilhard drew from his discovery and which underlay his work—of a single progressive axis of human evolution that emerged from a single source— was wrong, as was the model on which he drew of a neatly bifurcating evolutionary branching tree.[16] This standard scientific model of human evolution is what Darwin had sketched in his notebook with the appended comment "I think," but the emerging model based on new genetic information is of a complex web of species branching and then recombining periodically over a period of two million years. As the geneticist Josh Akey of the University of Washington says, "Take a pen on a piece of paper and start making squiggly lines: that's human history."

Redemption as liberation

The theological implications of all this for any grand theodrama of redemption are profound. It was with the imagery of a counterpoint between the First and Second Adam that St. Paul constructed his doctrine of salvation when writing to the Romans; the original sin that lead to universal death now being offset by the sacrifice of the new Adam. But if there is no first Adam, there is no second, and the whole soteriological edifice collapses. All the core theological themes that hinge on the putative historical actions of a primal couple—the fall, original sin, the subsequent unfolding of Salvation History, and the role of the Church in salvation—are now to be viewed as no more than fanciful mythological constructs. The value that can be extracted from them is less than the deception they foster, whatever a consistory of cardinals may say to the contrary!

So, we return to the original starting point of this reflection: the man who died on a cross outside Jerusalem nearly two thousand years ago. What must we say of him? Once the traditional grand theodrama is stripped away to reveal the original teachings of Jesus (something the "Jesus Seminar" has been engaged in) we are still left with a significant historical figure: a Jewish

15. Douglas, "Our Asian Origins," 35–37.

16. de Chardin, *Phenomenon,* 213 (diagram 4).

preacher and prophet whose ethics and example remain a monumental challenge. The Latin American theologian Jon Sobrino elucidates this in his *Christology at the Crossroads*: "Over against the notion of God as power Jesus sets the notion of God as love."[17] In his compelling study of the nature of power and God (*God and Empire*), the eminent scripture scholar John Dominic Crossan makes a persuasive case for what he terms the "radicality" of scripture expressed in the teaching of Jesus.[18] Crossan contrasts the message of John the Baptist anticipating the coming of the kingdom of God with that of the teaching of Jesus about the kingdom of God: for the former it was a case of waiting to see what God did (which never happened) but for Jesus the kingdom of God is happening now through what *we* do.

The focus of the challenge of Jesus was not in his nature, who he was, but in his message of what is expected of us. It was something he himself challenged: "Why call me 'Lord' yet refuse to do what I say?" (Luke 6:46). In this perspective much of the history of the church has been little more than a massive distraction, with its emphasis on hierarchy, submission to the truth, conformity and conversion. All this took precedence over the dominical ideals which are noted then set aside—do good to those who persecute you, love your enemies, give without expectation of reward, seek the humbler place of service . . . an inquisitor preparing an *auto-da-fé* in Dostoyevsky's searing parable of The Brothers Karamazov had no time for the return of Christ!

This new perspective of redemption, which immersed the significance of Jesus in the ongoing social needs and politics of the day, came to characterise the Liberation Theology that emerged in Latin America after the Vatican Council. Among the many distinguished voices the Jesuit Jon Sobrino (Why are they always Jesuits?) stands out in demanding a new view of salvation which is not just about orthodoxy (belief) but orthopraxis: "Following Jesus means taking the love that God manifested on the cross and making it *real* in history."[19] Paradoxically, he notes that "it was 'religion' that killed the Son" and that what triumphed with the cross "is the end of people's subjugation by other human beings in the name of

17. Sobrino, *Christology*, 214.

18. Crossan, *God and Empire*.

19. Sobrino, *Christology*, 227.

religion."[20] The history of Golgotha is now being lived out in the world of the poor and the search for humanization.[21]

Amongst contemporary theologians there have been many such voices—most of them silenced and crushed in the interest of the centralized power of Rome, like the charismatic bishop Dom Helder Camera. These voices argue that where love, peace, and justice take place on earth there is already the beginning of the final eschatological state, an "identification without total identity" between redemptive salvation and political liberation. This narrative of commemorative solidarity with Christ is ongoing.

But to draw this reflection to a close I would like to end with reference to the philosopher of "post-Christianity," Don Cupitt, who over many works has argued for a respect for the extraordinary "ordinariness" of life and an ethics of "solarity." This latter is the core of his vision of a redeemed world, for what he calls "solar living"—that constant outpouring of generosity and giving, like the sun which is the benign source of life for all. This was characterized above all in the life and teaching of Jesus, the Son of Man. It is this which now constitutes the grand theodrama of the crucified God for our times.

20. Sobrino, *Christology*, 209.

21. Cf. Sobrino, *Eye of the Needle*.

Chapter 8

A Conflicted Beginning

The genesis of Christendom and the West

AMONG THE BOOKS I have been reading during lockdown is Michael Goulder's *A Tale of Two Missions*. This is not a new book—it was written in 1993—and Michael Goulder has now passed away (in 2010). Goulder was a widely respected scripture scholar and even though not among the "superstars" of the trade his publications are notable for the penetrating forensic skill he brought to the analysis of scriptural texts—source criticism. It was only a few years ago that I became aware of his work when an Anglican friend suggested I may find his work of interest and it is only now that I have gotten round to reading some of it.

And what a revelation it has been. In fact, it has been quite a shock to me that after a lifetime reading and studying, being taught about the scriptures and teaching them to others, I realize how much I have missed or never knew. This is particularly true of the New Testament, which obviously underpins the Christian belief we know—or think we know today—and our understanding of the church. In my case, coming from a Roman Catholic background, this has come with the unequivocal conviction of a great tradition that, as Cardinal Newman so memorably put it, has grown as an oak out of an acorn. In this view the story of the church—for him the Roman Catholic Church—is one of a continuous unfolding "development" that has been taking place under divine guidance from the outset. Though there have always been many reasons and no shortage of people willing to contest this metanarrative I never really realized until reading Goulder how questionable the foundation of such a view really is and that there was in fact no inevitable beginning.

It is as if a window has been opened onto a world I had only partially glimpsed, echoes of which provided little more than background noise to a much more dramatic setting of the inevitable rise and triumph of Christianity in the classical world. Goulder's study in *A Tale of Two Missions* covers the period between 48 CE and 130 CE, when the New Testament was being composed and at a time when there were two clear foci in the communities that claimed to be followers of Jesus: one was in Jerusalem, under the leadership of Peter and the sons of Zebedee (later James), and the other among a diaspora of gentile converts made by Paul in towns of Asia Minor (now eastern Turkey), prominent among which was Ephesus. These are the "two missions"—Petrine and Pauline—of Goulder's book.

What emerges is that these two missions had very different understandings of a whole range of issues—the validity of the Jewish dietary laws; whether the kingdom of God had arrived; the place of work, sex, and money in daily life; the nature and place of the "gifts of the spirit" within church governance; and also the nature of Jesus' divinity. As the years passed these divisions deepened to a point of outright hostility and enmity between members of the two missions so much so that we find one denouncing the other as "the devil's seed" (2 John 7). And this was among members of, reputedly, the same church (1 John 2:19).

The Pauline mission was focused on reaching out beyond the constraints of Judaism to the gentile world. In practical terms this meant abandoning specifically Jewish practices such as circumcision and kosher regulations (two issues over which he had to return repeatedly in his letters) together with the rituals associated with the distant temple in Jerusalem in favour of domestically-based and lay-led celebrations and not of the sabbath but *kyriakon* (Day of the Lord). All this was inspired by the transformative vision Paul had had of the resurrected Christ through which he became convinced that God had intervened in history through Jesus in a decisive way and that the end of time was imminent. Though he had never met Jesus there was never any doubt in Paul's mind as to his pre-existent divine status.[1]

In contrast, the Petrine mission based in Jerusalem had a somewhat different view. Though recognizing Jesus as a *hasid* (holy one) of whom an angelic power called Christ had taken hold at baptism (Mark 1:11) and who had shown himself to be a son of God, particularly through his Resurrection, this was a church whose members had known Jesus and his family

---

1. Ehrman, *How Jesus became God,* 251–69.

and whose brother, James—yes, brother, not "brother" or "cousin"!—was a leading figure. For this church, whose members continued to practice the Jewish rituals and attend the temple services, a new eschatological dimension had been added to life that recognized this was indeed the prophesied end of days which called for a radical new way of communal living in which all wealth was shared and the more mundane realities of life such as work and marriage could now be dispensed with.

Two types of faith

What one sees here is not only two missions and types of church but something even more fundamental to the future of Christianity and the West: two types of faith. The significance of this was noted by Martin Buber in his celebrated work *Two Types of Faith*, in which he explored not only the difference between the Hebrew word for faith, *emunah*, and its Greek translation, *pistis,* but also the vast difference in worldviews they implied. In the former case it was a matter of trust in the context of a community relationship; in the latter it was a matter of individual intellectual assent to truth, *of individual conversion and saving one's soul.*[2]

This view, and the difference entailed by the two concepts, has been more recently enunciated by the former chief rabbi of Great Britain, Jonathan Sacks. The common understanding of religion in the West is shaped by personal belief in God, of saving one's soul and finding an eternal reward—a very Pauline view. But, as Sacks noted for Jews, holiness lays "in our relationships and social structures." It is not preoccupied with the next world but this one, emphasising how best to live with each other through compassion, kindness and mutual respect—a very Petrine view! It is in these contrasting views of faith and religion that one can see the basis of a divide opening up between Christianity and Judaism that would characterise two thousand years of history. But at the very beginning of the church's existence, it was a latent division *within* the church that was still a movement within Judaism.

This brings us to the crucial difference between the ways that Jesus and his teaching were understood among his early followers. Throughout the letters of St. Paul and the Acts of the Apostles we find repeated indications of tensions and even open conflict between Paul and the Jerusalem church under the leadership of Peter and Jesus' brother James. Likely

2. Buber, *Two Types of Faith*, 7.

enough the New Testament accounts of these differences have been intentionally smoothed over and harmonized—particularly the account found in the Acts of the Apostles—to present a pleasing and monolithic narrative that unfolds in accordance with divine design, much as Newman opined. That this account is now thought to have been written over sixty years after the events and by a source we now call Luke who was a companion and apologist for Paul is all of significance. Still, it is clear that his irenic account of the so-called Council of Jerusalem (c. 48 CE) written about 115 CE varies from Paul's more abrasive account in Galatians 2 written some sixty years earlier.[3] In this letter Paul also refers to "two missions," one to the gentiles, whom he sees as being entrusted to him, and the other to the Jews, entrusted to Peter. But can two very different understandings of Christianity have been competing with each other?

Once one becomes aware of this underlying dynamic, something more significant begins to emerge. It is not sufficient to read the various texts as if it was just a matter of different authors taking a personal view of things with various nuances and theological perspectives. What such an approach to the narrative does not reveal is that the New Testament texts give precisely this impression because they were selected to do so by what would ultimately become the dominant or winning mission, the Paulines. The way the life of Jesus has been presented and the theological reflection that this has given rise to are the consequence of the fundamental difference of the "two missions" that would determine everything that follows. As the winners get to write the history, what history has bequeathed to us is a book that consist of the Epistles of Paul (and his followers), four Gospels, two of them ultra-Pauline and two (Matthew and Luke) building bridges to Jerusalem and the Petrines.

The New Testament itself spans a trajectory of views from Mark's Gospel—with no birth narrative and a ministry that begins with the baptism of Jesus as the Son of God (a Petrine position using a traditional Jewish metaphor)—to the ultra-Pauline position of John's Gospel which also has no birth narrative but a statement of divine preexistence using Greek philosophical conceptualization. What has been remembered is also what is re-membered.[4]

3. The dates of many events and texts related to the New Testament are the subject of ongoing academic discussion. This date of 115 CE was accepted as the most likely by the Jesus Seminar of scripture scholars based on the work of Richard Pervo.

4. Ehrman, *Jesus before the Gospels*.

The year 70: the end of the beginning

At a crucial point in the emerging story of the church an event took place only vaguely alluded to in the New Testament but which would have seismic implications for the future of the church: the catastrophic invasion of Judea by the Roman army to supress a Jewish revolt. As a result, the population of Jerusalem was massacred, with those who could fleeing to what safe havens they could find further afield in Syria and the Middle East. Included in this were the survivors of the Petrine church based in Jerusalem. Until this point this church seems to have been remarkably successful—with even "many tens of thousands" of members (Acts 21:20)—and its influence even gaining ground further afield in Asia Minor among the churches founded by Paul and challenging his teaching. It is these "missionaries" to his churches who provoked such dissension that gave rise to the ire reflected in his letters. Such was their growing influence that on his travels Paul sometimes even had to avoid his own churches (Acts 20:16)—the explanation that he was in a rush is unconvincing given that he had time to call the elders to Miletus and await their arrival and it is quite possible that when he did visit Jerusalem (in 58 CE) members of the church there were responsible for his being reported to the temple authorities. His subsequent arrest ultimately led to his execution.

After the Roman devastation of 70 CE from being on the back foot, the pro-Roman, pro-gentile, post-ritualistic Paulines with their high Christology of Jesus as a preexistent divine figure found they had the field to themselves. Their subsequent history could now be presented with an air of providential inevitability (as by Luke) that would provide the core of what would come to be known as "Roman" Christianity or Catholicism. And a crucial move in this historiography was to annex the narrative of the authority of Peter. Though there is no clear evidence that Peter ever wanted to or would have any reason to go to Rome and about whose death we know absolutely nothing (other than from later apocryphal works), and regardless of the fact that the Roman church was in existence before the arrival of Paul—and was a church where women had a foundational and significant role (Rom 16:1–2)—regardless of all this, Peter and Paul have been presented as the twin foundational figures of this church ever since. What triumphed was a Pauline view of Christianity.

But this is not without qualification. When one considers the early creedal affirmation echoed in Galatians 3:28, which disallows discrimination against Jews, slaves, and women, what is surprising about this teaching is how soon it would be forgotten! By the end of the century the texts of the New Testament had become marked by their antisemitism, accommodation of slavery, and anti-feminism.[5] In the apologetics of Justin Martyr (c. 100–165 CE) we see how a new Hellenic philosophical/theological understanding shaped by a belief in a preexistent *logos*, hidden word, stripped the Bible of its historical context and deemed the "old" covenant of God with the Jewish people to be replaced with a new covenant (testament) with Christians.[6] Now in place was the Hellenic "high" Christology of the Pauline churches reflected in the divine *logos* of St. John—a doctrine that had come to replace the Hebraic "low" Christology of the Petrine churches.[7] Christianity, as we have come to know it, had arrived.

Though the subsequent history of Christianity in Syria and the Middle East can only be inferred with difficulty from questionable sources, one thing that characterizes it is its profusion of practices and beliefs.[8] It is this that would provide the context for the ensuing controversies over Christology with which the later "Christian" Roman emperor, Constantine, would engage in a battle for "orthodoxy" over "heresy." In fact, when we look more closely at these theological conflicts, what we see is a resurgence of those differences between the Petrine tradition and the Pauline tradition in which the latter, affirmed at the Council of Nicea (325 CE), was now presented as incontrovertible orthodoxy. It is this creed that would be would be imposed on the western Roman world with the authority of the emperor.

But there is something else about how Western Christianity became so distinctive. In his fascinating book *Inventing the Individual* Larry Siedentop has charted in great detail how a sense of individuality and the importance of the person emerged as one of, perhaps the most, distinctive characteristic of Christianity.[9] The sense of the moral equivalence of all before God that was proclaimed by St. Paul in his letter to the Galatians, regardless of status or class (Gal 3:28), amounted to "an intellectual revolution" that turned the world upside down.[10] This emphasis on the individual's moral agency—of the individual answerable to and under the scrutiny of God—replaced the

5. Crossan, *God and Empire*, 143–90.

6. van Hagen, *Agnostic*, 78–60.

7. Goulder, *A Tale of Two Missions*, 99–106, "The Messiah Christology," and 107–13, "The Possession Christology."

8. Ehrman, *Lost Christianities*.

9. Siedentop, *Inventing the Individual*.

10. Siedentop, *Inventing the Individual*, 51–66.

family as the focus of mortality and in doing so marked a decisive break with the mores of the ancient world.

The rise of monasticism and Western Christendom

To this unfolding narrative another twist is presented by the rise of an important new movement within the church: monasticism. It has always intrigued me, particularly as a result of my own monastic experience, what exactly were the origins of a movement that had seemingly so little in common with the church in which it appeared, shunning the urban centers where the Christian communities had first taken root,[11] rejecting the authority of bishops with their embracive cultural views, opting for a solitary life, despising women and sex, radical in its rejection of all earthly wealth in pursuit of an other-worldly asceticism. All these practices have been given numerous circumstantial historical explanations. But underlying them is another explanation, betrayed above all by one of the places of its origin in the remote wilderness of Syria. It is exactly to such places that the Petrine remnant of Jerusalem fled.

Notable among these were a group that has been called Ebionites or *'Ebionim,* the Poor—a term often used in the Psalms for God's faithful, persecuted remnant. When the bishop Epiphanius of Salamis in Cyprus asked some of them about the origin of their name in about 370 CE, they replied that they were descended from the Jerusalem church and their forebears had become poor by sharing their money in the days of the community recorded in the Acts of the Apostles. The alternative view (of the bishop), reluctant to accept such an explanation, was that they were the followers of a heretic, Ebion: but there was no such historical person! Rather their radical views on the sharing of wealth, giving up sex for ascetic reasons, believing that Jesus was possessed by the Spirit at his baptism in the dessert wastes of the Jordan valley, we have a strand of tradition reaching back to the very origins of Christianity. In other words, monasticism is in its genesis heir to the Petrine mission.

I say this is ironic because, in a further twist of the historical maze, it is the monasticism that was imported to Europe from the east that would come to be the savior of the church in the West in the so-called Dark Ages and provide the foundations for Medieval Christendom. Though Benedict of Nursia (c. 480–547 CE) and his Benedictine order are perhaps the most

11. Meeks, *First Urban Christians.*

famous, he was not alone. Of particular note was the rule of St Augustine of Hippo that he wrote in 338 CE while living in his hometown of Tagaste (now in Algeria).[12] This is the oldest monastic rule of the Western church and was adopted or adapted by numerous renewal movements across the centuries, such as the Order of Prémontré (or Premonstratensians—the order to which I belonged) founded in 1121 by St. Norbert of Xanten. The Rule of Augustine cited as its foundational ideal the passage in the Acts of the Apostles where the whole community was said to have held everything in common (Acts 4:32). Together with a routine of continued liturgical observance this was the main characteristic of the Petrine community of Jerusalem.

The monastic roots of secularism and science

The monastic ideal rapidly spread across Europe, transforming the Pauline understanding of the church that, apart from its pro-gentile orientation, had in origin been urban, with inclusively lay- and female-led communities, into something very different. With its all-male celibate clerical cast, rigorous sexual prudery, ascetic denunciation of wealth and worldliness, remote locations, elaborate ritualism, grandiose liturgical architecture, and highly structured way of life, the monasticization of the church created an institution almost beyond recognition from these earlier domestic roots. In particular it assumed a division of the church between members and ministers. This had once been quite fluid, but was now two very distinct tiers: the secular laity and religious clergy, a division that would have been anathema to Paul and all that he taught.

This whole process of re-formation culminated in the eleventh century with the reforms of Gregory VII—known as the Gregorian Reform (c. 1050–80 CE)—that imposed clerical celibacy, insisted on the complete separation of clerical appointments from lay investiture, and affirmed the primacy of the papacy as the supreme authority over the emperor. The determination of Gregory—himself a monk of the influential abbey of Cluny—made the distinction between the two worlds, secular and clerical, absolute and led to the famous conflict with the Holy Roman Emperor, Henry IV. The consequence of this epochal clash, in which the emperor was humiliated at Canossa, would be momentous for the future

---

12. This rule or canon for groups of clergy (canons) living together was taken to Europe after the collapse of the Roman province to the Visigoths and is reflected in the influential canonical rule of Archbishop Chrodegang of Metz, 755 CE

of Europe in a perhaps unexpected outcome. As the theologian Charles Davis wrote, "The victory of Pope Gregory VII in excluding the Emperor from ecclesiastical investitures caused the first separation of State from Church . . . .The Emperor as Emperor was now thrust out of the Church, and the Empire became a secular reality."[13] Here lies the origin of the modern Western secular state.

The advent of monasticism, with its ascetic practices given to scrupulous self-examination—of which the development of confessional practices and penitential rituals were an outcome—had further unforeseen consequences for the formation of Western society. In a fine chapter on "Scrupulosity" in his book *The Meaning of the West,* the philosopher Don Cupitt notes how "a scrupulous, rigorous self-examination in the quest for inner truthfulness" also created the psychological background to Europe's scientific revolution.[14] At first sight this may sound incongruous, but in the lives of such figures as the Franciscan friar Roger Bacon (c. 1220–92 CE), with a dedication to empirical observation, reflection, and experimentation (he was even regarded as a wizard), we see the emergence of a distinctive new manner of critical thinking and analysis that in time would become the basis of the scientific method and a distinctive feature of Western culture.[15] Noting this development, with reference to such towering geniuses as Newton and Darwin, Cupitt writes: "Religious, even perhaps neurotic, scrupulosity is turned outward so that it becomes *intellectual* scrupulosity—with startling results."[16]

The ensuing historical drama of this development was galvanized and given an extra level of complexity in the thirteenth century with the introduction of Aristotelian thinking—via the Islamic world—into the universities of Europe. This naturalistic philosophy was initially seen as a threat to the traditional teaching of the Roman Catholic Church but was eventually incorporated into the body of teaching that came to be known as the scholastic or Thomist synthesis, after its greatest exponent St. Thomas Aquinas. Regardless of the actual truth of what Aristotle taught and was accepted in the scholastic synthesis—much of which was eventually proved to be wrong—the most important consequence was that it directed human inquiry towards the natural world that was understood to be comprehensible

13. Davis, *Religion*, 3; Siedentop, *Inventing the Individual*, 192–207.

14. Cupitt, *Meaning*, 94–101.

15. Whitehead, *Science and the Modern World*, 14–15.

16. Cupitt, *Meaning*, 97.

according to reasoned inquiry.[17] Originally such naturalistic understanding was seen as a way to understanding the nature of the Creator, as in the *Summa contra gentiles* of Thomas Aquinas, but in time the development of the experimental method—such as by Roger Bacon—led to the realization that the natural world was an intelligible totality governed by its own internal laws.[18] Thus from medieval theology came the possibility not only of science but a secular understanding of the world that is "incarnational": as the philosopher A. N. Whitehead wrote, "faith in the possibility of science . . . is an unconscious derivation from medieval theology."[19]

One monastic innovation, if not invention, that neatly joins the two aspects of the genesis of secularism and science is one that perhaps more than any other is at the heart of the modern world: the clock. Some historians have seen this development as a fundamental element in the creation and characterization of modern industrial society: as Sally Dugan wrote on *The Roots of the Industrial Revolution,* "The regular rhythm of the demands of God was a foretaste of the more strident stroke of the Machine Age."[20] The first clocks were beginning to appear in the fourteenth century: by 1350, Richard of Wallingford was constructing a complex astronomical clock at the monastery of St. Alban's and a clock tower was installed in Norwich cathedral. Soon this useful spiritual accessory for regulating the many monastic times of prayer was moving beyond the confines of the cloister to the market place. Here it slowly but surely began to impose the discipline of time on the populace at large. Not only the sacred order but the secular order came to be increasingly characterized by time keeping. Cambridge historian, Simon Schaffer, thinks the growing awareness of personal time was critical to the creation of a new kind of European society: "I see a very strong relationship, which emerges between the 1300s and the 1500s, between mechanical clocks and an individualization or privatization of time."[21] Freedom to arrange one's affairs and go about one's business began to underpin a new kind of secular order or state which is implicitly neutral and democratic.[22] For this new development

17. Weinberg, *To Explain the World,* 131.

18. Crombie, *Robert Grosseteste.*

19. Whitehead, *Science and the Modern World,* 16.

20. Dugan, *Day the World Took Off,* 104.

21. Quoted in Duggan, *Day the World Took Off,* 107.

22. Siedentop, *Inventing the Individual,* 349, argues that the new image of society as an association of individuals—a state—began to emerge in the fifteenth century as an unintended consequence of feudal monarchies with their centralising regimes: "The monarchs not only created states, but also the foundation for a 'public' or 'national'

it is important to look away from the monastic kind of coordinated world to one in which individuals could arrange meetings, plan what to do and measure what others were doing. As the influence of the clock spread it became a prod to personal achievement and productivity: "Eternity ceased gradually to serve as the measure and focus of human actions."[23] In time, personalized time became the concomitant of personal freedom.

This drama spans centuries but became turbo-charged with the Reformation and rise of Protestantism.[24] Though this seismic event can in some ways be seen as a very "Pauline" reaction to centuries of "Petrine" domination, Luther's anguished search for justification to ensure salvation would be quickly followed by the rise of Puritanism in the sixteenth century. A distinctive practice of Puritanism was again the scrupulosity of self-examination and attempts to discern the will of God in daily events that led to practice of detailed diary-keeping as a religious exercise observing and recording "the movements of the spirit" and signs of providential action. This practice led to the careful observation of the natural world exemplified by the works of clergymen such as the botanist John Ray and naturalist Gilbert White, whose observations opened up whole new areas of knowledge.[25] It was from the ranks of such "diarists," many of whom were clergymen, that would emerge the proto-scientists and (in England) the foundation of the Royal Society for the Improvement of Natural Knowledge (1660). Thus, the long tradition of monastic asceticism provided not only the psychological but the religious foundation of science and secularism that have come to be defining features of Western civilization.[26]

The outcome of Pauline Christianity

But to this mentality and enterprise there is also a deeper theological foundation. It is an expression of the fundamental Christian (Pauline) belief in the

---

opinion." The beginnings of this process were to be found in the Investiture Controversy of the eleventh century. Soon monarchs were having their "divine right" challenged by individuals, as with King John and the imposition of the Magna Carta in 1215, the seminal document of modern society.

23. Quoted in Duggan, *Day the World Took Off*, 106; Mumford, *Technics and Civilization*.

24. Henrich, *Weirdest People*.

25. Thompson, *Watch on the Heath*.

26. Spencer, *Evolution of the West*, 94–109.

uniqueness of the Incarnation, of God becoming human, and the uniqueness of revealed truth. Among the many ways of understanding this belief is the view that the story of the Incarnation did not just depict a particular historical event but was a symbolic portrayal of the eternal spiritual process of the cosmos, involving both the humanization of God and the divinization of humankind.[27] For the nineteenth century German theologian Ludwig Feuerbach the Incarnation marked a turning point in history that over time gave birth to the idea that there was only one age or *saeculum*.

This idea was not itself original, as medieval writers and mystics like Joachim of Fiore (c. 1135–1202)—often deemed the most important millenarian thinker of the period—understood the unfolding of history to be in "three ages" with the final Age of the Spirit. This age would be characterized by a new religious "order" of spiritual men that would arise, making the hierarchy of the Church unnecessary. Such "incarnational" thinking that affirmed the indwelling spirit presaged the emergence of the modern secular state. As the Anglican scholar J. R. Illingworth wrote, "Secular civilization has cooperated with Christianity to produce the modern world."[28] He understood this to be the providential counterpart of the Incarnation and the Pauline vision of Christ in all things (Eph 1:3–14). This is an often-unacknowledged aspect of the Christian legacy.

As we look back over this convoluted history our perspectives continue to change. As Goulder acknowledged, "We can only interpret the things that happen to us through the categories of thought which our society and upbringing provide to us." So powerful are the categories of thought that are handed down to us that they often prevent us from seeing reality. Such traditionalism has been brought into question in our times not only by the findings of sophisticated scholarship but sensational discoveries, such as those at Qumran and Nag Hammadi, that cast new light on old issues. Other discoveries still have the power to surprise and shock, such as genetic finger-printing that has revealed some Palestinian ancestry going back to Jewish times indicating that they were survivors of the Roman holocaust who managed to remain attached to the land—much like the *anawim* of the Old Testament who survived the Babylonian

---

27. This was the view of Ludwig Feuerbach expressed in his book of 1841, *The Essence of Christianity*. Quoted in Geering, *Witness to Change*, 66.

28. Quoted in Geering, *Witness to Change*, 68.

deportation—through finding accommodation to subsequent regimes: they are still the true inheritors of the land.[29]

Conclusion

As at the beginning so in our own time there are deep and growing divisions within churches, between those seeking to retain old traditions and more liberal "modernizers," between fundamentalists and progressives. In some cases, this leads to a kind of paralysis of church governance or, like a car that has crashed its gears, unable to move forward or backwards—such is the recent agonizing of the RC church over whether to ordain married priests. But this just becomes a nuisance to others who want to get on with life. In a sense we are once again being challenged by the Pauline vision, willing to set aside scriptural precedent this time not about circumcision or dietary laws but the acceptability of gay relationships or the divorced and remarried, of an openness and willingness to accommodate the modern world without discrimination of Jew or gentile, rich or poor, male or female (Gal 3:28) with community-based churches led by local men and women—such as the church leadership of Phoebe (Rom 16:3).

That this is not always the case was the theme of the American scripture scholar, Stephen Patterson, in his book *The Forgotten Creed*. Writing of his experiences of the church in the United States, he states, "The church is the last truly segregated public space in America," and that "an ancient Christian credo declaring solidarity across ethnic lines, class division, and gender difference sounded a little unbelievable to someone who had come to see the Christian church as more a symbol of social ills than idealistic utopian dreams."[30]

But perhaps the most disturbing aspect of this story is that after two millennia the many distinctive Christian churches and traditions of the Middle East are now experiencing a final annihilation at the hands of those who would not so much rewrite or reinterpret history as obliterate it. For the future what is now needed is something of the radical Pauline vision and energy rather than Petrine equivocation. Of course, there are those who will argue that both are needed rather than some mythic monolithic structure. But then that's how it all began.

---

29. Sands, *Invention of the Jewish People*, 186–89.
30. Patterson, "Forgotten."

Chapter 9

Will the Sphinx Ever Smile?

Power, abuse, and ministry in the Roman Catholic Church

THE TABLET IS A well-regarded UK Catholic weekly journal that covers religious and international affairs in an informed and enlightened manner. Having said that, though I still have an archive of memorable articles collected from *The Tablet* over the years, I stopped reading it some twenty-three years ago! That was the point at which I parted company with the Church, having become increasingly exasperated with the reactionary and autocratic pontificate of John Paul II. Before that I had spent a similar length of time, twenty-three years, serving as a priest in various roles but mostly in an inner-city parish seeking to bring about something of that renewal of the Church envisaged by Vatican II. Ultimately the gap between life and faith became unbridgeable.[1]

That was then. Now the news is that things are different under a different pope. Indeed, the new film *The Two Popes*, pulling in five star reviews, portrays a genial and compassionate man whose warmth offsets the darker shadows of his predecessor, Benedict XVI. But have things really changed? Can they change? Other news from inside the Vatican closet, such as that by Frederic Martel, with its chronicle of salacious scandal, suggests otherwise.[2] Recently, for example, the Vatican has been found to have funded—with the donations intended by Catholics for good works—the biographical film about Sir Elton John, *Rocketman*, showing graphic gay sex. In view of the vigorous denunciation of homosexuality by the church, is this a further example

1. Kirkham, *From Monk to Modernity*.
2. Martel, *In the Closet of the Vatican*.

of hypocrisy or just bad investment management? The shadows remain. Even Pope Francis has rather ruefully quipped that changing things in the Vatican was like trying to clean the Sphinx with a toothbrush.

Though I no longer read *The Tablet,* which reports on such affairs, from time to time a friend and former colleague—who has a theological background and was a teacher at various Catholic institutes—sends me copies of items that have struck her. Invariably they are about scandals of clerical abuse and Vatican corruption. Her accompanying letters betray a sense of weary resignation and dissillusionment with an instituion that has been an important part of her life; she complains about the clerical culture of "do as I say, not as I do" and Pastoral Letters of "pious, rambling rubbish." Going on to say, "For myself I stopped listening years ago." Words symptomatic of a wider demographic, she represents a growing penumbra of Catholics who also feel disillusioned with a church to which they haver an increasingly tenuous allegiance. Such people struggle to remain committed, disgusted with the endless revelations of yet more scandals of abuse by the clergy and the shameful record of what the UK Independent Inquiry into Child Sexual Abuse called "a culture of cover-up and denial." This also seemed to be the tenor of the recent report by the former editor of *The Tablet,* Catherine Pepinster, in the forlornly-titled "Another Breach of Trust."[3] This concluded with the hope that things may change but with the rather damning caveat that the Church cannot be trusted.

This is indeed a sad state of affairs. But it seems only part of, or a symptom of, a wider dissatisfaction with clerical posturing and platitude on a whole range of issues that at heart are about the exercise and nature of power. In short, a state of affairs summed up by the word "clericalism." This word came into vogue in the 1860s when the *Saturday Review,* in 1864, fulminated against the inability of the Roman clergy to comprehend the movement of modern intelligence and who were characterized by "clericalism, obscurtatism, and adminstrative despotism."[4] This may be seen as a peevish criticism if it were not that decades before a pious and loyal Italian priest, Antonio Rosmini (1797–1853)—he was beatified in 2007—had been even more strident in his criticism. In his 1832 book *Of the Five Wounds of the Holy Church*—which rather graphically likened the damage being done to the Church by the clergy to the wounds inflicted on Christ at the crucifixion—he wrote of the lack of sympathy between clergy

3. Pepinster, "Another Breach."
4. Chadwick, *Secularization of the European Mind.*

and people, of pastors who treated their flock as vassals or dependants, of bishops who were wordly schemers out for their selfish interests . . .[5] As a result Rosmini—no surprises here!—was suspended from his priestly duties, exiled to a remote village in the Italian Dolomites, and the book was put on the index of forbidden works.

Should one be inclined to think that this was long ago and that things have since changed, then the recent shocking and scandalous treatment of the distinguished Irish theologian and pastor, Fr. Sean Fagan suggests otherwise. Here was a man of similar character and charism to Rosmini who joined a religious order, the Marists, in Dublin in 1950, with the ideal of bringing something of the kindness and compassion of Christ into the world. He would go on to become an able administrator, for a time based in Rome, and a widely respected lecturer in moral theology. One thing he was keen on was in holding authority to account and in the second edition of his popular 2003 book *Does Morality Change?* wrote of "the need for a radical examination of the clerical culture" that enabled abuse to occur and "the mindset which prompted the disastrous attempts at cover-up."[6]

It seems that a rather unremarkable letter to *The Irish Times* (July, 10, 2008) about the shortage of priests that was brought to the attention of the Congregation for the Defence of the Faith (CDF) is what triggered a reprisal. In his letter Fr. Fagan had mentioned, in passing, "The 'official' Church may not be ready yet for married priests and women priests, but they will come in God's good time."[7] The mere mention of such a taboo subject, of the possibility of ordination for either married or women priests, crossed a red line of prohibited topics set down by John Paul II and rigorously enforced by Cardinal Ratzinger, the prefect of the CDF, who not for nothing was given the sobriquet, "the Vatican rottweiler."

The details of what happened next have now been published posthumously by Angela Hanley in *What Happened to Fr. Sean Fagan?* They make for disturbing reading. The salient points of the case are that without any representation or clear understanding of the charge(s) against him Fr. Fagan was forbidden to write, told that his latest work, *What Happened to Sin?* should be withdrawn from sale and all copies be destroyed, failure to

---

5. One can read more on Wikipedia. I read the book some fifty years ago at the seminary, which happened to be next door to a Rosminian college and my philosophy lecturer was an inspirational Rosminian priest.

6 Hanley, *What Happened to Fr. Sean Fagan?*

7. Hanley, *What Happened to Fr. Sean Fagan?*

cooperate by his superiors would lead to their dismissal (something that was beyond the canonical power of the CDF), and he was threatened with immediate expulsion from the order and from the priesthood should any mention of this be made public. Fr. Fagan died in 2016, a broken man at the hands of the Church he dedicated his life to serving. This, despite theological flummery to the contrary, is how clericalism functions and the Church exercises power. Rosmini would not have been surprised.

But that is not the whole story. Fr Fagan's ruthless nemesis at the CDF was Cardinal William Levada, who was appointed by Cardimal Ratzinger to replace him when he became pope, a man with a track record of covering for paedophile priests and refusing to cooperate with investigative authorities into clerical abuse in his previous dioceses of Portland and San Francisco. It was this perhaps more than anything else that affected Fr. Fagan in that the Church was so obviously willing to cover up abuse and excuse corruption in its own ranks yet was ruthless in crushing an exemeplary pastor with an unblemished record who raised genuine questions about the nature of morality and ecclesial authority. Fr Fagan, following in the foorsteps of Rosmini, found how little things change over time in the Church.

The totalitarian mindset

While reading the story of Fr. Fagan I happened to be reading, by coincidence, another life story—that of the great Russian writer Vasily Grossman, a new biography of whom had just been published.[8] His great work *Life and Fate* has been compared to Tolstoy's *War and Peace,* and Grossman himself ranked alongside Pasternak and Solzhenitsyn as one of, if not the, outstanding Russian writer of the twentieth century. The fact that he is perhaps not so well known was his fate: his work was supressed by the Soviet authorities as it was being prepared for publication in 1960 and remained unpublished in his lifetime.

Grossman was a well-regarded war correspondent who had reported on the battle of Stalingrad and the "liberation" of Eastern Europe from the Nazis in 1943 by the Red Army. He was among the first to record the horrors of what he found not only of the devastation of Ukraine and annihilation of the Jewish population—which included his own own home and mother—but also the extermination camp of Treblinka. His reports were used in the Nuremburg trials as evidence of genocide. But Grossman

8. Popoff, *Grossman.*

struggled to comprehend the sheer brutality and inhumanity of it all and as he wrote reports the themes of his great work, *Life and Fate*, began to emerge: the need for freedom as the basis of life and humanity, the power of love and compassion compared to violence and hate, the importance of conscience in defining a person and, perhaps above all, the importance of each individual human life. What also became apparent to Grossman was that the greatest threat to humanity was totalitarian ideologies with their abstract ideas indifferent to actual people. And thus he was led into "heresy," stating that the fascist state of Hitler and the socialist state of Stalin were in essence no different; they simply mirrored each other.

At first Grossman suppressed an overt statement of these beliefs in his works, though the censors became increasingly sucipious of his "anti-Soviet" and bourgeois tendancies, and he was lucky not to be arrested. Forbidden to write, publicly shunned, Grossman was left an isolated and broken man. He died soon after in 1964 still insisting on the neeed for brotherly love and unity in the face of totalitarian divisivness. As I read the life of Grossman I began to realize something: his life and fate was almost a perfect parallel to that of Fr. Sean Fagan! Here were two lives from totally different worlds that seemed to mirror each other. Each had sought to serve the instutions they had grown up with, either party or church; each strove to enhance their reality through focusing on the importance of humanity and individual dignity; each had realized the rich variety in life that cannot just be compressed into one doctrinaire view; each came to question the coercive use of power for ideological or dogmatic ends. Because of such views each had come to be seen as a threat to the established orthodoxy; the views of each outraged apparatchiks of either party or church; each came to be seen as a troublemakers who should be silenced and their presence erased from the public domain. And the procedures used to achieve this were also remarkably similar. The record of Grossman's interactions with the state censor, ironically known as the "gray cardinal," reads almost as a cypher of Fr Fagan's interactions with a very real cardinal.[9] Two worlds—one of an atheistic ideology and the other of a revealed religion—that appeared so inimical yet acting with such congruence. Two very different lives but in so many ways identical!

9. Popoff, *Grossman*, 274–76

Spiritual Stalinism

But to properly understand this outcome it is necessary to broaden the historical perspective and dig deeper. Like so much of the life of the Church the roots and character of the CDF lie deeply embedded in the past. It is an institution formed in a very different time to ours—at the Lateran Council III with the bull *Ad abolendam* (1184)—that has changed little in the mentality of its executors and how through it the Church exercises power. Over the centuries it has remained secretive and unnacountable, annonymous and remorseless in its workings, without the right of appeal or even to question the basis of any judgement, refusing to respond to inquiry or divulge anything of the basis for its actions, inimical to human rights. An institution previously known under its more notorious name, the Inquisition, it has changed its name but not its nature: the shadows of Torquemada and Savanarola still linger. This was the institution with its medieval mindset that trapped Fr. Sean Fagan. Predicated on the belief that one's authority and actions are beyond question in the pursuit of a self-evident truth, it is this that finds repeated expression in "clericalism" and underlies clerical abuse. It is this that is the real heart of darkness in the Church for which no apology or ammendment has ever been made.

The work of reform and the agenda of renewal set out for the Church in the modern world by Vatican II—which so enthused Fr. Sean Fagan—was very much about changing this legacy and exorcising those ghosts of the past: reaching out to the wider society in a spirit of openess and dialogue, of engagement with other religious communities and a reappraisal of pastoral norms more sensitive to personal diversity. Until, that is, the clock was switched back by the resurgence of traditionalism under Pope John Paul II. Here was a man who had grown up in a Polish culture where two absolutist ideologies, Catholicism and Communism, fought for dominance; a man who resolutely refused to countenance the notion of a deep-seated culture of clerical abuse within the church—and even promoted some of its practicioners—because it contradicted the underlying premise of all his thought that the church was in essence a perfect society. Stalin had a similar ideological view of the pure socialist state.

This view reached its most forceful expression in the encyclical *Veritatis Splendour,* of which the distinguished moral theologian Bernard Haring wrote, "Almost all real splendour is lost when it becomes clear that the whole document is directed above all to one goal: to endorse total assent and submission."[10] One bishop was more scathing, calling it "spiritual Stalinism."[11]But its greater significance was that it revealed the core conviction on which clerical obduracy rests; that the Church was in essence pristine, the deposit of faith immutable and any flaws were the result of individual deviance not institutional deficiency. The reality for the post-conciliar church was now that nothing had or would change—or rather, as the Italian writer, Giuseppe Lampadusa once famously wrote (in *The Leopard*), things changed only to remain the same.

The medieval matrix

As with the roots of the CDF/Inquisition it is a wider historical spectrum that enables us to better understand why all this should be so but also unacceptable. For this we must return to the twelfth century, a pivotal momement in European history. The revolutionary changes that took place at this time reshaped the social and ecclesial structures of Europe leading to what has been called the Twefth Century Renaissance.[12] Among its most formative elements was the papal-led Gregorian Reform under Pope Gregory VII (1015–85). Gregory was an extreme and fanatical figure who makes any modern Vatican rottweiler look like a cuddly puppy—think rather Ayatollah Komeini or Abu Bakr al-Baghdadi—who, in the words of the distinguished Austrian historian and Catholic Friedrich Heer, "kindled more hatred in Europe than any other ruling figure since the days of the Neronian emperors."[13] A similar view was taken by the great English historian H. A. L. Fisher who wrote, "To this stern and implacable idealist we may principally ascribe the spread through Europe of a theocratic philosophy as menacing to the nascent state of the eleventh century as in our times is the communism of Lenin" (He published his *History of Europe* in 1936).[14] With its centralization of clerical power in the papacy—papal elections would now be in the hands of the college of cardinals—and the monasticization of the church expressive of Gregory's own background as a monk. This was most

10. Though Haring lived through the Nazi era in Germany where was twice hauled in for intterrogation, later in life he would have to face the CDF. When asked if he had to choose between the two what his choice would be he replied in favor of the former!

11. Smithson, "The Nature of Moral Authority," 1–7.

12. Moore, *First.*

13. Heer, *Holy Roman Empire.*

14. Fisher, *History of Europe.*

graphically expressed in the imposition of compulsory clerical celebacy, emphasizing a hierachy set apart and above all others—a reality reflected in the novel papal tiara of two, and later three, crowns that symbolized the supreme temporal and spiritual power of the pope and the church.[15] Gregory's reforms set the template for the creation of medieval Christendom that for traditionalists is still the normative expression of Christianity.

This was all in rather stark contrast to another reform movement that sprang up at the same time but among the towns of the Rhineland known as the Apostolic movement. This also would become a formative element in subsequent centuries, but unlike the centralizing papal reform imposed from the top down, this would be an emergent lay movement from the bottom up. Often manifested in marginal groups on the periphery of the "official church," this movement was primarily reacting to the perceived venality and corruption of the clerical establishment.[16] It was comprised of many uncoordinated strands of similar-minded, devoutly religious people forming catalytic groups, much as the Green Movement and Extinction Rebellion do in the secular milieu of today. It also provided the root from which the Protestant Reformation ultimately sprang.

The central ideal of the Apostolic Movement was to return to the way of life associated with the first followers of Jesus who lived together and held everything in common, as recorded in the Acts of the Apostles (2:42–45). Such groups were seen as a threat to the official church and had a choice of either conformity or being crushed—it was at this time that the heresy trials began, leading to unprecedented mass burnings and culminating in the murderous slaughter of the Albigensian Crusade: the idea of a crusade to enforce conformity was another of Gregory's conceptualizations.[17] And this was not the only or even most significant aspect of the church's war on heresy. In doing so it created the judicial structures of what the medievalist R. I. Moore saw as the foundations of a persecuting society whose functioning would be the true characterization of medieval Christendom and would become a distinctive feature of European civilization.[18]

15. Pope Boniface VIII (1294–1303) added the second crown into the tiara and Benedict XI (1303–04) the third.

16. Sheldrake, *Spirituality,* 65–90.

17. Moore, *War.*

18. Moore, *Formation.*

The early church

In this brief foray into the past we may better understand why a radical re-evaluation of the historical tradition of the church was necessary at Vatican II. This it sought to achieve through its twin goals of *aggiornamento* (keeping abreast of the times) and, more significantly, *approfondimento* (deepening and returning to origins). In this it was, perhaps unknowingly, resurrecting the hopes and agenda that had previously characterized the Apostolic movement of the twelfth century. It is the context of this now-often-only-partly-remembered past that I believe offers clues to the resolution of the problem of present scandals associated with the clerical abuse of power.

To discern this we are led to the place of origin—to the Apostolic fount, the radicality of the Gospels and of what Jesus really preached and who he was. In this modern scripture scholarship, such as that of the Jesus Seminar and John Dominic Crossan, have shown how even by the time the Gospels were being written the radicality of Jesus was being compromised and written out.[19] In particular the speed with which the emphasis changed from his teaching to his regal nature, interpreted through the medium of the Roman imperial cult which divinized its holders, is startling: *Quibus imperavit Augustus, imperavit Christus*—the only legitimate successor to Augustus (Caesar) is how Christ would soon become in the normative teaching of the church.[20] But this was a travesty of the tradition from which Jesus came, which was rooted in the sapiental Judaism that is recorded in the later writings of scripture (such as Qoheleth and Ecclesiates). Here was a profound humanitarianism reflected in the teachings of sages such as Hillel the Elder: "That which is hateful to you, do not do to your fellow" as being the summation of the Torah.[21] It is this spirit with its radical ethic of service that is the distinctive characteristic of the ministry of Jesus.

This spirit was reflected in all that Jesus did and taught. It is a point that Fr. Sean Fagan also made in his writing, that "clerical references to 'Church teaching' focus exclusively on words and documents, forgetting that Jesus taught in word and deed—and his deeds were often more powerful and more revealing than his words." Here we may pay closer attention to the word that has been recurrent throughout this narrative: power. A word full of ambiguity and hence its problematic nature. There is the

19. Crossan, *Power of Parable.*

20. Crossan, *God and Empire.*

21. Geering, *Christianity without God,* 101–16.

power of Rome, in Latin *potestas,* that crushes all opposition, imposing conformity, and the power of being, in Greek *ousia,* that is the fullness of being, wholeness, and individuality. The same word, two very different meanings, but it was noted of Jesus that when "power went out of him" (Mark 5:30) it was to heal and raise up. Similarly with faith: in Greek *pistis,* it is knowledge, logical persuasion and reason, but in Hebrew it is *emunah,* which is the innate conviction that transcends reason leading to deeper personal understanding and empathy.[22] It is the latter, not the former, that Jesus would have known.

It is through exploring such subtle differences of historical interpretation (or misinterpretation), when we strip away the accretions and return Jesus to his original Jewish culture, that we begin to better appreciate the radicality of his teaching and his profound humanitarianism. It was this that led to the radically different communal life (communism!) envisaged in the Apostolic way, where all things are held in common and where there is no difference between Jew and Greek, slave and free, male and female (Gal 3:28). That this original credal statement of "ortho-praxis" was almost completely marginalized in later church history by theological "ortho-doxy" would have profound consequences to this day.[23] It was the original reality reflected in the *agapes* that brought together people regardless of race, class, or gender in a moral equality. This was the radicality of the first Christian communities where there were no distinctions of power and privilege; where clericalism had no place and was in fact the very antithesis of all the gathered community, *ecclesia,* stood for. A fact reflected in the celebrations that would be presided over by both men and women (Rom 16:1–5).

The recovery of the original sense of the community of the faithful, the *consensus fideliem,* was at the very heart of the renewal that Vatican II hoped to achieve. It was this that in their own way both Rosmini and Fr. Sean Fagan were also seeking to achieve. At the conclusion of the letter which was to cause him so much grief Fr. Fagan wrote, "Inspired by the early history of our Christian communities and the division of ministries, we should be free to devise a healthy and human re-organization that could revitalise our parishes." I believe nothing less will address the scourge of clericalism and address its abusive use of power.

But, like Vatican II, these are pastoral aspirations to be persued with empathy, *emunah.* In contrast the medieval paradigm of "Christendom"

22. Buber, *Two Types of Faith.*
23. Patterson, "Forgotten."

that stands in its way has a history of enforcement with unsparing brutality and violence, reflected in an absolutist and abusive ministry. The twelfth-century conflict between the Apostolic life and a centralized clericalism continues to be played out. Will this ever change? At its heart this is a question of how difficult it is to change cultures and socieities built on enforced violence. It is a question that today confronts us across the globe in states such as Russia, Syria, and Iraq. Will/can brutalized societies or communities ever reform and change? Will the Sphinx ever smile?

Chapter 10

The Religious Engagement with History

Thinking about "religionsgeschichte" today

I HAVE RECENTLY BEEN thinking about *religionsgeschichte* (a German word for the study of the history of religions, though here I use it in the broader sense of religious history). This is not an everyday word and not one you might expect to come across very often. In fact I doubt if most people ever come across it at all! But in a time of fake news and post-colonial controversies raging over the memory and interpretation of the past, not to mention the many marginalized and minority groups vying for attention, it is perhaps worthwhile pausing to reflect on what benefit, if any, history can be to us; of how the past is to be understood and why it is often so controversial. After all, understanding the present always starts with coming to terms with the past.

Of course, history as memory or record of the past has itself quite a long history. From Herodotus to Holinshed inquisitive minds have sought to record the past; chroniclers have listed events and people but viewed from the understanding of their own "present," just as medieval illuminators illustrated biblical kings and battles as in the knightly contests they were familiar with. But history as an understanding of the past as "a different sort of place," that previous cultures had outlooks and beliefs that defy our easy comprehension, is not so old. In fact it is a rather modern European idea, one that owes much to the thinkers of the Enlightenment era of the seventeenth and eighteenth centuries, in particular Giambattista Vico (1668–1744).[1] The son of a Neapolitan bookseller, Vico became a doctor of law and developed a

1. Israel, *Radical Enlightenment*.

lifetime interest in how societies are organized and structured. His leading idea was *verum esse ipsum factum*, "What is true is what is made." In other words, what humans have created, or the "facts" of the past, should be the focus of historical study. The word "fact" came into usage in the sixteenth century and perhaps more than any other word epitomises the new empirical "scientific" attitude to the world.

Of course, Vico was an heir to the legacy of the Renaissance. This great cultural ferment was inspired partly by a rediscovery and reappraisal of ancient Classical texts that became more readily available after the migration of scholarship and manuscripts from Constantinople after its fall in 1453. With a renewed sense of the past went the call for a renewed understanding of the scriptures by going back to the sources. In this the new humanists realized the human capacity for error: "By going back to the earliest possible version of any given text, they hope to get 'behind' these errors of copying to get as close as possible to the original text, and therefore the original meaning."[2] Scholars such as Erasmus were concerned that the scriptures were correctly translated and understood, which was not necessarily the same as handed down by ecclesiastical tradition. This became a key point of contention in the Reformation, which only added further impetus in the search for a rediscovery of the past.

Whatever the constraints Vico may have later perceived in his education as a Jesuit scholastic, emerging out of his understanding of Divine Providence, we can see a mind grappling to understand the past as a historical process that, as he describes it, shepherds mankind from barbarism to a more settled, orderly state. At different points in this process—or as others would say, "progress"—things are different. As Vico's modern biographer, Sir Isaiah Berlin, describes it, "Vico perceived a revolutionary truth when he asserted, before Herder or Hegel or Marx, that to each stage of social change there correspond its own types of law, government, religion, art, myth, language, manners . . . and that this pattern is the life of a society."[3] A consequence of this change is that as we move from one period to another it becomes difficult to understand the previous period as it was understood by the people of that time. This presents a profound obstacle to historical understanding that is quite often overlooked.

Exploring this theme in his book *Christianity Medieval and Modern*, the theologian Dennis Nineham showed how the way we understand

2. Spence, "Humanism."

3. Berlin, *Vico and Herder,* 68

what we may think to be the same beliefs as previous generations can in fact be completely different.[4] For example, the word "transubstantiation" is still used, particularly by Roman Catholics, to refer to the change of the Eucharistic elements into the body and blood of Christ, yet our modern understanding of substance is entirely different from that of the medieval scholastics whose own understanding was based on an Aristotelian physics and metaphysics that has long since been discredited and abandoned.[5] Going back to before the scholastics the dominant matrix of Christian thinking for a thousand years had been Platonism. For Plato the essence of a thing precedes its existence. Whilst the essence is eternal, perfect, and changeless, what we see in this world is contingent, defective, and transient. In this essentialist view there are two worlds, of which one is the shadow of the other. This dualist way of thinking is the context for all early Christian doctrine but it is not a view of reality that we now recognize as anything more than an elaborate fantasy. And all this was quite different from the previous cultural matrix of Judaism which provided the context for the teaching and ministry of Jesus. Just how different this was to the later Greek interpretations—and how misleading these have been—has become apparent in recent decades.[6] Thus, looking back to the past from our present can become something like a game of charades: pretending it is something that it isn't.

Until Vico it was the Bible which provided the basis for an understanding of history and the gold standard for all chronology. For example, Samuel Shuckford's *The Sacred and Profane History of the World Connected* (1728) confidently assimilated all non-biblical traditions (paganism!) to scripture in order to provide an understanding of the past that was contingent on the Bible. In this "euhumerist" reading of pagan myths and gods they were actually Noah and his sons in disguise.[7] But, as always when it comes to scriptural interpretation, there were dissenting views. One particularly contentious issue in attempting to distinguish a natural, rather than sacred, history was language. If language was, as Genesis stated, God's

---

4. Nineham, *Christianity Medieval and Modern*.

5. Weinberg, *To Explain the World*, 22–30.

6. Vermes, *Jesus in the Jewish World*.

7. The Greek philosopher Euhumerus, who lived in the fourth century BCE, taught that the gods were simply the heroes of the past who over time had become deified with the exaggerated retelling of their stories.

gift to Adam, how could it have been so necessary for its fragmentation at the destruction of the Tower of Babel (Gen 11:6)?[8]

Even from these snippets it will perhaps be becoming clear that history is not so much about collecting facts about the past (which is what antiquarians did) as understanding a process of change, how things have been constructed (*factum*) in different ages. In history humans are not merely spectators, as in the natural sciences, but actors who shape their own destiny; which is why Vico called his *magnum opus* "The New Science," *Scienza Nuova* (1725). In this revolutionary understanding of the workings of history without the intervention of God humans create society through their irrational drives, fears, and ideals.[9] Indeed, one can go further and say that humans do not just observe and invent things but also invent themselves and in doing so reinvent the societies in which they live.

By the eighteenth century this growing historical awareness had helped to generate a new form of consciousness which, allied with the rise of nationalism, led to a search for historical roots in the idylls of past epochs—step forward Sir Walter Scott, who almost single-handedly invented the genre of the historical novel. Also of note is the suffix "ism," which I have just used in the word national*ism*. The presence of this noun suffix, which only came into use in the eighteenth century, was itself an expression of the new historical awareness and consciousness that should alert us to a new conceptual understanding not previously present: a warning to us that our usage for a description of previous ages is itself a fabrication, or, as Vico would have said, something "we have made."

That all this thinking took place within the matrix of an engagement with a biblically-based culture, Christianity, should be noted.[10] And the controversies this generated provided the catalyst for further thought. Which brings us once more to *religionsgeschichte*, a school of thought which arose in nineteenth-century Germany and which emphasized the degree to which the Bible had been shaped by its cultural milieu. In particular it sought to show how the religion of ancient Israel reflected distinct historical traditions and how Christianity emerged over time in response to a variety of social and cultural factors.

8. Porter, *Enlightenment.*

9. Israel, *Radical Enlightenment,* 664–70.

10. Zamoyski, *Holy Madness.*

An "old" and "new" testament

This new approach to the Bible raised a whole host of problems for both Judaism and Christianity, not least because the so-called "Old Testament" had been handed down as part of a canon of sacred Scripture that was unquestionable in its veracity. Yet for Jews the Hebrew Bible, the Tanakh, was never "old," and for the early followers of Jesus their movement was a part of Judaism for a hundred years before anyone thought of either calling themselves Christian or their writings "new." Here one may note that, according to recent scholarship, the earliest use of the word *Christianus* was in a letter that Pliny wrote to the emperor Trajan in 111 CE and not, as is often said, the Acts of the Apostles (Acts 11:26), which was written about 125 CE nor the First Letter of Peter (4:16) written about 175 CE.[11]

But the fact that divine authorship was deemed as valid for the Old as well as the New Testament itself presented a tension as to how one had emerged from the other. This in turn generated a formidable body of scholarship reaching across a century seeking to evaluate the status and meaning of the scriptures. The task, in the words of one scholar, Theodore Vriezen, was "to offer a history of the religion of Israel with respect to not only its historical development but of its essence and inmost character as well."[12] Many notable works by outstanding scholars addressed this issue, such as von Rad's *Old Testament Theology*, Eichrodt's *Theology of the Old Testament*, Knight's *A Christian Theology of the Old Testament*, Snaith's *Distinctive Ideas of the Old Testament*, to name but a few.

But there is a problem with all of this. The underlying presumption of such works was that the "new" testament of Christianity provided a sort of cypher with which to interpret the "old" testament of Judaism. Conversely, texts were examined on the basis of their predictive value, of "promises" and "fulfilment." According to the modern scripture scholar Thomas Thompson, this was all quite unsatisfactory: "The past century's efforts of Bible scholars to use the Bible for constructing a history of Israel have failed miserably. Much of the reason for this failure lies in a brand of scholarship that was more apologetic and theological than critical and historical."[13] The consequences were that "understanding the Old Testament as a history related to Christian origins has resulted in the theological orientation of the Bible

11. Scott, "If Not Christian, What?"

12. Vriezen, *Religion of Ancient Israel*, 7.

13. Thompson, *Bible in History*, 228.

being largely ignored."[14] What Thompson is advocating is very much the agenda of Vico, that the prime challenge to scholarship is to understand the text in its context, or as it was understood in its formative period, and how biblical epochs were differentiated and distinctive.

And there was a further problem: to categorize the presumed Word of God as "old" was itself derogatory and demeaning. Who said it was "old"? When did it become "old" and how did the relativizing concept of "oldness" arise? The categorization just seemed to be accepted as standard with its controversial origin often overlooked. It was Marcion of Sinope (c. 85–160 CE), the disaffected son of a bishop, who came up with the very strange idea that the Jewish scriptures, which he described as a "testament," *testamentum,* presented God as a demiurge who had nothing to do with Jesus. For this view he was denounced and excommunicated. He was also very selective about the few Christian writings of which he approved which prompted a further controversy as to what constituted an orthodox canon of scripture, a problem which has never been fully resolved. It was in the context of this controversy that the bishop Melito of Sardis (d. 180) coined the phrase "the old testament." But this would only entrench a division based on the deranged speculation of a heretic.

At the beginnings of the church there was no such distinction. The translation of Pliny's term *Christiani,* as "adherents or party of *Christus*" suggests that he saw them as no more than a Judean sect who were followers of a *Christus.* A little later, at a time of ascendancy for the new faith of Christianity, the assumption of "newness" was a charge made by snooty pagan philosophers, such as Celsus, who in *The True Word* (c. 175 CE) derided this new religion as having neither temples, priesthood, sacrifices, nor scriptures like the proper religions of old. In any case larger collections of scriptural writings, both Jewish and Christian—such as the *codex vaticanus* which probably originated in Egypt in the fourth century—were all written in a specific form of common Greek, *koine,* that was used in the translation of the Jewish scriptures in what is called the Septuagint. That this specific form of language was adapted and shared is something we now better understand from the discovery of ancient papyri at Oxyhrynchus and elsewhere in Egypt.

The concept of a clearly divided canon of scripture only became established in the cultural void which opened up with the collapse of the Western Roman Empire and ensuing Dark Ages in Europe. With the collapse of

14. Thompson, *Bible in History,* 230.

classical civilization monks were eager to preserve the essential teachings of their faith. It is in this context that the equally radical division of time into two epochs—"before" and "after" Christ—also came into being. It was a division that would make little sense to the wide swathes of humanity that lived beyond the confines of the Western world or even pagans within it.

A Jewish perspective

It has taken the near-collapse of European civilization in our own time with the cataclysmic wars of the twentieth century—in which antisemitism and the Jewish Holocaust were distinctive features—to make us question what exactly this Christian legacy of "old" and "new" testaments really is. This is reflected in the work of scholars such as Geza Vermes, whose parents perished in the Holocaust and who himself became a Catholic priest joining a religious order (The Congregation of Our Lady of Zion which had been founded by two Jewish brothers who themselves had converted from Judaism) but which he later left to re-embrace his Jewish identity. The focus of Vermes's work on the historical Jesus reminds us of the blindingly obvious, that Jesus was a Jew, that Christianity was an aspect of Judaism, and that Christian scriptures are meaningless outside a Jewish context—a point emphasized by another contemporary scholar, W. D. Davies, who summarized his work on *Paul and Rabbinic Judaism* as being that "the Gospel for Paul was not the annulling of Judaism but its completion."[15]

Davis published his work in 1948, a year after the sensational discovery of the Dead Sea Scrolls. What the scrolls revealed was exactly what the *religionsgeschichte* school had intimated, that behind the surviving literary relics from the past (such as the Bible) lay diverse and dynamic societies in which beliefs were shaped by distinctive social and political circumstances. The scrolls, which contained scriptural fragments, revealed a wide diversity of texts that indicated (according to the scholar Frank Cross) three textual families had developed over the five centuries before the time of Christ based on different traditions.[16] It was a situation remarkably reminiscent of what Julius Wellhausen a century before had surmised about the original composition of the Pentateuch.

What Wellhausen's work suggested, in his celebrated documentary hypothesis of the Pentateuch, was that the Bible was not a monumental

15. Quoted in Nicholls, *Pelican Guide*, 201.
16. Shanks, *Mystery and Meaning*.

monolith but a tapestry composed of many strands which had grown from different contexts and later been artistically woven together. In a similar way we can view the many books which comprise the Bible as a vast evolutionary diorama to which transformations have been made in the light of later understanding. Thus, we see, for example, Exodus 6:3 stating that God was not known to the patriarchs by the name of Yahweh but then in Genesis 15:7 we read of Abraham addressing God by that very title. All of which is further complicated in translation by the later European import of the word "God" which becomes a ubiquitous characterization covering all previous nuances like the icing on a layered cake. The scripture scholar Bart Ehrman has written extensively on the way the single term "God" has come to subsume a whole multitude of divine names and beings that appear in the Bible but have been written out in translation and common memory.[17]

The consequence is a certain opacity which was well-described by the literary savant Harold Bloom: "Archaic Judaism is all but totally unknown to us. We know the rabbinical Judaism that has been dominant since the second century CE, and we know, more or less, what that Judaism judged to be the chain of tradition that extended from Ezra the great Redactor to the Pharisees and then on to Akiba . . . What we do not know is the Judaism that was available to the Yahwist . . . All I can see is that the Yahweh of the Yahwist has very little to do with the God of Ezra or the God of Akiba."[18] I have often pondered this profound and challenging passage which summarises what I have so often found; just how difficult a book the Bible is to read and how its fluent literacy so easily beguiles and misleads us.

History as a basis for faith

At the heart of the Bible is the understanding that the events it records, its historical narrative, are an expression of an encounter with God. The Exodus, for example, is not just about the escape of some Hebrew slaves out of Egypt but presented as an act of God that delivers these slaves for his own purposes. In other words, it is an existential encounter that is interpreted in the light of the understanding of the people at the time. The process of understanding its significance is ongoing and one that leads to

17. Ehrman, *How Jesus Became God.*
18. Bloom, *Book of J,* 31.

ever more exalted claims, from what von Rad called "a critically assured minimum" to "a theological maximum."[19]

For many it has been the hope that greater background knowledge provided by archaeology would help to bridge this gap between actual historical events and the truth of the Bible narrative. But this hope has not been fulfilled. If anything, the opposite has become apparent: the more one investigates the more impenetrable things seem to become; the more material evidence, the more questionable the theological construct.

A case in point is the notorious fate of Sodom and Gomorrah. A recent report, published (October 2018) after more than ten years of investigations in the area by a team of archaeologists and geologists, concluded that 3,700 years ago there was a meteorite strike that devastated a 25-square-kilometer area around the north of the Dead Sea in an event reminiscent of the Tunguska meteorite strike that was observed in in Siberia in 1908.[20] The widespread presence of iridium and sulphur nodules are key indicators of such an event—the "fire and brimstone" of Genesis 19:24—to which the biblical writer attributed "a theological maximum" interpretation. But to the unfortunate people on the ground who experienced this event the "critical minimum" was that it was just bad luck!

Nor was this the only such event. Going back further in time another ten thousand years, a more significant comet exploded over Anatolia in 10,950 BCE, ushering in the mini ice age of the Younger Dryas period that lasted over a thousand years, devastated the hunter-gatherer societies of the Old Stone Age, and eventually kick-started the new farming communities of the Neolithic Period.[21] These distant events found their echo in the biblical stories of the expulsion from the Garden of Eden and ensuing life of drudgery tilling the soil and to which humanity was prevented from returning by the cherubim with the flaming sword (Gen 3:22–24).[22] The text we have from some ten thousand years later encases these distant and mythologized events in a very different moral narrative. By this time the snake, in particular, has suffered reputational damage, being transformed from a symbol of fertility and life to one of evil that seduces Eve. In this version the snake has been separated from Eve, whose name in Hebrew, *chava*, is more or less identical to the word for snake; this is a reminder of

19. von Rad, *Old Testament Theology*, 108.

20. Seidel, "Bible's Sodom and Gomorrah."

21. Sweatman, *Prehistory*.

22. Collins, *Gobekli Tepe*, 225–58

an earlier time when across the Middle East the snake goddess was seen as responsible for the creation of humanity. Such was the invective against such beliefs in the Bible—where all such images are simply dismissed as *asherah* or shame—that femininity itself came to be seen as the corrupted locus of evil, temptation, and sin.[23] As the scripture scholar Lloyd Geering summarized, "The advent of monotheism annihilated the goddesses of nature so successfully that the Hebrew Bible does not contain a single word meaning 'goddess.' One or two personal names of ancient Canaanite goddesses have survived; we find Ashtoreth, goddess of fertility, but only after the name has been deliberately disfigured by replacing its vowels with those of the Hebrew word for 'shame'—an ancient example of what we might term 'theological correctness.'"[24]

Whereas the moral interpretation of the destruction of Sodom would provide the exemplar for the approbation with which gay relationships are still viewed by many, the mythology of Eve and "the fall" would prove even more devastating for the status of women in the Christian era.[25] But perhaps a more significant example of a mythologized past is the Exodus event itself, for which in this case it is the lack of archaeological evidence that has been a key factor in recent research. The distinguished Israeli archaeologist Israel Finkelstein writes, "There is no mention of such an event in any New Kingdom Egyptian source, and there is no trace of the early Hebrews in Egypt," before going on to list a whole range of features related to the geography of the Exodus, such as the place names, which firmly locate this narrative in the seventh and sixth century BCE, over half a millennium after the events purported in the Bible.[26] In the end all that can be said is "that the Exodus story is based on some remote memories rooted in the reality of the thirteenth century BCE."[27] The association of the revelation of monotheism with this putative event makes it perhaps the most significant piece of literary fiction ever written.

If this is the case, it opens up a whole new perspective as to why and how such a national epic came to be created. A likely scenario, indicated by the dating of place names and vocabulary, is that at a time when Jews returning from the Babylonian exile sought to reaffirm their national identity and

23. Olyan, *Asherah*.

24. Geering, *Coming Back to Earth*, 101.

25. Pagels, *Adam*.

26. Finkelstein and Mazar, *Quest*, 52.

27. Finkelstein and Mazar, *Quest*, 61

reclaim their ancestral lands, the Passover epic was attached to the ancient harvest festival of Azymes, or the feast of Unleavened Bread (Genesis 12, 39). Or, as another scripture scholar put it, the bondage in Egypt becomes a paradigm for bondage in Babylon: "The story of the Exodus from Egypt and the memories of the return from exile influenced each other in a reciprocal way."[28] Such an understanding challenges much of the commonly-accepted biblical structure and leads inevitably to a radical reassessment of the Bible in terms of its real historical actuality.

This sort of reappraisal of the past is much as Vico would have expected from his "new science" of history, revealing the different epochs in which social transformations gave rise to different ways of thinking. Whereas the Hebrew scriptures show this happening over millennia, the Dead Sea Scrolls offer a much more focused insight into this happening in one particular epoch which had become distinctly apocalyptic. For example, the text called "4Q246," or the Aramaic Apocalypse, talks of the coming of the divine sonship in almost identical terms to that which would be applied to Jesus in the Gospels as "the Son of God." As Herschel Shanks wrote in a detailed appraisal of the situation, "Jesus' divine sonship thus occurs within a cultural context that is related both to history and to the contemporaneous world in which Jesus lived; to this extent Jesus' divine sonship is by no means unique."[29]

History today

A historical understanding enables us to see not only that events may not have happened as recorded but that a mythologized rendering of the past actually helped to create them. The creative role of memory in the transmission of the past has been extensively studied in a pioneering book by Bart Ehrman, *Jesus before the Gospel*, that shows how memory does not just recall the past but recreates it.[30] Which leaves us in a quandary, one that confronted Albert Schweitzer in his *Quest of the Historical Jesus*. At the close of his book, he was resigned to the fact that the quest was in vain and poignantly affirmed that Jesus, "comes to us as One unknown." It was a view echoed by R. H. Lightfoot in his 1935 *History and Interpretation in the Gospels*, that "for all the inestimable value of the Gospels, they yield us little

28. Finkelstein and Mazar, *Quest*, 52.

29. Shanks, *Mystery and Meaning*, 73.

30. Ehrman, *Jesus before the Gospels*.

more than a whisper of his voice; we trace them in but the outskirts of his ways."[31] And this is true for the Bible as a whole.

Many years ago, I remember a talk given by Rabbi Lionel Blue to his rabbinical students, at a time when he was chair of the Beth-Din and professor at Leo Baeck College, reminding them of how intangible the foundations of the Bible really were; a chance encounter, a dream in the night, an unexpected guest. People sought to make sense of their experiences and life situation just as we do today in the light of their own cultural assumptions. Just as the many generations of the past interpreted and recorded their past in the light their own needs and experiences, so we must be no less bold in affirming an understanding which reflects our situation, knowing that our understanding of the past will reflect our experience of the present.

This was the outlook of one of the most formidable modern biblical scholars, Rudolf Bultmann. Following the philosophy of his friend Martin Heidegger, Bultmann assumed an existential position in which to exist (to "stand out") a person must realize by decisive choice his own possibilities. This is the basis of discipleship. "If he makes no such existential choice or decision his existence is unauthentic, determined by factors within the grip of which he is in a spiritual sense dead."[32] For Bultmann faith must not and cannot just depend on conviction about the historicity of certain events in the past, it is rather a present response to the teaching of the gospel, the *kerygma*. The ethical standards it presents are still as challenging as any since and set the standards that define our humanity. What we make of it is up to us.

In this brief discourse I have focused on the Judeo-Christian religious tradition, but I am aware that the issues raised regarding the engagement between ancient religious texts and modern understanding affect all religions. This is particularly true of Islam, where religious authorities have vehemently sought to prevent any such approach to its sacred texts or religious tradition as that taken by the *religionsgeschichte* school. A case in point is Nasr Hamid Zayd, an Egyptian Qur'anic thinker and one of the leading theologians in Islam. While not denying that the Qur'an was of divine origin, Zayd argued that it was a "cultural product" that had to be read in the context of the language and culture of the seventh century Arabs, and could be interpreted in more than one way. As a result, in 1995

31. Quoted in Nicholls, *Pelican Guide*, 257.
32. Nicholls, *Pelican Guide*, 334.

an Egyptian Sharia court declared him an apostate, which led to death threats and his having to flee from Egypt.

Others, such as Raif Badawi in Saudi Arabia, who sought to open up a website forum for debate, have been similarly charged with apostasy and imprisoned. The recent fate of Jamal Khashoggi was meant as a stark warning to others who might want to adopt a critical disposition to a theocratic ordering of the state. To Islamists any concession to a modern mentality of critical reflection is anathema. As a result, their "mythical world picture," as Bultmann would have put it, continues to grate with modernity, just as Vico's views once grated with the religious authorities and the Inquisition. Clearly the appeal of a homogenized past, with its simple storyline and definitive truths, is as beguiling as ever. For this reason, the challenge of *religionsgeschichte* is ongoing.

Chapter 11

The Global Challenge

Religious conflict or a new humanitarianism?

I WAS RECENTLY ENGAGED in an animated discussion with my Sikh neighbor. This is in fact quite a common occurrence, as we get to grips with the nature of religious belief, what's wrong with the world, and how to put it right. But what most intrigues us most is how much we agree. Though we come from completely different cultural backgrounds—he from Singapore where his father was relocated by the British Raj at a time my grandfather was helping to build that self-same raj, and I from the Western Roman Catholic tradition—our minds are as one. His core conviction is simple: if religion doesn't help people to lead better lives then it's pointless.

What prompted our exchange was my rather facetious comment on the coronation of "King Modi," the Indian Prime Minister. Of course, I was exaggerating, as he has not been crowned king, at least not yet! But he is getting closer. On August 6, among great jubilation by his Hindu followers, he laid a forty-kilogram brick of silver as the foundation stone for a new temple of Ram to be built at Ayodhya on the site of the ruins of the old Babri mosque that was torn down by Hindu fanatics in 1992. That was the trigger for an outburst of pent-up religious enmity, a settling of ancient grievances, and a reasserting of national pride that left thousands dead, mostly Muslims. Such recent events constitute only the latest act in a drama that is threatening to tear India apart in an orgy of religiously-fuelled violence.

And Modi thrives on it! Listen carefully to his words: "Tens of millions of Indians cannot believe this day has come . . . the fight for the temple is like the fight for freedom . . . the construction of the Ram temple is an instrument to unite the country." In other words, it is part of the

139

agenda of Modi's BJP to create a sectarian Hindu state. This is all about rolling back the secular state inherited from Neh and erasing the memory of the British Raj. Plans are already afoot to abandon the grand seat of government in Delhi designed by Sir Edward Lutyens for a new, "more appropriate" Indian complex. As Modi went on to say, "The wait of centuries is at an end." And the crowds hailed their "Hindu King" as "the greatest Indian leader of the last five hundred years."[1]

And he isn't alone. During the previous week Turkish President Recipe Erdogan staged a similar dramatic event in Istanbul: the rededication of the Hagia Sophia as a mosque.[2] The inaugural call to prayer attracted over 350,000 people. Here as in India we witnessed an ambitious political leader appealing to religious nationalism to bolster his poll rating, rolling back the secular state while appealing to ancient traditions and past glories, and in this case aspiring to restore the caliphate.[3] Again, increasing numbers of people loved it. It is the same path that Vladimir Putin has chosen to follow by employing his militant Russian Orthodox nationalism to fill the void left by the failed ideology of the Soviet state. Yes, today as in past ages religion is a powerful and destabilizing political weapon.

A clash of civilizations

So, what are we to make of all this? Some twenty-five years ago a controversial book by Samuel Huntington predicted that some such pattern of events was inevitable as history set forth on a new course. The title of the work summed up his thesis: *The Clash of Civilizations and the Remaking of World Order.*[4] Many people are now familiar with the geological notion of "tectonic plates"—those half-dozen or so vast segments of the earth's crust that carry the continents. These "plates" are in constant motion, grinding against each other, sometimes creating such spectacular effects as earthquakes and volcanoes. Huntington proposed a similar scenario for a

1. Tomlinson, "Modi is hailed as the Hindu king."
2. This is only one of many such events. Cf. Barchard, "Turkey."
3. This was already implicit in Erdogan's naming of a new bridge over the Bosphorus in 2013 as Sultan Selim the Grim Bridge. This was the sultan (1512–20) who extended Ottoman control over Egypt and Arabia to create a new caliphate. The name of one of his captains, Oruc Reis, has been given to a survey ship currently exploring for oil and gas off the Greek islands and Cyprus in an act of provocation that has brought Greece and Turkey to the brink of war.
4. Huntington, *Clash.*

political understanding of the modern world, for he saw it divided into some half dozen great "blocks," or cultural entities—Chinese, Hindu, Islamic, Orthodox, the West (including Europe and the Americas), and Africa. And he proposed that the future could be understood only in terms of the conflicting interests of these entities.

Huntington had a rather Spenglerian view of "the fading power of the West," a view that has continued to gain ground.[5] By uncoupling Modernization and Westernization—"the world is becoming more modern and less Western"—he attributed greater future significance to other civilizations, particularly in view of their more rapidly rising populations. If this diversity has now replaced the Cold War polarization of the world into two armed camps, it has also disturbed the notional reference points that spelled out who we are, for—in Huntington's thesis—who we are is defined in terms of who we are against: a state's place in the world is defined by its friends and enemies. With such a view of the world it is not surprising that his scenario should end on a rather apocalyptic note with the possibility of civilization yielding to barbarism and a global Dark Age descending on humanity.

In a later chapter I refer to Tolkein's *The Lord of the Rings* and its amazing popularity that wrong-footed all its critics. Perhaps there is something subliminal going on here. The kind of world that Huntington envisions has much in common with the woes of Middle Earth where friends and enemies, good and evil, are clearly depicted and everyone is very clear whose side they are on. No doubt something of the appeal of this fantasy world is that it does indeed make for clear identities and reassures us with the triumph of the values we cherish. It is a worldview of great value to politicians because it ensures popular support for clear agendas drawn on nationalist, cultural, or religious grounds. We have seen the results in Bosnia, Chechnya, Kashmir, Israel and, on a larger scale, "The Axis of Evil" of George Bush. Now, with China, the USA, India, and Turkey involved, the scale is dangerously enlarged. In this worldview of identity politics everyone is either a friend or enemy, the latter are endlessly demonized, and everyone is clamoring to be "great again." But it is crucial to remember that this is a fantasy world, the dream of narcissists and "supermen" (yes, note it is always men), and a rather puerile illusion at that.

Those inhabiting the real world of ordinary humanity have more limited horizons and though they live beneath the banners of political strongmen they can be found to be striving for remarkably similar things:

5. Spengler, *Decline of the West*; also Koch, *Suicide of the West*.

food, clothes, a living wage, a home, domestic security, freedom to develop talents, a cultural form that gives meaning to life and that can be shared with neighbors. As Aleksandr, a striking worker in Minsk, Belarus, put it, "People are tired of lies, of not having freedom of speech. We just want to live in a civilized society with the rule of law."[6] We have heard survivors of Iraq's multifaceted conflicts yearning for a similar outcome. This may rightly be called a humanist view, for it sees a shared humanity as the basis of life and foundation for everything else.

As the world is now awash with migrants seeking a better place to live—a recent estimate has put this number at seven hundred million people—there is no better place to get a sense of this common human longing than in the migrant camps that now proliferate along the borders of Europe. Typical is the so called "jungle" just outside Calais on the Channel coast where Kamal Sadeghi, 39, a Christian convert from Iran, and his wife Niki Karimi, 33, and their daughter, Sava, were recently interviewed by *The Times*: "The boat is our only chance for a new life in a safe country," Mr. Sadeghi, a singer and carpenter, said in desperation, "I am too tired to carry on. If they try to stop us I will drown myself."[7] He fled Iran after his wife's family objected to their marriage. They sought sanctuary in Slovenia but were placed in a prison with three hundred single men and lost their savings to the "mafia." "We have lost everything since we left Iran three years ago," he said; his wife, a lawyer who is suffering from depression because of their ordeal, said: "We need just a normal life."

In this moving interview we see a snapshot of the world humanity craves. Normality. Freedom. Security. Opportunity. Acceptance. Happiness. Life. No doubt the political strong men would say that is exactly what they are trying to deliver. But the way they go about it seems at best questionable. They build vast military arsenals and undertake prohibitively expensive vanity projects such as being the first to land humans on Mars—and aren't we all eager to go there? They siphon off billions of dollars of the national wealth for personal aggrandizement while imposing draconian laws that create a surveillance state where no one is free to move unquestioned, a so-called "sovereign democracy." And they are never short of words or reasons as to why things should remain as they are. But what is most needed is least likely: a world of greater humanity, diversity, justice, and hope.

6. O'Reilly, "200,000 gather."
7. Brown, "We'll drown."

And such a world is exactly what Lorenzo Simpson called for not long after Huntington's; a world guided by what he called "dialogical humanism." The world depicted in *The Unfinished Project: Towards a Postmetaphysical Humanism* provides a renewed basis for multicultural politics.[8] If the idea of a common humanity is to be salvaged from political Manichaeism, then we must reimagine the concept of *the other*. The framework for this he describes as "situated cosmopolitanism" characterized not by monolithic allegiances or absolute options, but by the fluid interchange of opinion with its own ongoing dynamic. Involving disputation and critique, this process seeks the reshaping of one's preconceptions of the *other's* difference through mutual interaction that challenges preconceptions. As a radically humanitarian approach in its allowances for cultural osmosis, this seems an altogether more hopeful agenda than the uncontrollable violence released by the political demonization of *the other*.

The role of religion

At the heart of this agenda, however, remains an intractable problem: the role of religious belief—or, more specifically, the institutionalized structures that give it expression and the religious authority that defends it. In the wake of the divisive wars of religion that ripped Europe apart in the seventeenth century, this was the issue that confronted Enlightenment thinkers. The central choice then was between a society founded on reason, as expressed democratically by ordinary citizens, or one founded on revelation, as mediated through authoritarian elites. The idea of a universal humanism championed by Enlightenment thinkers has been largely discarded because of its overreliance on a fixed conception of individuality, which all too often involves an idealized essence based on a white, masculine, and rational view of the world. But it is a choice still at the heart of the struggle within the various civilizations of the world.

In this matter Huntington is rather dismissive of the West, seeing it as the only civilization that has never generated a major religion and quoting favorably the view of the historian Christopher Dawson that "the great religions are the foundations on which the great civilizations rest."[9] But this rather sweeping view of religion as an undifferentiated category in which all are pretty much alike can be misleading in view of the great

8. Simpson, *Unfinished Project*.
9. Huntington, *Clash*, 47.

diversity that exists within this category and also the stages of human consciousness that different religions reflect. The noted theologian Lloyd Geering takes a more nuanced view in his wide-ranging analysis of the human religious quest.[10] Crucial in his view is the threshold of religious consciousness that was crossed in the middle of the first millennium BCE. So significant is this period that it has been called the Axial Age or the Great Transformation, the title of Karen Armstrong's celebrated book devoted to the study of this period.[11] It was at this time that quite independently such major reformers as Zarathustra, Confucius, Lao Tsu, Buddha, Socrates, Mahavira, the prophets of Israel, and the writers of the Upanishads arose, to name but some.

The change in religious understanding reflected in the teaching of these prophetic figures seems to have gathered pace after the time of Zarathustra (variously estimated as between 1500 BCE and 600 BCE) and as a consequence of his teaching. This can be highlighted by contrasting the *Gathas*, which reflect the influence of Zarathustra's teaching, and the writings of the earlier Indo-European *Rigveda*. Writing of this contrast Shaul Shaked notes: "It seems possible to say that the main contrast between the Gathic and the Vedic religion consists in the Gathic expectation that each individual should make the right choice or the right distinction, while the Vedic religion, at least in the earlier portions of the Rigveda, regards communal performance of ritual and sacrifice as the highest religious achievement. In evolutionary terms . . . the Gathic religion seems to present a more reflective, more inward-oriented kind of religion than the Rigveda," or, as Geering notes, "Those individuals who pioneered the Axial Period manifested a greater degree of personal self-awareness than appears to have been the case hitherto."[12]

In other words, a change in consciousness can be seen to have taken place. This marked the change from the old religious traditions that emerged almost unconsciously in cultural groups—characterized by ritual enactment, ceremonial celebration and storytelling—to a more reasoned view of the purpose and meaning of life within a linear view of the history of the cosmos and humanity, leading from a beginning to a final point, and characterized by ethical standards of behavior applicable to all individuals regardless of their ethnicity or social status. Such was the view of Confucius

10. Geering, *Tomorrow's God*.

11 Armstrong, *Great Transformation*.

12 Shaked, "Zoroastrian Origins," 197.

who taught that one should treat others the way one would wish to be treated. This "golden rule," as it has come to be called, is now recognizable as the
lodestone of a worldwide religious consciousness.

Over two thousand years later, most are still trying to catch up with
the implications of this change of consciousness, particularly among followers of the various derivative religions. The violent assault of Buddhist
nationalists in Myanmar (Burma) on the Rohingya Muslims, for example,
flies in the face of all the Buddha taught and stood for. The whole purpose
of the leaders of the Axial change of consciousness was to raise people's
sights above cultural and ethnic diversity. As Geering noted, "With the
Axial Age came the birth of world religions in which people transferred
their ultimate allegiance from tribe, race, or nation to some reality or
truth that transcended ethnicity."

Of course, as Karl Jaspers, who coined the phrase "the Axial Age,"
himself noted, "The age that saw these developments . . . cannot simply be
regarded as a simple upward movement . . . When the age lost its creative-
ness, a process of dogmatic fixation and levelling down took place."[13] But
over the centuries the various traditions have produced inspired individuals who have sought to return to the inspiration of the founders to remind
us that a religion is meaningless if its followers fail to do this. One such
was the great Persian poet Saadi Shirazi (1210–1302), still venerated and
loved more than any other figure in Iran. In his famous poem *Bani Adam*
("Children of Adam") we find the words:

> *All human beings are members of one frame,*
>
> *Since all, at first, from the same essence came.*
>
> *When time afflicts a limb with pain*
>
> *The other limbs at rest cannot remain.*
>
> *If thou feel not for other's misery*
>
> *A human being is no name for thee.*

These words are now inscribed in the foyer of the United Nations head-
quarters in New York. It is a pity some of the ayatollahs and power brokers
in Iran—the guardians of the faithful—do not consider these sentiments
as they play at a coldly calculated blackmail with people's lives as pawns
in a political power game. Such is the fate of Nazanin Zaghari-Ratcliffe,

---

13. Jaspers, *Origin and Goal of History*, 5

among many others. Such is the reason migrants like Kamal Sadeghi and Niki Karimi are in the Calais "jungle."

A more hopeful and uplifting contemporary example is the teaching of the Indian spiritual leader Acharya Swamishree Maharaj (1942–2020), whose inspiring life and humanitarian message was based on the principle: "We haven't come to take, but to give."[14] His teaching that "one's service and benevolence are the greatest of life's rewards" is a refreshing contrast to the narrow enmity of the Hindu nationalists indicating the vast differences that can exist in the understanding and interpretation of a religious tradition.

The challenge of compassion

It is in this context that Karen Armstrong has been promoting a new global venture, the Charter of Compassion, challenging the great religious traditions of the world to recognise what they all claim in their better moments to be the core virtue of their faith: compassion. Her conviction is that by undertaking this common goal we can change the world for the better, for such commitment reflects the challenge that the founders and prophets of the Axial Age set before their people. Such was message of the Jewish prophet Jeremiah: "See, I am setting before you the way of life and the way of death . . ."(Jer 21:8)—his reprise of the commandment attributed to God in the Book of Deuteronomy 29:19: "I set before you life and death, blessing, and curse. Therefore, choose life so that you and your descendants may live . . ."

It is noteworthy that at the beginning of her career Karen Armstrong produced *Holy War*, a major TV series that offered an historical perspective on today's violent world. It seems ironic that the cockpit of this conflict and the focus of the TV series was the Middle East, the cradle not only of civilization but also of the world's great monotheistic religions. The series was accompanied by a substantial book, the disturbing and depressing text of which recounted a seemingly endless spiral of violence.[15] That was over thirty years ago. Since then, things have become immeasurably worse. Ongoing conflicts nurtured by fanatical religious groups and power-hungry men (always men!) have plunged the region into an abyss of suffering that has left millions homeless, their lives torn apart, their trauma unending, their memories a

14. "Acharya Shree Purushottampriyadasji Swamishree Maharaj."
15. Armstrong, *Holy War*.

nightmare of barely-imaginable horror. And so, it continues. Any hope we might have from the world religions may well seem overshadowed by the pessimism implicit in Huntington's clashing civilizations.

Ironically, part of the reason for this is that the great belief systems that emerged from the Axial Age have been so successful in shaping our world that it is difficult to think beyond them or envisage a different order of things. The inertia of established practice is an issue that even the founders struggled with: the death of Socrates was a consequence of his enlightenment, in being seen to challenge established religious piety; probably the same fate befell Zarathustra. Later, even where elements of the initial radical message survived it became embalmed in older cultic practices. So, for example, despite the Buddha's emphatic distancing of himself from the great cultic world of Hinduism[16] and the clear affirmation of the ethical Eightfold Way, his memory is sustained by great temples with monumental statues (of him) that are the focus of elaborate ritual—yet these are the very things that characterized the ancient religious worldview he renounced and that have now themselves become polarizing. As a humble ascetic seeking enlightenment he left behind the cultic world of temples and religious monuments for the open road, but his followers have simply rebuilt them in his name.

It is a story that would also be replicated in the institutionalization of the message of Jesus of Nazareth in an imperial ecclesiastical edifice. This transformation and the conversion of the pagan Roman Empire to a Christian empire is perhaps one of the most remarkable transformations in history. How this happened is a story that has been told in detail by Bart Ehrman but still remains problematic.[17] In particular is the issue of how a message of love and compassion could so quickly become one of brutal oppression, as happened as a result of various imperial edicts after the reign of Constantine, notably the Theodosian Code that prescribed a whole range of savage punishments and the destruction of pagan shrines: the destruction of the temple of Allat Palmyra in 385 CE reads like a prequel to the ISIS savagery of 2015. Why this should have happened Ehrman helps to make clear when he writes that a unique feature of Christianity that led to the rise of intolerance was "its heightened emphasis on true

---

16. The concept of "Hinduism" was only created in the nineteenth century in response to British influences. Bayly, *Birth*, 325–63.

17. Ehrman, *Triumph of Christianity*.

knowledge."[18] As he goes on to elaborate, unlike other religions, Christianity was not principally a sets of practices but proper belief. Doctrine, or "orthodoxy" (right thinking), was crucial to its identity and claims to eternal salvation. Wrong answers not only had eternal consequences but frustrated the perceived will of God and so could not be tolerated. Such a consequence is an implicit aspect of any belief system that makes "truth" claims as did the Axial religions.

But there are other aspects of the post-Axial religions that we now find problematic. One is their understanding of the status of women. The teaching of the Axial Age was located in a firmly-established patriarchal culture that had little or no regard for women, an attitude reflected in the laws of Sargon the Great that women should be veiled and silent in public. This misogyny, with its assumption of male privilege, is something that even Axial thinking failed to address, and it has subsequently become a feature of the great religious traditions. This was highlighted only recently (October, 2019) in an incident that took place on an Easyjet flight from Ben Gurion airport, Tel Aviv, when a woman was asked to move as two ultra-Orthodox male passengers objected to sitting next to a woman— apparently not an unusual occurrence. A similar case involved a retired lawyer and wife of a rabbi who told her fellow passenger that there was nothing in the Torah forbidding him sitting next to a woman to which the response that it was "a general principle that a person should not put himself in a dangerous situation." This reveals the presumption in favor of male privilege common to all forms of religious ultra-orthodoxy. In the Roman Catholic Church even discussing the role of women as celebrants was forbidden by Pope John Paul II despite ample scriptural evidence. In Islam the position of women is even more contentious. Clearly traditional religious orthodoxy is rooted in fear of women.

Even more problematic is the goal to which Axial thinking directs religious consciousness. The meaning and purpose to life is seen as deriving from its presumed final goal that the theologian Paul Tillich described as *theonomous*, indicating that *theos*, God, established *nomos*, order, in all things. Unfortunately, however, when the supernatural element is challenged, many people understandably become extremely disturbed and agitated as the whole meaning and purpose of life seems threatened. It is from such that the followers of Modi and Erodogan come. And it likewise provides the seed bed of fundamentalism, in which people reject any

18. Ehrman, *Triumph of Christianity*, 266

modern views and seek refuge in the imagined certainty of a past that seems threatened by modernity. That these are powerful objections to any program of renewal can be seen in the example of the Roman Catholic church: the great renewal agenda of Vatican Council II, once hailed as a new beginning but now regarded largely a failure, was frustrated by powerful traditionalist elements within the church with which the present pope Francis still struggles to compete.

A new consciousness

What makes today's global world so different from previous times and the belief systems of the Axial Age is a change of consciousness. Again, I invoke the work of Lloyd Geering, who has charted these waters with great acumen. He writes, "As a result of the globalizing process of modern times [the] diverse ways of being human are losing their distinctiveness and a common way of being human is slowly emerging."[19] It is a point that particularly animated my Sikh friend to observe that all those ostensibly religious actions—like building a temple in Ayodhya—amount to no more than as a personal pastime if they are detached from our identity as human beings; that so-called "religious values" are in essence human values common to all or they are nothing.

This change of consciousness is partly a consequence of the change being promoted by the mass media and internet that is now accelerating at an alarming rate. It is part of what the visionary palaeontologist Teilhard de Chardin referred to as the *noosphere*, a new layer of knowledge created by humans that now encloses the *biosphere* (the natural world of planetary life) and the *lithosphere* of the earth's rocks. One estimate of the speed of growth manifested by this world of information and knowledge proposes that if we assume one bit of information is the size of an atom then in a hundred years the combined mass of information will be greater than the size of the earth!

What this new creation reflects is the widening and maturing of human consciousness into what may be called global consciousness. The advent of this global world may well usher in the greatest revolution of human history and will surely constitute a new reality. It reflects a threshold of consciousness and change as great as that of the Axial Age. Indeed, our present era could even be referred to as a New Axial Age. For as Geering further notes:

19. Geering, *Witness to Change*, 76.

"As the Axial Period gave rise to our cultural traditions which have provided the meaning systems for humankind for more than two thousand years, the advent of the global world, which is currently threatening those traditions, is the great new event of human history." Nor is this merely a cerebral change. International travel and migration also play an important role, as people increasingly represent a blending of races, ethnic backgrounds, and a complex cultural heritage. It is clear that any attempts to prevent this flood of change by creating safe havens of tradition—or building walls!—will prove as futile as Canute ordering the tide to retreat.[20]

Such a transformation will have profound implications for our understanding of the meaning of life. In the Axial Age the great thinkers directed our gaze beyond this world to a transcendent realm that gave a purpose and meaning to life. In many ways their thinking was dualistic, for it presupposed an ontological difference between the natural world and a supernatural sphere of reality: as Robert Bellah noted of the new religions of the Axial Age, "The historic religions are all in some sense transcendental."[21] In the new understanding we are not just in transit through this world but are an integral part of it. As the Dutch theologian van de Pol wrote: "The contrasts between supernatural and natural, this-worldly and other-worldly, have lost their meaning for modern mankind. Modern mankind no longer knows anything of a God who dwells somewhere and exists in himself, quite apart from the total reality of humans and their world."

The new religion of life

This has become the context for what the Cambridge theo-philosopher Don Cupitt called "the new religion of life"—a theme he has explored in many of his books.[22] In his view life is everything. It is the total expression of the natural world in which we live; it has no future dimension, it is now. It is not demanding, it is enabling—we are what we are and can make of ourselves what we wish. Life is not selective or discriminatory, but universal—the sun shines on all alike, rich or poor, good or bad. Therefore, to make the most of it we too must live like the sun, pouring out warmth, enabling growth,

20. I have often stood on the exact spot in the charming Sussex village of Bosham where this celebrated event is reputed to have taken place. The tide still comes up the High Street, for nature remains unchanged but the cultural world of Canute is long gone!

21. Quoted in Stramousa and Schulman, *Axial Civilizations*, 6.

22. Cupitt, *New Religion of Life*; Cupitt, *Creative Faith*.

benefiting all—what Cupitt called "solarity," living like the solar orb on which our lives depend. This is indeed a challenge!

In some ways this global consciousness of life may seem a return to the pre-Axial consciousness that did not differentiate between the human and natural worlds, when people saw themselves as integral to the great life-giving world of *Gaia*, the great earth mother. Now people are rediscovering—particularly in our post-COVID situation—a renewed sense of belonging to the natural world and being dependent upon it—being integral to life. This change of consciousness can also be seen in the re-emergence of an interest in paganism, now said to be the fastest growing "religion" in the UK. Perhaps that too is a reaction to or recognition of the technological hubris that led us to believe our future depended entirely on ourselves and the machines we had invented. Whatever the reason this new consciousness reflects a profound new re-engagement with nature and a renewed appreciation of life.

With this goes a new sense of appreciation for ancient tribal and indigenous cultures such as that of the Australian aborigines who see themselves as part of the land: "We do not own the land [as in the West's material culture], the land owns us." Similarly, they see the land and animals as worthy of respect and having "rights": the Maori of New Zealand consider the Whanganui River in the north island to be a place of special spiritual significance, and it has become (in March 2017) the first river in the world to be recognized as a living entity with its own rights and the legal status of a person. Similar rights are being sought in legal challenges on behalf of primates and whales: Chaokoh, the Thai coconut milk producer, recently lost most of its supermarket contracts when people learned it was using chained "monkey slaves" to gather the coconuts.

"Dadirri"

Having briefly mentioned the Australian aboriginal consciousness I would like to pause before hurrying on, because *not* hurrying on is at the heart of this consciousness and message. "We don't like to hurry. There is nothing more important than what we are attending to. There is nothing more urgent that we must hurry away from . . . we are river people. We cannot hurry the river. We have to move with its current and understand its ways." These words were part of reflection delivered by Miriam-Rose Ungunmerr-Baumann, a distinguished indigenous elder and in 2021 named Senior

Australian of the Year. She was talking about the concept of "dadirri."[23] This is inner, deep listening and quiet, still awareness, she explains: "When I experience dadirri, I am made whole again. I can sit on the riverbank or walk through the trees . . . I can find peace in this silent awareness . . . In our Aboriginal way, we learnt to listen from our earliest days. This was the normal way for us to learn—not by asking questions. We learnt by watching and listening, waiting and then acting. Our people have passed on this way of listening for over forty thousand years . . ."

Reading these words reminded me of something John Muir wrote as he contemplated the destruction of the American wilderness in the mid-nineteenth century by the remorseless advance of Westernized settlers for whom nature was merely a resource to be exploited. For Muir nature was not something separate from our selves, as he wrote in "Moutain Thoughts":

The sun shines not on us, but in us.

The rivers flow not past, but through us.

Thrilling, tingling, vibrating every fibre and cell of the substance of
our bodies, making them glide and sing.

The trees wave and the flowers bloom in our bodies as well as our
souls, and every bird song, wind song, and tremendous storm song
of the rocks in the heart of the mountains is our song.

What Muir was saying was that we can only live as a part of nature. Nature is not an "externality," and to forget this makes our life impossible. Muir, a nature mystic who was said to have saved the American soul from materialism, formulated the concept of preserved areas, or national parks, to protect the wilderness that led to the creation of Yosemite National Park in 1890. But it is also remarkable that what he was saying was exactly the same as the ancient Aboriginal understanding of life and *dadirri*. This ancient people and their wisdom had been treated with contempt, as savages, by Western powers. That this should have been so is testimony to just how self-destructive this Western culture had become. At least the realization has now at last offered the possibility of healing and hope.

This transformation of worldview by an ecological sensitivity is something that we can perhaps better perceive in our present predicament as we struggle with the calamitous implications of climate change and the COVID pandemic. *There seems to be a growing sense that we cannot go on as*

23. Living Water, "Dadirri."

we are, that things must change, that we must change. Again, there is a shift in understanding, epitomized in the distinction between religion and spirituality, between the publicly-organized events and private state of mind, in the reappraisal of the natural world *and our place in it* as the source of *health and healing,* even awe and transcendence rather than merely the antechamber of some supernatural world beyond.[24]

A "new normal"

In the narrative of "axiality" the ancient cosmological mythologies gave way to transcendental "reflexivity" in the passage from ritual enactment to religious ethical behavior, from *ecological,* cyclical time to linear, *structural* time—and with these changes comes the possibility of history. This happened in the aftermath of the great civilizational crisis of the twelfth century BCE. Palaeo-anthropologists have found that such collapses are not uncommon in human history. One thinks, for example, of the pre-Columbian civilizations of South and Central America such as the Chavin, Mocha, and Olmec, and the mysterious abandonment of Teotihuacan (though the narrative of "axiality" does not embrace the Americas where the understanding of time and transformation was very different to that of the West).[25] Under extreme duress people can lose confidence in the belief systems that have sustained their societies and abandon them. This is what seems to have happened on Rapa Nui (Easter Island) with the "toppling" of the Moai and the emergence of the "birdman" cult.

The question for us now is whether such a collapse with a consequent change of consciousness is happening in our global society in response to a deluge of climatic, epidemiological, economic, ecological, and demographic stresses? We have a growing sense that "normality" as we knew it will never return; that things will be different in the future.[26] But what will be the "new normal"?

In the original axial age, the answer was fashioned in transcendental terms with the conviction that another world is possible, a better world not only in the future but in "the beyond," after life. Karl Jasper's original Axial

24. McCarthy, *Consolation of Nature.*

25. D'Altroy, *Incas,* 138–44, "(Space-)Time": "Crucially, the Incas thought that it was both possible, and sometimes desirable, for humans to change the past and reset time."

26. Numerous newspaper articles now elaborate this theme, particularly business columns. Wighton, "Short-Termism."

Age had to do with the creation and institutionalization of a tension between the transcendental/heavenly and mundane/earthbound orders. Plato would have phrased this as an escape from the cave of unreality in which we are confined and thus established the dualistic thinking that has shaped the West ever since. But this "escape" no longer convinces and this whole view has become a fiction. Our understanding of reality is different: in place of a fixed order, we see nothing but the quantum world of chance and probabilities within a cosmos largely composed of unintelligible "dark matter" that by its nature will remain forever incomprehensible.

So, we are thrown back on the uncertainty of the present moment—a situation that brings with it the need for both a new sense of urgency to act in that present moment and the demand for immediacy focused on what must be done. Such a form of consciousness is perhaps reflected in the contrast now made between "religion," as organized and structured belief systems, and the more personalized spontaneity of "spirituality." When people affirm the latter while distancing themselves from the former—as is increasingly the case—this seems to reflect a change of self-understanding reminiscent of the earlier axial transformation.[27] Yet spirituality is a hard concept to pin down. It can be any of a list of things: a form of self-affirmation, an awareness of the singularity of life, a sensitivity to others and the natural world, a sense connectedness to nature, an inwardness and restraint in the pursuit of ambition and possessions.

A phrase that captures the need and timber of our times is the title of one of the great spiritual classics of the eighteenth century, translated as *The Sacrament of the Present Moment.*[28] To be sure, this clandestine work by the French Jesuit Jean Pierre de Caussade (1675–1751), suppressed in his own lifetime as an expression of "Quietist" heresy, was written with a sense of abandonment to a greater, transcendental providence; but its title also captures that sense of awareness of an all-embracing natural world with which people so earnestly seek to reconnect in order to "save" not only themselves but the planet. It conveys a sense of the ultimate contingency of the present moment and the opportunities it presents. These are just some of the elements of an emergent narrative designed to give new meaning to life.[29] The Pilgrim Fathers invoked an ancient narrative in their journey to an unknown land; we today need not so much a new home as a new narrative.

27. Hunt, "Old Tree," 3–8.

28. This is one translation of the title of *L'Abandon,* Muggeridge.

29. Cupitt, *Ethics.*

Chapter 12

Survival

───────────

The illusions of civilizations
and the lessons of COVID-19

ONE OF THE UNFORESEEN benefits of the COVID pandemic has been time: time on our hands, time to stop and think, time to live a different daily routine, time to reflect on what is really important and what the future may hold. This newfound reality has even been given a name, the Great Pause, and scientist have a new word for it: anthropause (Not to be confused with the andropause, the male equivalent of the menopause—but let's not get into that debate!). That this has happened at the beginning of a new era of human planetary domination now called the Anthropocene is not without its significance

People have been filling the newfound time on their hands by taking up surprising new interests such as home baking, a fad indicated by the unexpected rocketing demand for flour and baking materials. People's sensory world also seems suddenly to have expanded with a renewed appreciation of nature: listening to birdsong, looking at the night sky, experiencing the silence and fresher air as traffic disappears, and even animal behavior has been responding to the changed circumstances and the demand for kittens is up 120 percent. Now we have time to reflect on what exactly is the nature of the world we have created: Where is it leading and what do we need to change? That our global civilization has been forced to pause for thought could be a blessing in disguise.

Usually, civilizations just keep running until a military or natural catastrophe overwhelms them, sometimes with spectacular and unexpected abruptness. Take for example the Aztecs. A lockdown TV documentary series focused on the fate of Tenochtitlan, the capital of the Aztec empire with its magnificent temples to the Sun and Moon whose ruins are being reexcavated at the heart of modern Mexico City. Everything about this place was monumental. Probably the largest city of its time, it held a quarter of a million people housed on *chinampas,* the reclaimed marshland of the lake surrounding the gleaming white temple complex that rose seventy meters into the sky.[1] The skill and craftsmanship, the mathematical and astronomical knowledge, the engineering ingenuity, that lay behind this achievement is breathtaking, even down to the quarrying and transportation of thousands of tons of stone over 40 kilometers, and all by human physical effort. When the Spanish Conquistadores arrived in 1519, they were spellbound that such a place could exist. Here was a successful and sophisticated civilization, yet its very existence was based on an illusion.

Fundamental to the nature of the Aztec civilization was a belief in the efficacy of sacrifice: that the gods who controlled human destiny, climate, and the fate of the world had to be constantly placated though human sacrifice. The beating heart of the city and civilization was literally the beating hearts plucked out of countless victims, the relentless provision of which drove the expansion of the Aztec empire. The sudden demise of the city at the hands of the Spanish came about not only through a combination of violence and the effects of rampant new diseases but also a fatalism. The beliefs that inspired Aztec civilization were based on a view of life that was always hovering on the brink of destruction by the gods who—as personifications of the forces of nature—were believed to have sacrificed themselves so that the world and humanity could exist. As the Mexican writer Carlos Fuentes eloquently put it: "For ancient Americans the forces of the universe were a constant source of danger as well as a constant source of the very survival they menaced. This ambiguity was resolved in sacrifice, which was no more in doubt for them than the formula $E=mc^2$ is for us today."[2]

The myths of the peoples of Mesoamerica were born of a sense of catastrophe in which the cosmos repeatedly collapsed into chaos and the gruesome savagery with which the gods were portrayed reflected this nadir. When the statue of Coatlicue, the earth goddess, was first discovered, people found it shocking beyond belief, if not incomprehensibly terrifying—it still is. The French poet Charles Baudelaire could only say that such works were the expression of a "barbaric art," barbaric in the sense of totally alien to the

1. Cervantes, *Conquistadores,* 148.
2. Fuentes, *Buried Mirror,* 94.

concept of personality.[3] The beliefs that inspired it were an expression of the heart of darkness that lies within the human psyche, the black hole that exists in the center of the civilizations humans create.

A pattern of denial

Of course, societies and civilizations are often unaware of the real reasons for their demise. The great cities of ancient Sumer arose in Mesopotamia thanks to clever irrigation that allowed the growth of abundant crops. But it was this same irrigation system that slowly leached the soil, forming subterranean salt pans that made farming impossible and turning the land into the desert it is today.[4] Similarly the fourteenth-century Viking settlers in Greenland had no inkling of climate change but it decided the fate of their society. And while Edward Gibbon wrote his famous six-volume history of *The Decline and Fall of the Roman Empire,* he entirely overlooked what may have been the crucial environmental factors: some have argued that the empire never really recovered from the Antonine plague of 165–80 CE. Will the same be true of us?

Nearer to our own time we have another graphic example of a society based on an illusion that grew then collapsed with spectacular suddenness: the Soviet Union. This is the story that President Putin is now currently busily engaged in rewriting as he cobbles together a pastiche of virulent nationalism. The reality is somber. From its outset in 1917 this state was the expression of a utopian ideal according to which all people would be equal and private wealth abolished and shared for the good of all by one centralized party. To ensure that such a utopia did indeed come to pass, especially among those who resisted, it was necessary from the outset to organize work camps of forced labor under a government agency, *Glavnoe Upraveniye Lagerei,* better known by its acronym GULAG, which was later uncovered by the novelist Alexander Solzhenitsyn in *The Gulag Archipelago.*[5] Here was a hidden and unrecognized world that underpinned the illusions of Soviet reality.

3. Fuentes, *Buried Mirror,* 107.

4. Wright, *Short History of Progress.* When Sir Leonard Woolley first started excavating Ur he wondered at the "well nigh incredible . . . contrast between past and present" and why "the very soil lost its virtue?"

5. Applebaum, *Gulag.*

Ironically the first camp was, like the gleaming white island city of Tenochtitlan in its surrounding lake, set on an island (Solovetsky), from which the spires of an old white-walled monastery rose above the surrounding icy waste of the White Sea. Both were stunning to behold. And the underlying similarities didn't stop there. The victims of the Red Terror were as necessary for the achievement of the new socialist utopia as the human sacrifices consumed in industrial quantities on the altars of the Aztecs. These were drawn from the neighboring tribes they oppressed just as the network of Soviet camps that developed would be fed by the expansion of the Soviet empire to include further victims: Ukrainians, Poles, Balts, Tartars, Khazaks . . . .in all over thirty million people, whose only realistic expectation of release was death. Their doleful reality was captured in the final letter of the poet Osip Mandelstam who wrote, "I am treated like a dog. I am a shadow. I do not exist. I only have the right to die."[6] Insofar as barbarism is a denial of personality then, as with Buadelaire's judgement on the earth goddess, Coatlicue, here also is a barbarism at the heart of civilization.

The Nazi Germans took note of this system and coined a remarkably concise and cynical epithet for their own imitation: *Arbeit macht frei*, "Work makes free." Again, the same black hole of which Ruth Kluger wrote and Hans Lochmann portrayed opened up in the heart of civilization. Yet many Russians still think such actions were necessary for victory in the Second World War. An opinion poll run by the Levada Center in Moscow in 2019 revealed that 46 percent of Russians thought the "human casualties suffered by the Soviet people during the Stalin era" were justified and 70 percent favourably viewed Joseph Stalin, the chief architect of the Gulag.[7] Recently he was voted (in Russia) as "the most outstanding figure" in world history. There have even been calls to restore the statue of Felix Dzerzhinsky, founder of the KGB and an architect of the Red Terror, to his plinth outside the infamous Lubyanka building where so many thousands simply disappeared, as if into a black hole.

A flawed past

In 1989 the Soviet empire collapsed. By this time few viewed the utopian communist ideology as anything other than an illusion—or more critically

6. Quoted in Merridale, *Night*, 256.
7. Reyner, "Levada Poll."

by Solzhenitsyn, "The Lie"—and its demise was as rapid as that of the Aztecs. In the face of an overwhelming indifference to individual lives when protest movements like Solidarity in Poland did erupt their message was simple: "We matter."[8] This was all part of the increasingly destabilized civilization of the West. Coming to our own tim, the COVID pandemic has not only shut down much of our global civilization but has coincided with a number of disturbing events that have thrown into stark relief the illusions we live by. It is a remarkable coincidence that the virus should cause a malignant respiratory failure that destroys the lungs of its hapless victims who in their final moments experience an inability to breathe—a condition also voiced by George Floyd in his last moments. The words "I can't breathe" would soon echo around the world as a cry to recognise the "virus of racism." Its covert presence seemed everywhere. In scenes similar to the toppling of statues of Lenin and Stalin at the collapse of the Soviet Union, statues of anyone linked to racism or slavery began to be toppled across the world. The message again was simple: "Black lives matter."

Suddenly it seemed as if the whole story of Western civilization was being picked apart. Not only had the narrative largely erased or never really acknowledged trade in slaves, but its subtext was an illusion of moral superiority, entrepreneurial endeavour, and progressive enlightenment. What is clear from lives such as that of the seventeenth-century Bristol slave trader Edward Coulston, whose statue was unceremoniously toppled into the harbour from whence his slave ships sailed, is that the vast sums of money made from the African slave trade, was money that was used not only to finance entrepreneurial activity that would facilitate the Industrial Revolution and the rise of Great Britain but also to fund both extravagant lifestyles, and ordinary incomes, across the country.[9] One vicar noted with confusion that his eighteenth-century church extension had been funded from the profits of the slave trade and wondered if it should now be knocked down!

That the National Trust should have found one-third of its historic homes have links to the slave trade is no surprise and probably a conservative estimate. And the more one looks the more one finds the corrosive tentacles

8. At a private meeting in April 1982 with the charismatic leader of Solidarity, Lech Walesa, while he was under house arrest, told me that he saw Solidarity not just as a political movement but spiritual one that affirmed human rights and in which his role model was Mahatma Gandhi.

9. Curiously, if not untypically, the "celebrated and seminal text" on the Industrial Revolution by Mathias, *First Industrial Nation*, makes no mention of the vast wealth the slave trade made available for crucial bank capitalization that transformed society.

of slavery embedded in our whole way of life. In one typical vignette the church of St. Botolph without Aldgate in the City of London recently removed a bust to Sir John Cass, a politician and philanthropist whose wealth came from the slave trade, though his name is also borne by the local school at which until recently he was presented a "a role model." But the roots of slavery go deeper still. St. Botolph himself was a seventh-century Saxon noble at a time when trade in slaves was not only common (one thinks of stories of St. Patrick and later Viking slave traders) but often associated with the wealth of powerful elites; the medieval church struggled to eradicate this practice. The Archbishop of Canterbury, Justin Welby, now thinks the time has come to be more radical and "decolonize" white Jesus: "The way the Western church portrays Jesus needs to be thought about again."

Nor is slavery, in its general sense of a denial of personal rights, a thing of the past. A UN report of 2019 identified 40 million people as being enslaved today, a quarter of them children, and their numbers are "only likely to increase."[10] Modern slavery exists under our noses, in our cities and in many guises: forced labor, domestic service, human trafficking, the *kafala* "sponsorship system." Sweat shops around the world underpin the global economy and feed our consumer habits like a shadow GULAG with an Aztec appetite for humanity. Once again, the practice forms part of an illusion we are generally happy to live with. One of the criticisms levelled at the leading abolitionist William Wilberforce by social reforms like William Cobbett was his indifference to the "factory slavery" that existed on his own doorstep and his opposition to worker's rights as a "general disease of our society"; the essayist William Hazlitt wrote that Wilberforce "preaches vital Christianity to untutored savages and tolerates its worst abuse in civilized societies."

And all this leads to the even more disturbing thought that in our narratives of the past civilization and slavery are symbiotic, the one sybaritic of the other, and have been since their beginnings in ancient Mesopotamia. Amongst the earliest cuneiform texts to have survived from those times is one from Lagash, an important Sumerian city during the middle of the third millennium BCE. Here we find a class of *ir* (slaves) and also *namra-ak* (captive women and children) who were kept in concentration camps called *kara* ("the place where people die"). Records indicate that many of

10. ILO, "Forced Labour." It is estimated that a staggering 45% of Africans are exposed to some form of modern slavery.

the *namra-ak* starved to death while others were sent to colonize foreign lands.[11] How prescient is this of the twentieth century?

An ecocidal epoch

The whole saga of civilization is often presented as a glittering spectacle of achievement, monumental creations, abundant prosperity, and conspicuous consumption—all sustained by the limitless cornucopia of nature. COVID-19 has very effectively challenged this illusion of how we live. The debate over whether the virus was man-made or a natural phenomenon is moot; the reality seems to be that in the man-made environment of the food market of Wuhan it was humans who facilitated its transference across the species barrier by the appalling mistreatment of animals. In a sense the virus is "nature's revenge" on humanity. The illusion of ever-greater supplies of exotic foods to supply insatiable human appetites, of an unsustainable lifestyle with an acceptable right, has been called into question and found wanting. The challenges that the presence of humanity on the planet presents to other creatures and life forms has now become overwhelming and to the grim record of modern times to the concept of genocide has now had to be added another neologism, ecocide.

Now in his ninth decade, Sir David Attenborough, perhaps the world's most famous naturalist, is given to reflecting on the changes he has witnessed over his lifetime, in particular the scale of environmental destruction. There is an increasing note of anguished desperation in his voice as he pleads for a change in our ways to save ourselves as well as the world's ecosystems and the myriad life forms, particularly animals, many of which are at critical levels of survival as their numbers plummet. The scale of this human-induced "ecocide" is unprecedented in human history. Who would have thought, for example, that the largest life form in the world, the Australian Great Barrier Reef, with all the life forms it supports, could be on the point of total destruction as a consequence of human activity?

The driving force behind this ecocide has been something many are loath to recognize and that even Sir David regrets for not having emphasized earlier: the explosion of the human population. To put this into perspective, in the 1930s the human population stood at about two billion. It had reached this number after the two million years since our hominid ancestors first appeared on earth. By 1974 this had doubled to four billion.

11. Charles River Editors, *Sumer*, 104.

By our present time it is on the point of doubling again to eight billion. These numbers are staggering. They are also unsustainable, and the environmental stresses of providing for such numbers of people beckons a civilizational collapse such as happened previously on a regional scale to a number of civilizations.[12]

But population numbers are not the only issue driving this ecological crisis. Also crucial is the human mindset. And here an inconvenient truth is that Christianity has been instrumental in bringing us to this point. Why and how this has come about has been explored in detail by numerous writers such as the New Zealand theologian Lloyd Geering in his wide-ranging book *Coming Back to Earth: From Gods, to God, to Gaia*.[13] Central to this issue has been the mentality towards the earth that arose from biblical teaching. By presenting "man" as distinct from the animals and possessing domination over them, the Bible depicts "man" as created in the image of an absolute God and sharing "his" dominating power. As the historian Arnold Toynbee wrote, "Some of the major maladies of the present world—in particular the recklessly extravagant consumption of nature's irreplaceable treasures . . . can be traced back to a religious cause, and this cause is the rise of monotheism . . . Monotheism, as enunciated in the book of Genesis, has removed the age-old restraint that was once placed on man's greed by his awe."[14] Nor was this all. Toynbee went on to assert that it was from this matrix that emerged not only secularization but a scientific mechanism that "robbed nature of its divine mystery and has broken its spell." In short, biblical theism has had the effect, whether intended or not, of encouraging the exploitation of the earth.

More recently, Thomas Berry has been an eloquent exponent of the same theme. Both an ecologist and a Roman Catholic priest, Berry has been particularly critical of the failure of traditional religious leaders to grasp what has been happening. He identifies the cause of the problem as the lack of "an understanding of the developmental (evolutionary) character of the universe."[15] The Judeo-Christian view of nature as an "externality" for our use and disposal is at the root of our present malaise. Because this has been particularly true of Christianity, he reminds us that "the present disruption of all the basic life systems of earth has come about within a culture that emerged

12. Diamond, *Collapse*.
13. Geering, *Coming Back to Earth*.
14. Toynbee, *Genesis of Pollution*.
15. Berry, *Selected Writings*.

from a biblical-Christian matrix. It did not arise out of the Buddhist world, or Hindu or Chinese or Japanese worlds or the Islamic world, it emerged from within our Western Christian-derived civilization."

In real time just how frightening can be the consequences of such a legacy can be seen with reference to the USA. It is here that we see powerful Republican politicians whose Bible-based evangelical fervor is matched only by their contempt for environmental concerns. As Congressman Tim Walberg said in 2017, "As a Christian I believe that there is a creator in God who is much bigger than us. And I am confident that if there's a real problem, he can take care of it." Others just see it as God's plan to just "blow the lot" before being "raptured" up to heaven. The American naturalist E. O. Wilson sees such attitudes a reflection of "the mood of Western civilization [that] is Abrahamic. The explorers and colonists were guided by a biblical prayer: 'May we take possession of this land that God has provided and let it drip milk and honey into our mouths for ever.'"[16] This too is a part of the Christian legacy.

The understanding of Nature as an entity in itself governed by its own internal laws is quite different from the biblical idea of creation governed by a deity. In the Hebrew Bible there is no understanding or reference to "nature" as such, and the nearest in Greek translations is the word *physis*, matter, which is rare. What humankind now needs is a new and greater sensitivity to the natural world, a new way of perceiving it, and the recognition that we are all part of what ecologist Thomas Berry called an "Earth community" of life. We need a style of thinking that acknowledges us to be more than semi-detached occupants of a natural world; that sees respect for the natural order as the basis for any sustainable way of life; that places nature's rights ahead of ours; that requires our appetites for both consumption and procreation to be restrained.

A different "normality"

One of the effects of COVID-19 is that it has challenged the long-standing hubris that we can manipulate nature for our benefit. It has also reawakened an awareness of the significance of the natural world for many suffering under the restraints of lockdown. Not only have many remarked on the way nature has responded to our absence—clearer skies, fresher air, starry nights, sweeter bird song—but there has been a growing sense among

16. Wilson, *Future of Life*, xxii.

people of the importance of natural spaces such as parks and gardens, of the health benefits of just being able to walk under the trees—the so-called "green prescription" that can save the NHS millions. There has even been a resurgence of neo-paganism with its appreciation of the natural rites and rituals attuned to the seasons of the year; of the natural forces or "goddesses" so effectively excoriated from the biblical record.

But even here there is an ambivalence so characteristic of all human activity. The priority in the pandemic has been human survival and the provision of personal protective equipment (PPE). The result has been vast increase in disposable, but indestructible, plastic items that had until the pandemic been the focus of reduction. Whereas pre-lockdown UK households had got down to an average of 99 pieces of plastic waste a week, now it has shot up to 129 items. Worldwide a staggering 194 billion disposable masks and gloves are being used a month. This is on top of a resurgence in the use of such items as disposable coffee cups that in the UK is running at 2.5 billion a year. Much of this plastic waste ends up in the oceans (two trillion tons and growing), being ingested by all forms of life in the food chain down to the smallest plankton.[17] So prevalent now is the plastic in nature that it is predicted that in millions of years to come all that will remain of the evidence of the human presence on earth will be a sedimentary layer of petrified plastic.

Whatever the "new normal" of the future may be, it will differ greatly from the past normal. COVID-19 has given a whole civilization a rare moment for pause, a chance to reconsider the illusions it lives by and to change, lest it descend into the final abyss. The present moment of history demonstrates a curious conjunction of significant events and deep historical currents: a global pandemic, a growing ecological crisis, a new sense of the evils of racism, the recognition that all lives matter and a disenchantment with the creed of greed. From the outset of the pandemic the focus has been on the priority to save lives, the insistence that life matters above all else.

One of the most positive features of the lockdown has been a new sense of generosity, a spirit of solidarity, a willingness to support others, an appreciation for those who help us not only in hospitals but also in stores and public services. This new spirit is perhaps best epitomized by the card

17. When the *Deepsea Challenger* made its decent into the Mariana Trench, the deepest part of the Pacific Ocean in 2021, among the first things the cameras picked up on the sea bed was a piece of plastic!

that the British Red Cross has put out: "Kindness will keep us together." In this we can perhaps discern the spirit of "the new normal"; of the path that civilization must now take, one that leads beyond slavery, the illusions of totalitarian ideologies, and human and ecological exploitation. COVID-19 may in fact prove to be the beginnings of a better future.

Bibliography

"Acharya Shree Purushottampriyadasji Swamishree Maharaj, 78: Humanitarian Leader Known to All as 'Bapa.'" *The Times*, August 29, 2020.

"Discovery of 750 More Graves at indigenous School Shocks Canada." *The Times*, June 25, 2021.

Aaronovitch, David. "QAnon Cultists Go to War with 'Evil.'" *The Times*, January 8, 2021.

Abrams, M. *Natural Supernaturalism: Tradition and Revolution in Romantic Literature.* London: Norton, 1973.

Applebaum, Ann. *Gulag: A History of the Soviet Camps.* New York: Doubleday, 2003.

Armstrong, Karen. *The Great Transformation.* London: Atlantic Books, 2007.

———. *Holy War: The Crusades and their Impact on Today's World.* London: Macmillan, 1988.

Arnason, Johann P., et al, eds. *Axial Civilizations and World History.* Leiden: Brill, 2005.

Baigent, Michael, and Richard Leigh. *Inquisition.* London: Penguin, 2000.

Baggini, Julian. *The Godless Gospel: Was Jesus a Great Moral Teacher?* London: Granta, 2020.

Barchard, David. "Turkey Embraces a New Iconoclasm." *Tablet,* August 18, 2020.

Barras, Colin. "Genes of the Undead." *New Scientist: The Collection* (2018) 74–77.

Bate, Jonathan. *Radical Wordsworth: The Poet who Changed the World.* New Haven: Yale University Press, 2020.

Bayly, C. A. *The Birth of the Modern World, 1780–1914.* Oxford: Blackwell, 2004.

Bede. *The Ecclesiastical History of the English People.* London: Penguin, 1990.

Bennetts, Mark. "Activist Charged over Plaque for Stalin." *The Times,* July 16, 2017.

Berlin, Isaiah. *Vico and Herder: Two Studies in the History of Ideas.* London: Hogarth, 1992.

Berry, T. *The Dream of the Earth,* San Francisco, Sierra Club books, 1988.

———. *Selected Writings on the Earth Community,* New York: Orbis, 2014.

Blakely, Rhys. "Dead Sea Scrolls analysis pieces the past together." *The Times,* June 3, 2020.

Bloom, Harold. *The Book of J.* London: Faber, 1991.

Brown, David. "We'll Drown if You Stop Us, Migrants Warn Britain." *The Times,* August 12, 2020.

Brown, Hanbury. *The Wisdom of Science: Its Relevance to Culture and Religion.* Cambridge: Cambridge University Press, 1986.

Brown, Peter. *Authority and the Sacred: Aspects of the Christianization of the Roman World*. Cambridge: Cambridge University Press, 1997.

Buber, Martin. *Two Types of Faith*. New York: Syracuse University Press, 2003.

Burgess, Kaya. "Church's Mea Culpa on Anti-Semitism." *The Times*, April 21, 2019.

Carroll, James. *Christ Actually: The Son of God for the Secular Age*. London: Collins, 2014

CathNews New Zealand. "Nazi Germany Bishops Criticised by Their Successors." *CathNews.co.nz*, May 4, 2020. https://cathnews.co.nz/2020/05/04/nazi-germany-bishops-holocaust/.

Cervantes, Fernando. *Conquistadores: A New History*. London: Allen Lane, 2020.

Chadwick, Owen. *The Secularization of the European Mind in the Nineteenth Century*. Cambridge: Cambridge University Press, 1975.

Charles River Editors, *Sumer*. London: Create Space Independent Publishing Platform, 2018.

Christiansen, Eric. *The Northern Crusades*. London: Penguin, 1997.

Clark, Christopher. *Iron Kingdom: The Rise and Downfall of Prussia 1600–1947*. London: Penguin, 2007.

Cohn, Norman. *The Pursuit of the Millennium*. London: Secker & Warburg, 1957.

Cohn-Sherbok, Dan. *Holocaust Theology*. London: Lamp Press, 1989.

Collins, Andrew. *Gobekli Tepe: Genesis of the Gods*. Rochester, VT: Bear and Company, 2014.

Crombie, A. C. *Robert Grosseteste and the Origins of Experimental Science*. Oxford: Oxbow, 1953.

Cronin, Vincent. *The Wise Man from the West*. London: Hart Davis, 1955.

Crossan, John Dominic. *God and Empire: Jesus against Rome, Then and Now*. London: Harper Collins, 2007.

———. *The Power of Parable: How Fiction by Jesus Became Fiction about Jesus*. London: SPCK, 2012.

Cupitt, Don. *Creative Faith: Religion as a Way of Worldmaking.* Santa Rosa, CA: Polebridge, 2015.

———. *Ethics in the Last Days of Humanity*. Santa Rosa, CA: Polebridge, 2016.

———. *The Meaning of the West: An Apologia for Secular Christianity*. London: SCM, 2008.

———. *The New Religion of Life in Everyday Speech*. London: SCM, 1999.

D'Altroy, T. N. *The Incas*. Hoboken, NJ: Wiley, 2015.

Davidson, Robert, and A. Leaney. *The Pelican Guide to Modern Theology Volume 3: Biblical Criticism*. London: Penguin, 1970.

Davie, Martin. *New Dictionary of Theology: Historical and Systematic*. 2nd ed. London: InterVarsity, 2016.

Davis, Charles. *Religion and the Making of Society*. Cambridge: Cambridge University Press, 1994.

Dawkins, *Unweaving the Rainbow*. London: Penguin, 1999.

de Chardin, Pierre Teilhard. *The Phenomenon of Man*. London: Collins Fontana, 1965.

Diamond, Jared. *Collapse: How Societies Choose to Fail or Succeed*. London: Penguin, 2005.

Dodd, C. H. *The Founder of Christianity*. London: Harper Collins, 1971.

———. *The Parables of the Kingdom*. London: Fontana, 1961.

Douglas, Kate. "Our Asian Origins." *New Scientist: The Collection* (2018) 35–37.

Dugan, Sally, and David Dugan. *The Day the World Took Off: The Roots of the Industrial Revolution*. London: Channel 4 Books, 2000.

Ehrman, Bart. *Forged: Why the Bible's Authors Are Not Who We Think They Are*. London: HarperOne, 2012.

———. *How Jesus Became God: The Exaltation of a Jewish Preacher from Galilee*. London: HarperOne, 2014.

———. *Jesus before the Gospels: How the Earliest Christians Remembered, Changed, and Invented their Stories of the Saviour*. London: HarperOne, 2016.

———. *Lost Christianities: The Battles for Scripture and the Faith we Never Knew*. Oxford: Oxford University Press, 2005.

———. *The Triumph of Christianity: How a Forbidden Religion Swept the World*. London: Oneworld, 2018.

———. *Whose Word Is It? The Story Behind Who Changed the New Testament and Why*. London: Continuum, 2006.

Elliot, J. H. *Imperial Spain*. London: Penguin, 1970.

Erichsen, C., and D. Olusoga. *The Kaiser's Holocaust: Germany's Forgotten Genocide*. London: Faber, 2011.

Fernandez-Armesto, Felipe. *Columbus*. Oxford: Oxford University Press, 1991.

———. *Before Columbus: Exploration and Colonization from the Mediterranean to the Atlantic 1229–1492*. Philadelphia: Univ. of Pennsylvania Press, 1987.

Feuerbach, Ludwig. *The Essence of Christianity*. London: Trübner, 1841.

Finkelstein, Daniel. "Next Time I'm Asked How Anti-Semitism Started, I'll Say: Go to This Exhibition." *The Times*, March 20, 2019.

Finkelstein, Israel, and Neil Silberman. *The Bible Unearthed: Archaeology's New Vision of Ancient Israel and the Origin of its Sacred Texts*. New York: Free Press, 2001.

———. *David and Solomon: In Search of the Bible's Sacred Kings and the Roots of the Western Tradition*. New York: Free Press, 2006.

Finkelstein, Israel, and Amihai Mazar. *The Quest for the Historical Israel*. Atlanta: SBL, 2015.

Fisher, H. A. L. *A History of Europe*. London: Edward Arnold, 1936.

Frankl, Viktor. *Man's Search for Meaning: An Introduction to Logotherapy*. London: Hodder & Stoughton, 1959.

Fuentes, Carlos. *The Buried Mirror: Reflections on Spain and the New World*. London: Andre Deutsch, 1992.

Funk, Robert. *The Five Gospels: What Did Jesus Really Say? The Search for the Authentic Words of Jesus*. New York: Harper, 2007.

Geering, Lloyd. *Christianity without God*. Santa Rosa, CA: Polebridge, 2002.

———. *Coming Back to Earth: From Gods, to God, to Gaia*. Santa Rosa, CA: Polebridge, 2009.

———. *Tomorrow's God*. Wellington, NZ: Bridget Williams, 1994.

———. *Witness to Change*. Petone, NZ: Steele Roberts, 2018.

Gilk, Paul. *Picking Fights with the Gods: A Spiritual Psychoanalysis of Civilization's Superego*. Eugene, OR: Wipf & Stock, 2016.

Glyn, Parry. *The Arch Conjuror of England: John Dee*. New Haven: Yale University Press, 2013.

Goodman, George. *Fatal Colours: The Battle of Towton, 1461*. New Haven: Phoenix Press, 2011.

Goulder, Michael. *Five Stones and a Sling: Memories of a Biblical Scholar*. Sheffield, UK: Phoenix, 2009.

———. *A Tale of Two Missions*. London: SCM, 1994.

Grumett, David. "Let His Fire Burn." *Tablet,* June 2, 2018, 7–8.

Gutinontov, Pavel. "Pobeda Pred'yavlyaet Schyot." March 22, 2017. https//www. novayagezeta.ru/articles/2017/03/22/71864-pobeda-pred-yavlyaet-schet.

Hanley, Angela. *What Happened to Fr. Sean Fagan?* Dublin: Columba, 2019.

Harvey, Nicholas Peter. *The Morals of Jesus.* London: DLT, 1991.

Heer, Friedrich. *The Holy Roman Empire.* London: Phoenix, 1996.

———. *The Medieval World: Europe 1100–1350.* London: Weidenfield & Nicolson, 1961.

Hengel, Martin. *Studies in Early Christology.* London: T. & T. Clark, 1995.

Henrich, Joseph. *The Weirdest People in the World: How the West Became Psychologically Peculiar and Particularly Prosperous.* London: Allen Lane, 2019.

Hochschild, Adam. *King Leopold's Ghost: A Story of Greed, Terror and Heroism in Colonial Africa.* London: Picador, 2019.

Hodes, Aubrey. *Encounter with Martin Buber.* London: Allen Lane, 1972.

Hunt, Rex. "Old Tree, Stardust, and Moments of Wonder." *The Fourth R* 33.6 (2020) 3–8.

Huntington, Samuel P. *The Clash of Civilizations and the Remaking of World Order.* New York: Simon & Schuster, 1997.

International Labour Organization. "Forced Labour, Modern Slavery, and Human Trafficking." https://www.ilo.org/global/topics/forced-labour/lang--en/index.htm.

Israel, Jonathan. *Radical Enlightenment: Philosophy and the Making of Modernity 1650– 1750.* Oxford University Press, 2001.

Jaspers, Karl. *The Origin and Goal of History.* New Haven: Yale University Press, 1969.

Kee, Alistair. *The Roots of Christian Freedom: The Theology of John A. T. Robinson.* London: SPCK, 1988.

Kirkham, Dominic. *From Monk to Modernity.* 2nd ed. Eugene, OR: Wipf & Stock, 2018.

———. *Our Shadowed World.* Eugene, OR: Wipf & Stock, 2019

Kluger, Ruth. *Landscapes of Memory: A Holocaust Girlhood Remembered.* London: Bloomsbury, 2004.

Knohl, Israel. "Axial Transformations within Ancient Israelite Priesthood." In *Axial Civilizations and World History,* edited by Johann P. Arnason et al., 201–24. Leiden: Brill, 2005.

Knox, Ronald. *Enthusiasm.* London: Collins, 1987.

Koch, Richard. *Suicide of the West.* London: Continuum, 2007.

Komonchak, J. A. *The New Dictionary of Theology.* Dublin: Gill & Macmillan, 1987.

Koonz, Claudia. *Mothers in the Fatherland.* London: Methuen, 1986.

Kung, Hans, and Julia Ching. *Christianity and Chinese Religions.* London: SCM, 1988.

Lawson, Tom. *The Last Man: A British Genocide in Tasmania.* London: Tauris, 2014.

Living Water. "Dadirri our greatest gift to Australia, says Indigenous elder and 2021 Senior Australian of the Year." *TheLivingWater.com.* http//blog/dadirri-our-greatest-gift-to-australia-saysindigenouselder-and-2021-senior-australian-of-the-year.

Longley, Clifford. *Chosen People: The Big Idea that Shaped England and America.* London: Hodder & Stoughton, 2003.

Lovelock, James. *The Revenge of Gaia: Earth's Climate Crisis and the Fate of Humanity.* New York: Penguin, 2007.

MacCulloch, Diarmaid. "Church's Apology for Historical Antisemitism." *The Times* November 22, 2019. https://www.thetimes.co.uk/article/times-letters-churchs-apology-for-historical-antisemitism-8jbv60557.

———. *A History of Christianity.* London: Allen Lane, 2009.

MacDonald, Nathan. "John William Colenso (1814–1883): Archetypal Heresiarch?" *The Eagle* 96 (2014) 24–28.

Martel, Frederic. *In the Closet of the Vatican: Power, Homosexuality Hypocrisy.* London: Bloomsbury, 2019.

Mathias, Peter. *The First Industrial Nation: The Economic History of Britain 1700–1914.* London: Routledge, 1969.

Mazower, Mark. *Dark Continent: Europe's Twentieth Century.* London: Penguin, 1999.

McCarthy, Michael. *The Consolation of Nature: Spring in the Time of Coronavirus.* London: Hodder, 2020.

McKie, Robin. *Ape Man.* London: BBC, 2000.

Meeks, Wayne. *The First Urban Christians: The Social World of the Apostle Paul.* New Haven: Yale University Press, 2003.

Merridale, Catherine. *Night of Stone: Death and Memory in Russia.* London: Granta, 2001.

Miller, R. J. *Born Divine: The Births of Jesus and Other Sons of God.* Santa Rosa, CA: Polebridge, 2003.

———. *Discovering Indigenous Lands: The Doctrine of Discovery in English Colonies.* Oxford: Oxford University Press, 2010.

———. "Free Rain." *The Fourth R* 34.1 (2021) 3–6.

Miłosz, Ceszłow. *Native Realm: The Search for Self-Definition.* London: Penguin, 2017.

Moore, R. I. *The First European Revolution, 970–1215.* Oxford: Blackwell, 2000.

———. *The Formation of a Persecuting Society: Authority and Deviance in Western Europe 950–1250.* 2nd ed. Oxford: Oxford University Press, 2007.

———. *The War on Heresy: Faith and Power in Medieval Europe.* London: Profile, 2012.

Muggeridge, Kitty. *L'Abandon.* New York: Harper, 2009.

Mumford, Lewis. *The City in History: Its Origins, Its Transformations and Its Prospects.* London: Penguin, 1961.

———. *Technics and Civilization.* New York: Harcourt, Brace & Co., 1934.

Nadler, Steven. *A Book Forged in Hell: Spinoza's Scandalous Tretise and the Birth of the Secular Age.* Princeton: Princeton University Press, 2014.

Nicholls, William. *The Pelican Guide to Modern Theology.* London: Penguin, 1971.

Nineham, Dennis. *Christianity Medieval and Modern.* London: SCM, 1993.

Olusoga, David. *Black and British: A Forgotten History.* London: Pan, 2017.

Olyan, Saul. *Asherah and the Cult of Yahweh in Israel.* Atlanta: Scholars' Press, 1988.

O'Reilly, Johnny. "200,000 Gather to Show Dictator They Are No Longer Afraid." *The Times*, August 17, 2020.

Paabo, Svante. *Neanderthal Man: In Search of Lost Genomes.* New York: Basic, 2014.

Pagels, Elaine. *Adam, Eve and the Serpent.* London: Penguin, 1988.

———. *The Gnostic Gospels.* London: Vintage, 1979.

Parry, Glyn. *The Arch Conjuror of England: John Dee.* New Haven: Yale University Press, 2012.

Patterson, Stephen. "The Forgotten, Unbelievable Creed." *The Fourth R* 32.6 (2019) 10–12.

Pepinster, Catherine. "Another Breach of Trust: The Abuse Inquiry's Damning Report on Ealing Abbey and St. Benedict's School." *Tablet*, October 31, 2019.

Perkins, Pheme. *Introduction to the Synoptic Gospels.* Gradn Rapids, MI: Eerdmans, 2009.

Pigott, Stuart. *Ancient Britons and Antiquarian Imagination.* London: Thames & Hudson, 1989.

Popoff, Alexandra. *Vasily Grossman and the Soviet Century*. New Haven: Yale University Press, 2019.

Porter, Roy. *Enlightenment*. London: Penguin, 2000.

Pottan, Ed. "We're Not Slavish to History. We Don't Think It Tells the Story Well Enough." *The Times*, January 2, 2021.

Reyner, Solange. "Levada Poll: Majority of Russians View Stalin as Favorable." *Newsmax. com*, April 17, 2019. https://www.newsmax.com/newsfront/joseph-stalin-dictator-levada-center-approval/2019/04/17/id/912174/.

Richards, Hubert. *The First Christmas: What Really Happened*. London: Fontana, 1973.

Robinson, John. *Honest to God*. London, SCM, 1963.

Roux, Geoges. *Ancient Iraq*. 3rd ed. London: Penguin, 1992.

Sacks, Jonathan. *The Dignity of Difference*. London: Continuum, 2002.

Sands, Philippe. *East West Street: On the Origins of Genocide and Crimes Against Humanity*. London: Weidenfeld & Nicolson, 2016.

Sands, Shlomo. *The Invention of the Jewish People*. London: Verso, 2009.

Sanghera, Sathnam. *Empireland: How Imperialism Shaped Modern Britain*. London: Viking, 2021

Santos, Laurie. "The Happiness Lab." https://www.happinesslab.fm/.

Sarmiento, Domingo. *Facundo: Civilization and Barbarism*. London: Penguin, 1998.

Saward, John. *The Mysteries of March: Hans Urs von Balthasar on the Incarnation and Easter*. New York: Harper Collins, 1990.

Schmandt-Besserat, D. *Before Writing, Volume 1: From Counting to Cuneiform*. Austin: University of Texas Press, 1992.

Schuster, I. *Illustrated Bible History of the Old and New Testaments*. 13th ed. Freiburg: Herder, 1913.

Schwarz, Howard. *Reimagining the Bible: The Storytelling of the Rabbis*. Oxford: Oxford University Press, 1997.

Schweitzer, Albert. *The Quest of the Historical Jesus*. London: A & C Black, 1910.

Scott, Bernard Brandon. "If Not Christian, What?" *The Fourth R* 34.1 (2021) 13–18.

———. "Jesus the Lord: It's Dangerous." *Westar Institute, Praxis Forums*, February 2021. https://www.westarinstitute.org/blog/jesus-the-lord-its-dangerous.

Shah, Abidan. *Changing the Goalpost of New Testament Textual Criticism*. Eugene, OR: Wipf & Stock, 2020.

Shaked, Shaul. "Zoroastrian Origins: Indian and Iranian Connections." In *Axial Civilizations and World History*, edited by Johann P. Arnason et al., 183–200. Leiden: Brill, 2005.

Shanks, Hershel. *The Mystery and Meaning of the Dead Sea Scrolls*. London: Random House, 1998.

Sheldrake, Philip. *Spirituality and History*. London: SPCK, 1995.

Seidel, Jamie. "Bible's Sodom and Gomorrah destroyed by an exploding asteroid, says archaeologists." *News.com.au*, November 22, 2018. https://www.news.com.au/technology/science/archaeology/how-an-asteroid-destroyed-sodom/news-story/.

Siedentop, Larry. *Inventing the Individual: The Origins of Western Liberalism*. London: Allan Lane, 2012.

Simpson, Lorenzo. *The Unfinished Project: Towards a Postmetaphysical Humanism*. London: Routledge, 2013.

Smithson, Alan. "The Nature of Moral Authority." In *Veritatis Splendor: A Response*, by Charles Yeats, 1–7. Norwich: Canterbury, 1994.

Sobrino, Jon. *Christology at the Crossroads*. London: SCM, 1978.
———. *The Eye of the Needle: No Salvation Outside the Poor*. London: DLT, 2008.
Soza, Felippe. *Official Handbook*. Santiago, Chile: Niceye, 2007.
Spence, Martin. "Humanism as Translation." *Sofia* 139 (2021) 94–109.
Spencer, Nick. *The Evolution of the West*. London: SPCK, 2016.
Spengler, Oswald. *Decline of the West*. New York: Knopf, 1926.
Stramousa, Guy, and David Shulman, eds. *Jerusalem Studies in Religion and Culture Volume 4: Axial Civilizations and World History*. Leiden: Brill, 2005.
Sweatman, Martin. *Prehistory Decoded*. Leicester: Matador, 2019
Thomas, Keith. *Man and the Natural World: Changing Attitudes in England 1500–1800*. London: Penguin, 1983.
Thompson, Keith. *The Watch on the Heath: Science and Religion before Darwin*. London: HarperCollins, 2005.
Thompson, Thomas L. *The Bible in History: How Writers Create a Past*. London: Jonathan Cape, 1999.
Tomlinson, Hugh. "Modi Is Hailed as the Hindu King of a Divided Nation." *The Times*, August 8, 2020.
Toynbee, A. *The Genesis of Pollution*. New York: Horizon, 1973.
Trudeau, Richard. "Making Sense of Cain and Abel." *The Fourth R* 34.2 (2021) 3–5.
Ullmann, Walter. *The Carolingian Renaissance and the Idea of Kingship*. London: Routledge, 2011.
van Hagen, John. *Agnostic at the Altar: Searching for Transcendence in the Story of the Prophets*. Eugene, OR: Wipf & Stock, 2019.
van Tilburg, Jo. *Among Stone Giants: The Life of Katherine Routledge*. New York: Scribner, 2003.
Vearncombe, Erin. "Gathered Around Absence: A First-Century Approach to the Text Known as 'Mark.'" *The Fourth R* 33.5 (2020) 19–21.
Vermes, Geza. *Jesus in the Jewish World*. London: SCM, 2010.
———. *Jesus the Jew*. Minneapolis: Fortress, 1981.
von Rad, G. *Old Testament Theology, Volume 1*. London: SCM, 2012.
Vriezen, Theodore. *The Religion of Ancient Israel*. Cambridge: Lutterworth, 1969.
Warner, Marina. *Fantastic Metamorphoses, Other Worlds: Ways of Telling the Self*. Oxford: Oxford University Press, 2004.
Weinberg, Steven. *To Explain the World: The Discovery of Modern Science*. London: Allan Lane, 2015.
Whitehead, A. N. *Science and the Modern World*. London: Free Association, 1985.
Wighton, David. "Short-Termism May Be Here for the Long Run." *The Times*, October 22, 2020.
Williams, Hywel. *Emperor of the West: Charlemagne and the Carolingian Empire*. London: Quercus, 2010.
Wistrich, Robert. *Antisemitism: The Longest Hatred*. London: Methuen, 1991.
Wilson, E. O. *The Future of Life*. London: Little, Brown, 2002.
Wood, Michael. *In Search of the Dark Ages*. London: BBC, 1981.
Wright, Ronald. *A Short History of Progress*. Edinburgh: Canongate, 2004.
Yeats, Charles, ed. *Veritatis Splendor: A Response*. Norwich: Canterbury, 1994.
Zamoyski, Adam. *Holy Madness: Romantics, Patriots and Revolutionaries 1776–1871*. London: Weidenfeld & Nicolson, 1999.

Index